A HUMAN CONDITION

The law relating to mentally abnormal offenders: Observations, analysis and proposals for reform

LARRY O. GOSTIN

Edited by:
Anne Ross

Volume 2

D1281995

Special Report published by:
MIND (National Association for Mental Health)
February, 1977

First published 1977 by
MIND (National Association for Mental Health)
22 Harley Street, London W1N 2ED

Printed in Great Britain by
Reedprint Ltd, Windsor, Berks.

ISBN 0 900557 32 X

Contents

Foreword

The metaphors of social management are many. Between, for example, a man confined to pace out his life within certain acres of ground and a section of an Act of Parliament that empowers another man so to confine him, lies a benign minefield of ideas – "Mentally abnormal offender", "offender-patient", "not guilty by reason of insanity", "diminished responsibility", and many others. These ideas, these metaphors, we invent, elaborate, discard and refashion in the unending quest for the human grail of justice: justice not as an absolute, but as a tested balance, at this moment of time, in this state of insight and awareness, of different and sometimes conflicting legitimate interests.

In that quest, the law is often a clumsy weapon, but it is the most handy, sometimes the only weapon that a democratic society possesses. Volume 2 of *A Human Condition* explores in fascinating detail the interaction between law, metaphors and experience in our social management of those whose acts are both so anti-social and so disordered as to earn for them the label "mentally abnormal offender".

The business of Volume 2 is therefore with the criminal aspects of mental health legislation. It thus complements its predecessor, Volume 1, which fully examined the civil law of mental illness. Volume 1 received a great deal of notice in the press, including a full page *Guardian Extra* and a leading article in *The Times*; it initiated the debate on mental health legislation in England and Wales.

The announced aim of the Secretary of State for Social Services, Mr David Ennals, to bring in a new Mental Health Act makes the completion of *A Human Condition* particularly timely. Already Volume 1 has been heavily quoted by the DHSS in a consultative document, itself the subject of further observations from MIND. We look forward, with the publication of Volume 2 of *A Human Condition*, to a constructive debate, a progressive White Paper and a new reforming Mental Health Act.

Charles Clark
Chairman, MIND (National Association for Mental Health)

Acknowledgements

I am indebted to more people than I could hope to name in a short space. I have sought assistance on every aspect of this report. I have had valued psychiatric advice from, among others, Dr Jim Glancy and Dr Tony Whitehead.

I have had legal advice from most of the members of our Lawyers' Group, particularly Oliver Thorold, Genevre Richardson, Louis Blom-Cooper, Q.C., Bill Bailey, Maggie Rae, William Bingley, Joe Jacob, Patrick Shepherd, Jim Michael, Bill Nash and Kieran Raftery.

I am also very much obliged to Jean Allison, Tony Gifford, A.H. Edwards and Douglas Miller. These four people made a substantial contribution.

Individuals at the Department of Health and Social Security, the Home Office, the Mental Health Review Tribunal Regional Offices, and the All Party Parliamentary Mental Health Group were very courteous and diligent in providing important information. I am most grateful to all of the individuals involved.

All of the staff at MIND deserve praise, because at one time or another, each of them offered much-needed assistance. Those who were particularly involved include Denise Winn, Ron Lacey, Mike Libby, Shelagh Robertson and Joanna Murray. Most particularly, I am very grateful to Janet Murdie, Legal and Welfare Rights Assistant, who very competently helped me with all aspects of the report.

The administrative staff at MIND were efficient and friendly throughout. I would like to thank them all individually: Jean Truslow, Shirley Barnett, Allan Salmon, Margaret Windsor, Rebecca Motala and Jacqueline West. I am especially indebted to Christine Jolly, who typed so many drafts of the various sections of this report that I have lost count.

Finally, if I may indulge myself, I would like to dedicate both volumes of *A Human Condition* to my father, Joseph Gostin, and my late mother, Sylvia. My only regret is that they are not here to share this experience with me.

Larry Gostin
London, December 1st 1976.

Notes on terms and some observations

Mentally abnormal offender. For the purposes of this report, a mentally abnormal offender is defined as a person who has been charged with a criminal offence and who, as a result of evidence of mental disorder, has been placed under legal custody or control for the purpose of receiving psychiatric care or treatment.[1] (The term 'mentally abnormal' has a pejorative implication, and therefore some authors have preferred the term 'offender-patient'.)

The mentally abnormal offender is nominally exempt from ordinary penal measures. Yet in practice, most procedures for dealing with abnormal offenders contain a penal element; while they excuse the offender from retributive punishment, they impose an indefinite period of control within a mental institution.[2] The abnormal offender can be admitted either to one of the four special hospitals or to a local NHS hospital.

Less often, he is required to receive treatment, care or supervision outside the hospital. This will result from a guardianship order, which confers on the local authority social services department (or some other person) all the powers it would hold as the offender's father if the offender were under 14 years of age.[3]* It may also result from a probation order with a condition of psychiatric treatment. Approximately one-half of the offenders given this order receive non-residential care.[5]†

Part IV of the Mental Health Act provides for compulsory admission to hospital (or into guardianship) under civil (as opposed to criminal) procedures. It is outlined and analysed in Volume I of *A Human Condition.*

Part V of the Mental Health Act provides for compulsory admission to hospital (or into guardianship) of patients concerned in criminal proceedings. It also makes arrangements whereby a prisoner can be transferred to hospital.[6] Most of the decisions under Part V of the Act are taken either by a court or by the Home Secretary. It is concerned not only with psychiatric treatment and observation, but also with custody and security.‡ This volume

*The courts very rarely exercise their power to make a guardianship order. In 1971, only 11 orders were made; 4 in 1972; 8 in 1973; and 7 in 1974.[4]

†In this report MIND is primarily concerned with those legislative provisions which may result in compulsory detention in hospital. Accordingly, we have not included a full analysis of psychiatric probation orders in the text; but Appendix 2 gives a brief exposition of the law on this subject.

‡It should be pointed out that the provisions in Part V which refer to restrictions on discharge do not necessarily mean that the patient must be placed under secure conditions. A restricted patient cannot be discharged without the consent of the Home Secretary; but he may be sent to a local NHS hospital which operates an open-door policy. On the other hand, if a patient is admitted under Part IV of the Act, he will not necessarily be placed in non-secure conditions; he may, in fact, be detained in a special hospital.

1

of *A Human Condition* presents an exposition and analysis of the criteria and procedures laid down in Part V of the Act.

Special hospitals. Under section 40 of the National Health Service Reorganisation Act 1973, the Secretary of State has a duty to provide and maintain establishments for persons subject to detention under the Mental Health Act who, in his opinion, require treatment under conditions of special security because of their dangerous, violent or criminal propensities. There are four such special hospitals: Broadmoor, Rampton, Moss Side and Park Lane (see Chapter 8).

The responsible medical officer (RMO) is the medical practitioner in charge of the treatment of a detained patient.[7] Sections 43 to 47 of the Act and the Mental Health (Hospital and Guardianship) Regulations 1960 refer, *inter alia,* to the functions of the RMO. He has certain duties, including the renewal of detention, granting of trial leave and discretionary decisions on the withholding of his patients' mail. The Minister of Health's Memorandum of Guidance (1960) states that all hospital patients should be under the clinical charge of a consultant or a senior hospital medical officer.

The Report of the Committee on Mentally Abnormal Offenders (The Butler Report). The Butler Committee was set up on 21 September, 1972 with, *inter alia,* the following terms of reference: To consider to what extent and on what criteria the law should recognise mental disorder in a person accused of a criminal offence as a factor in his liability to be tried or convicted, and his disposal. It was established in part because of the anxiety and concern felt by members of the public when serious offences were committed by people released from the special hospitals; the case in point was that of Graham Young[8] (often referred to as the 'St. Albans poisoner').

The Committee made an exhaustive report to the Home Office and Department of Health and Social Security. The Government is now reviewing the report, with a view to implementing some of its recommendations. Although MIND differs from the Butler Committee in some of our recommendations, where we have specified agreement we hope to add weight to the case for change in accordance with the Committee's proposals.

A hospital order is an order by a court that an offender be detained in hospital.

A restriction order is an order imposed by a superior court in addition to a hospital order, which has the effect of requiring the Home Secretary's consent on all questions of leave of absence, transfer and discharge.

A restricted patient is an offender-patient who is subject to a hospital order with restrictions.

References and Notes

1. For an exhaustive (but perhaps futile) attempt to define the term 'abnormal offender', see H. Prins, "The abnormal offender in the community", *Howard Journal,* vol. 13, no. 3, 1972, p. 220.
2. N. Walker, *Crime and Punishment in Britain,* 2nd ed., 1968, p. 288.
3. Mental Health Act 1959, ss. 33, 34.
4. *Report of the Committee on Mentally Abnormal Offenders,* Cmnd. 6244, October 1975, para. 15.4. (hereinafter cited as *The Butler Report).*
5. N. Walker and S. McCabe, *Crime and Insanity in England,* vol. 2, 1973, p. 66.
6. See also Mental Health (Hospital and Guardianship) Regulations 1960, regulations 13-18.
7. Mental Health Act 1959, s. 59(1).
8. *The Butler Report,* para. 4.1.

References and Notes

Part I
Admission of the abnormal offender into hospital

Introduction

Traditionally, mentally abnormal offenders have been exempt from ordinary penal measures on the grounds that they are not criminally responsible for their behaviour.[1] It is maintained in law that a person who does not have full comprehension when committing a criminal act cannot be held legally responsible for it. Thus, if medical evidence establishes that he was unable to appreciate the nature and quality of the criminal act (or did not know it was wrong), then the special verdict of "not guilty by reason of insanity" is applicable.[2] The court then has no choice but to make a hospital order with special restrictions and without limit of time.[3]*

Another traditional justification for exempting the abnormal offender from ordinary penal measures is that he is too mentally disordered to stand trial for the offence charged. Thus, if the defendant is unable to understand the course of the proceedings at the trial, he may be found unfit to plead.[4,5] The result of such a finding is that the defendant will not stand trial; instead, a hospital order will be made, together with a restriction order without limit of time.

In deciding whether the accused is fit to plead, the concept of criminal responsibility is not relevant; the medical evidence adduced must relate to his mental state at the time of the trial.

Offenders found not guilty by reason of insanity or unfit to plead accounted for only 3% of the total number of mentally abnormal offenders admitted into hospital in 1974.† These traditional legal procedures have largely been supplanted by a 'utilitarian' approach, introduced by the Mental Health Act 1959. Under section 60 of that Act, a magistrates' or Crown Court may make a hospital order if it finds (on the basis of two medical opinions) that the offender is suffering from a mental disorder of a nature or degree which warrants his detention in hospital for treatment.

A hospital order has a similar effect to an admission for treatment under section 26 of the 1959 Act. This means that the patient can be detained in hospital for one year; the authority for detention can be renewed for one further year and then for intervals of two years at a time. The patient can be discharged at any time by the responsible medical officer, a Mental Health Review Tribunal or the hospital managers. A Crown Court can make a hospital order subject to the special restrictions on discharge contained in

---

*The special verdict of not guilty by reason of insanity is one of the five instances where the mental state of the accused at the time of the offence is relevant. The other four are diminished responsibility, drunkenness, non-insane automatism and infanticide. These five are discussed in some detail in Appendix 1.

†According to the Criminal Statistics for England and Wales (Cmnd. 6168), three people were found not guilty by reason of insanity and 32 unfit to plead in 1974.

section 65 of the Act. This means that the patient can be discharged only by, or with the consent of, the Home Secretary. The order can be made for a fixed period or without limit of time; in 1974, 99% of all restriction orders were for unlimited periods.[6]

In making a hospital order, with or without restrictions, the court is not concerned with the criminal responsibility of the offender, or whether he is capable of understanding the proceedings of the trial (he has already been tried and convicted);* the only relevant considerations are his mental condition and his suitability for psychiatric treatment *at the time of sentencing.*[7]

Thus, contrary to popular belief, no causal relationship has to be established between the mental disorder and the criminal behaviour. Moreover, partial or complete recovery from the disorder will not necessarily reduce the offender's criminal propensity.[8] As the Butler Committee said: "A person may be cured of his mental disorder, but still be disposed to commit a crime."[9]

Dr. McGrath, Physician Superintendent of Broadmoor Hospital, aptly observed:[10]

"Under the old dispensation of 'not guilty by reason of insanity' there had to be established . . . a causal link between mental illness and the offence. The man committed the offence because he was mentally ill and suffering from this or that delusion. That is not so under the provisions of section 60 and 65 of the Act. All that has to be established is that (a) the offender-patient committed the act or the omission charged, and (b) he is so mentally disordered as to need hospital treatment. There need be no causal link between these two factors."

On another occasion Dr. McGrath said: "Treatment of a psychosis is by no means synonymous with 'cure', and the association of psychosis with gross anti-social activity does not mean that the two conditions mutually influence each other in the direction of curability".[11]

In several cases which have come before the Court of Appeal, the offender objected to a hospital order on the grounds that there was no connection between his illness and the offence committed. The court ruled that there need be no connection,[12] and that the offender's consent to the order was not required.[13]

After reviewing a large sample of cases that involved mentally abnormal offenders, Walker and McCabe reached the same conclusion:[14]

"Often, the offences were petty affairs committed without planning or skill, for food, small sums of money or minor saleable articles. Each of these could be ascribed to a motive which we regard as normal: hunger, desire for money, need for sleep and shelter. In these cases, it is hardly

---

*Under section 60(2) of the 1959 Act a magistrates' court can make a hospital order without recording a conviction. The court must, however, be satisfied that the defendant did the act or made the omission with which he was charged.

possible to say with confidence that the offender would not have done it if he had not been disordered, for they are indistinguishable from the acts of a large number of ordinary, if incompetent, people."

The implication is that some mentally abnormal offenders differ from 'normal' offenders only in their need for treatment. The psychiatric services therefore, may not be in a better position to predict or prevent future violent behaviour than the prison services or Parole Board.

Moreover, there is evidence to suggest that the population of "abnormal" offenders is not significantly different from other confined populations, and the label may, in some cases, result more from chance than from a reliable classification; the very term 'abnormal' suggests that norms of society are to some extent invoked. Numerous studies show that there is a substantial overlap between the populations of mental hospitals, prisons and reception centres. Conservative estimates indicate that anywhere between one-tenth and one-third of the prison population could be clinically diagnosed as "mentally abnormal".[15] In fact, a survey of the views of prison medical officers produced an estimate that some 500 prisoners would be better placed outside the penal system.[16]†

Transfers

A prisoner may develop a mental disorder *after* he has been sentenced to a term of imprisonment. Alternatively, he may have been mentally disordered at the time of sentencing, but it was not detected and he was therefore dealt with as an ordinary offender.

If a person serving a sentence of imprisonment is found to be "mentally abnormal" he can be transferred to a hospital. The Home Secretary must find, on the basis of two medical reports, that the offender is suffering from a mental disorder of a nature or degree which warrants his detention in a hospital for medical treatment. He must also be of opinion, having regard to the public interest and to all the circumstances, that it is expedient to make a transfer direction.[17]

A transfer direction has the same effect as a hospital order.[18] It can be made with or without restrictions on discharge. If it is made without restrictions, the offender is no longer subject to the prison sentence. He can therefore be unconditionally discharged from the hospital by the RMO, a tribunal, or the hospital managers. But if it is made with restrictions,[19] he cannot be dis-

---

†The 'utilitarian' nature of a hospital order is an important concept for the purposes of this report. The rationale for the use of indeterminate sentences for the mentally abnormal offender is that the psychiatrist can predict the recurrence of the offending behaviour. Given the fact that often there is no relationship between the offence and the disorder, it is unfair to expect the doctor to do this. It is preferable to offer treatment to the offender on a voluntary basis – either in hospital or in prison. If the offender requires treatment after the expiration of a definite period (based on the severity of the offence and his previous criminal record), he should be detained in pursuance of an "admission for treatment" under Part IV of the Mental Health Act. These issues are explored in detail in Chapter 5 *infra*.

charged without the consent of the Home Secretary. However, the restrictions on discharge automatically lapse after the expiry of the full term (without remission) of the sentence.[20]

The reader will notice from the short exposition of the relevant legislation presented above that the offender-patient is dealt with in different ways, depending on when his mental disorder arises (or else when it is detected). Table 1 (pp. 10-16) presents a summary of the legislation in chart form.

References and Notes

1. H. Fingarette, "Diminished mental capacity as a criminal law defence", *Mod. L. Rev.*, vol. 37, 1974, p.264; A. Samuels, "Mental illness and criminal liability", *Med. Sci. Law*, vol.15, no.3, 1975, p.198.
2. Criminal Procedure (Insanity) Act 1964, s. 1.
3. *Ibid.*, s. 5 and schedule 1.
4. Mental Health Act 1959, s. 73.
5. Criminal Procedure (Insanity) Act 1964, s. 4.
6. *Criminal Statistics for England and Wales for 1974,* Cmnd. 6168, pp. 240-241.
7. P. Fallon, *Crown Court Practice: Sentencing,* 1975, p. 123.
8. British Psychological Society, "Memorandum of evidence to the Butler Committee on the law relating to the mentally abnormal offender", *Bull. Brit. Psychol. Soc.,* vol. 26, 1973, pp. 331-342.
9. *The Butler Report,* para. 4.4.
10. P. G. McGrath, "The mentally abnormal offender", *Medico-Legal Journal,* vol. 41, 1973, pp. 4, 7.
11. P. G. McGrath, "The treatment of the psychotic offender", *Howard Journal,* vol. 10, 1958, p. 38.
12. R v McBride, [1972] *Crim. L. Rev.* 322; R v Hatt, [1962] *Crim. L. Rev.* 647.
13. R v Gunnee, [1972] *Crim. L. Rev.* 261.
14. N. Walker and S. McCabe, *Crime and Insanity in England,* vol. 2, 1973, p. 129.
15. Howard League for Penal Reform, "Procedure and resources for mentally abnormal offenders", report based on evidence given to the Butler Committee, 1975. The research cited by the Howard League follows: Whitehead and Ahmad (1970), Scott (1969) ("even among the selected populations of remand homes and prisons, the proportion of psychiatric problems is in the region of 15-20 per cent"), Taylor (1960), Sparks (1971). See also the statement by Dr. Robert Bluglass to the Annual Conference of the Royal Society of Health, *New Psychiatry,* May 13, 1976, p. 7.
16. *Interim Report of the Committee on Mentally Abnormal Offenders,* Cmnd. 5698, July 1974, paras. 7 and 13.
17. Mental Health Act 1959, s. 72.
18. *Ibid.*, s. 72(3).
19. *Ibid.*, s. 74.
20. *Ibid.*, s. 75.

Table 1 Mental disorder and the offender

Legislation	Criteria and evidence	Decision-maker (and burden of proof)	Effect	Recommendations of the Butler Committee
A. Mental disorder present at the time of the offence (See Appendix 1)				
1. Special verdict of not guilty by reason of insanity. Criminal Procedure (Insanity) Act 1964, s. 2.	M'Naghten Rules: the offender did not know the nature and quality of the act or did not know that it was wrong. No formal requirements – generally two medical opinions.	Jury (Defence raises evidence and bears the burden of proof to "a balance of probabilities".)	Hospital order made with restrictions and without limit of time (mandatory). See C(2) below.	Revised verdict: "not guilty on evidence of mental disorder". This would include a *mens rea* element and specific exemption would be given on evidence of severe subnormality or severe mental illness. Magistrates' courts should be allowed to return the special verdict. Wider powers of disposal should be given to the courts.
2. Diminished responsibility, which is a plea in mitigation of sentence. Homicide Act 1957, s. 2.	The offender suffers an abnormality of mind that impairs his mental responsibility. As A(1) above.	Jury As A(1) above.	Reduces charge of murder to one of manslaughter; thus it avoids the mandatory life sentence and allows the court a wide range of disposals.	Repeal of section 2; courts should be given wider powers of sentencing on a conviction for murder; *or*

				The defence should no longer bear the burden of proof – only the burden of raising the issue.
				Defence should be required to give advance notice if it intends to raise the issue of diminished responsibility.

B. Mental disorder present at the time of the trial (See Chapter 1)

1. Transfer direction before trial. Mental Health Act 1959, s. 73(2)(a).	The defendant must be suffering from mental illness or severe subnormality which warrants his detention in a mental hospital. Two medical opinions are required.	Home Secretary	Hospital order with restrictions and without limit of time (mandatory). See C(2) below.	There are no specific recommendations.

Legislation	Criteria and evidence	Decision-maker (and burden of proof)	Effect	Recommendations of the Butler Committee
2. Unfit to plead Criminal Procedure (Insanity) Act 1964, s. 4	The offender is unable to understand the proceedings so as to make a proper defence, to challenge a juror, and to understand the evidence. As A(1) above, except that in some cases only one medical opinion is put before the court.	Jury (If the defence raises the issue it has the burden of proof to the balance of probabilities. If the prosecution raises the issue, it has the burden, beyond a reasonable doubt.)	The facts of the original charge are not examined if the issue is raised at the outset of the trial; if trial proceedings have already started, they are abandoned when the issue is raised. The defendant must be detained in hospital, with restrictions on discharge imposed without limit of time – see C(2) below. The defendant may be remitted for trial at a later date.	The wording of the verdict should be revised to "under disability in relation to the trial". The criteria should be revised to: can the defendant understand the course of the proceedings, understand the substance of the evidence, give adequate instructions to advisers and plead with understanding to the indictment? The facts must be tried at the earliest possible time. Where there is any likelihood that the defendant may make an early recovery, the trial should be adjourned for not more than six

months; if there is no likelihood of recovery, the facts should be heard immediately.

The courts should be given a much wider discretion in regard to disposal.

C. Mental disorder present at the time of sentencing (See Chapters 2-5)

		Court		
1. Hospital order. Mental Health Act 1959, s. 60.	The defendant is suffering from mental illness, psychopathic disorder, subnormality or severe subnormality which warrants his detention in a mental hospital. Two medical opinions are required.		A hospital order has a similar effect to an admission for treatment under s. 26 of the 1959 Act; i.e. detention is initially for a period of one year, and the order may be renewed for a further year and then for periods of two years at a time. The patient may be discharged at any time by the RMO, the hospital managers or a Mental Health Review Tribunal.	One medical opinion should be obtained from the doctor who will be treating the patient, and his consent to the patient's admission should be obtained before the order is made. "Interim hospital orders" should be introduced, so that the suitability of the treatment available at the admitting hospital can be tested.

Legislation	Criteria and evidence	Decision-maker (and burden of proof)	Effect	Recommendations of the Butler Committee
2. Hospital order with restrictions on discharge with or without limit of time. Mental Health Act 1959, s. 65.	As C(1) above. The court must also consider that restrictions on discharge are necessary for the protection of the public. Magistrates' courts must remit to the Crown Court for a restriction order to be made. Opinions of two medical practitioners are required, and one must give oral evidence to the court.	Crown Court	Patients may only be discharged by, or with the consent of, the Home Secretary. A restriction order may be made for a fixed period or without limit of time.	As C(1) above. The consent of the treating doctor should be obtained before a restriction order is made, or before the patient is recalled to hospital on other than medical grounds. The legislation allowing the courts to impose a restriction order for a fixed period should be repealed. Regular reports on the progress of the patient should be made to the Home Office.
3. Probation order with a condition of psychiatric treatment. Powers of Criminal Courts Act 1973, s. 3.	The condition of the defendant must be such as requires and may be susceptible to treatment, but does not warrant his detention in a hospital.	Court	The patient must attend hospital for psychiatric treatment as an informal in- or out-patient.	There should be closer co-operation between the courts, the doctors and the probation officers involved in the care of the patient.

		The defendant must consent to the making of this order. Two medical opinions are required.		There must be a careful assessment of the individual offender's needs and suitability. Medical evidence should be given by the treating psychiatrist.

D. Mental disorder present after sentencing (See Chapter 6)

1. Transfer to hospital of a person serving sentence. Mental Health Act 1959, s. 72.	Home Secretary	As C(1) above. As C(1) above, but the Home Secretary must consider, having regard to the public interest, that the transfer of the prisoner to a mental hospital is expedient.	The prisoner is transferred from prison to hospital; an order made under s. 72 has the same effect as a hospital order under s. 60. As C(1) above.	As B(1) above. The patient should be allowed to apply for a Mental Health Review Tribunal hearing at what would have been his earliest possible date of release.

Legislation	Criteria and evidence	Decision-maker (and burden of proof)	Effect	Recommendations of the Butler Committee
2. Transfer from prison to hospital with restrictions on discharge.	As C(2) above.	Home Secretary	As C(2) above.	As D(1) above.
Mental Health Act 1959, s. 74.	As C(2) above.		The patient may be returned to prison if the Home Secretary is notified by the RMO that he no longer requires treatment; or he may be released on licence if he would have been so released on return to prison. The restrictions on discharge cease to have effect on the expiration of the offender's sentence. He is thereafter liable to detention as in D(1).	

1. Mental disorder at the time of the trial

Where a criminal defendant is suffering from a substantial mental incapacity such that it would be legally improper for him to stand trial, there are procedures under the Mental Health Act 1959 and the Criminal Procedure (Insanity) Act 1964 which can prevent him from being tried. In such circumstances, the defendant is said to be "unfit to plead" or, as suggested in the Butler Report, "under disability in relation to the trial" or, more simply, "under disability".

A determination that a person is under disability prevents him from being tried at all. Therefore it does not show that he is either innocent or guilty since there are no findings of fact.

The decision can be made by either the Home Secretary or a jury. The Home Secretary may have the accused transferred to hospital when he has been committed in custody for trial at the Crown Court. This will have the effect of either postponing the trial or preventing it from taking place.* The Home Secretary holds these powers under section 73 of the Mental Health Act 1959. He exercised similar powers under the old Criminal Lunatics Act 1884 only where "it would not be practicable to bring him (the accused) before a court, or that trial is likely to have an injurious effect on his mental state".

The basis for this practice as set out in the Report of the Royal Commission on Capital Punishment is presumably still applicable: "that the issue of insanity should be determined by the jury whenever possible and the power [of the Home Secretary] should be exercised only when there is likely to be a scandal if the prisoner is brought up for trial".[1]

In 1974, 12 people were transferred under section 73 of the 1959 Act; they represented 2% of the total number of persons subject to special restrictions who were received into hospital in that year.[2]

Where the accused is brought up for trial, he may be adjudged to be unfit to plead under the Criminal Procedure (Insanity) Act 1964. In pursuance of section 4 of that Act, the issue of disability is determined not by the Home Secretary, but by a jury. In 1974, 32 people were found unfit to plead under the 1964 Act; this represented 5% of the total number of persons subject to special restrictions received into hospital in that year.[2]

---

*It should be noted that the Home Secretary can only decide to transfer the accused to hospital. If the hospital reports that the patient is not going to be fit to appear in court, the clerk of the court is contacted. It is then for the court to decide what should be done with him. The court has the power in these circumstances, if it receives the necessary medical evidence, to make a hospital order, with or without restrictions, in the patient's absence (section 76). Alternatively, the court may decide to postpone the date of the trial under section 7 of the Courts Act 1971 in order to allow further time for the prisoner's mental condition to improve. See generally, J. C. Smith and B. Hogan, *Criminal Law*, 3rd ed., 1973, pp. 130-133.

A more detailed account of the procedures and criteria under which the accused may be found to be under disability follows.

Removal to hospital of persons committed for trial: Mental Health Act 1959, s. 73(2)(a)

The current law

Under section 73(2)(a) of the Mental Health Act, where a person has been committed in custody for trial at the Crown Court, the Home Secretary may, in certain circumstances, direct that he be transferred to hospital as if he were serving a sentence of imprisonment.* The Home Secretary must be satisfied by reports from at least two medical practitioners (at least one of whom must be approved for the purposes of section 28 of the Act as having special experience in the diagnosis or treatment of mental disorders) that the accused is suffering from mental illness or severe subnormality (not psychopathy or subnormality) of a nature or degree which warrants his detention in a hospital for medical treatment.[3]

A person who is subject to a transfer direction made in pursuance of section 73 of the Act must be admitted to the hospital specified in the direction within 14 days, or the direction will cease to have effect.[4]

A transfer direction has the same effect as a hospital order.[5] Under section 74 of the Act, the Home Secretary *must* also direct that an accused person who is transferred to hospital under section 73(2)(a) shall be subject to the special restrictions set out in section 65 of the Act.

A transfer direction under section 73(2)(a) will cease to have effect when the case is disposed of by the Crown Court, but this does not prevent that court from making a hospital order, with or without restrictions.[6]

The following provisions found in section 76 of the Act also apply to a person who is subject to a transfer direction under section 73(2)(a), but whose case has not yet been disposed of by the Crown Court as described in the preceding paragraph. At any time before he is brought to trial, the responsible medical officer may notify the Home Secretary that he no longer requires treatment for mental disorder. The Home Secretary may then direct that he be readmitted into custody for trial; upon his arrival back into custody the transfer direction will cease to have effect.[7] However, if the Crown Court decides that it is impracticable or inappropriate to bring him to trial, the court may make a hospital order, with or without restrictions, in his absence and without convicting him.[8]

The court can do this if it is satisfied, on the evidence of two medical practitioners (complying with section 62(1) of the Act) that the person is suffering from mental illness or severe subnormality of a nature or degree which warrants his detention in hospital for medical treatment. The court must also be of opinion, after considering any depositions or any other documents it may require, that it is proper to make a hospital order.[9]

*For a more comprehensive explanation of the complex provisions of section 73, see Appendix 3.

Observations and proposals for reform

A restriction order under sections 60/65 of the Mental Health Act has grave consequences for the offender-patient, and therefore strict safeguards are imposed on a court making such an order. In addition to the need for two medical recommendations, a court must determine beyond reasonable doubt that the accused committed an imprisonable offence. Furthermore, the restriction order can be made only if a Crown Court is convinced that it is strictly necessary for the protection of the public.

In contrast, the same restriction order can be imposed by the Home Secretary under sections 73/74 of the Act with relatively few safeguards; with fewer, in fact, than are available under the civil procedures of Part IV of the Act. No determination need be made by a court that the defendant committed the offence with which he is charged; and he need not be considered dangerous to himself or others. The only requirement is that the Home Secretary be satisfied, on the basis of two medical opinions, that "it is expedient" to make such an order. No social worker need be involved; the nearest relative has no right to discharge the patient; and there is no right of appeal to a Mental Health Review Tribunal.

Since a decision under section 73 is made by the Home Secretary rather than by a court of law, there is no hearing to determine whether the accused ever committed the crime with which he is charged. He may spend a long time in hospital, because the doctors and the Home Secretary must act on the assumption that he actually performed the dangerous act in question; this will necessarily affect the decision on when he may safely be released. (This issue is more fully discussed later.)

It is true that the restriction order will lapse when the court finally disposes of the case. But the defendant may remain in custody for many months before the court hears the case. One solicitor reported in a letter to *The Times*[10] that his client was still awaiting trial six months after being committed in custody. He also said that the accused's relatives had never been informed of the transfer; they arrived to visit him at H.M. Prison, Brixton, only to discover that he had been transferred to Rampton Hospital. Even the solicitor was not informed that a direction for transfer had been made.

Moreover, when the court does dispose of a case involving a patient who has been transferred under section 73(2)(a), it can do so in his absence and without convicting him. Accordingly, it need not make any finding of fact; it can make a restriction order† on the basis of the medical recommendations, with no reference to any evidence on whether the person actually committed the criminal act in question.

In MIND's view, it is improper to subject a person to a restriction order if no court of law has determined that he has committed an imprisonable offence. The full reasons for this are set out on pp.24-27 of this report. We do appreciate that when a person is awaiting trial in prison, it may be

†A magistrates' court cannot make a restriction order, but must commit the person to the Crown Court for this purpose.

appropriate that he be transferred to a therapeutic setting until he can be tried. The problem with section 73(2)(a) is that the transfer may result in an indefinite stay in hospital, without any findings of fact. We propose that when the time comes for the accused to stand trial (and this should not be postponed solely because of his disability, as seems to occur under section 73), the transfer direction should cease to have effect. After that, if the person is mentally competent, he should stand trial for the offence with which he is charged; and if he is convicted, the court has the option of making a hospital order, with or without restrictions, in accordance with the provisions of sections 60/65 of the Mental Health Act. If, on the other hand, the defendant is acquitted, the court has no jurisdiction over him, but he could then be civilly admitted to hospital if in need of treatment. Of course, the procedures under Part IV of the Act would then have to be followed.

The question of whether the defendant is under disability may arise, so that the trial cannot proceed. In this event, the issue of disability should be determined in accordance with the Criminal Procedure (Insanity) Act 1964 and the proposals stated for the reform of that Act, which follow.

Unfitness to plead: Criminal Procedure (Insanity) Act 1964, s. 4

Criteria

The existing criteria for determining whether a defendant is under disability are whether he can understand the course of proceedings at the trial in order to make a proper defence, challenge a juror to whom he might wish to object, and understand the substance of the evidence.[11] The Butler Committee, on the recommendation of H.M. judges, has proposed that the reference to capacity to challenge a juror should be omitted, and two criteria should be added: whether the defendant can give adequate instructions to his legal advisers, and can plead with understanding to the indictment.[11]

The meaning of the term 'mental disorder' in this context is considerably different from its meaning as used in the Mental Health Act 1959. Even if the accused is the proper subject of a formal admission to hospital, he is not necessarily under a disability in relation to the trial; although he suffers from a medically classifiable mental disorder, he may still be able to follow the proceedings in court and therefore be fit to stand trial.[12]

Nor do other forms of mental disability necessarily place the person under a legal disability in relation to the trial. For example, it has been held that neither hysterical amnesia* (where the defendant has no recollection of the alleged crime)[13] nor persecution mania (where the defendant is unable to act 'in his own best interest' at the trial)[14] constitutes sufficient basis for a finding of unfitness to stand trial. The finding of disability apparently turns upon the *capacity* of the defendant to comprehend the deliberations of the court; the

---

*The majority of the Butler Committee feel that the *status quo* should remain, i.e. that amnesia should not be regarded as equivalent to a mental disability of the kind traditionally accepted as a reason for barring trial. Professor Sir Denis Hill and Professor Nigel Walker take exception to this view (paras. 10.4 – 10.11).

content of the defence, i.e. whether or not the defendant can put up a good defence, is not relevant for this purpose.

Procedure

If the question arises during the trial whether the accused is under a mental disability which constitutes a bar to his being tried, the procedural provisions of the Criminal Procedure (Insanity) Act 1964 (which was based upon the Third Report of the Criminal Law Revision Committee, Cmnd. 2149) have effect.[15]

The issue of disability may be raised by the defence or the prosecution; or if neither party raises the issue, the judge should do so himself if he has doubts about the fitness of the accused. He may resolve his doubts by reading the medical reports, though it is not desirable that he should hear oral evidence.[16]

The burden of proof in such enquiries lies with the party that alleges disability.[16] If the defence raises the issue, then the standard of proof required is that on a balance of probabilities the accused is unfit to stand trial;[17] but if the prosecution alleges unfitness, it must be proved beyond a reasonable doubt.[14]

Section 4(3) of the Criminal Procedure (Insanity) Act requires that the question of disability be determined as soon as it arises;[18] under section 4(2) of the Act, however, the court (having regard "to the nature of the supposed disability" and if satisfied that it is "expedient so to do and in the interests of the accused") has discretion to postpone the inquiry until the case for the prosecution has been heard. This means that the court may require the prosecution to present its case, and the defendant may be acquitted if there is insufficient factual evidence to justify a conviction.[18] If the jury acquits the defendant, the question of disability will not be determined. If, however, the prosecution does present a substantial case showing that the accused is guilty on the facts, the issue of disability will immediately be determined by the jury.[19] Under section 4(2), the judge may postpone the determination of disability until the case for the prosecution has been heard only if it appears that the defence has a reasonable chance of success on the factual issues of the case.[20] This is so even where the disability is such that whatever the outcome of the trial, the accused is likely to be detained in hospital.[21]

Jury

Section 4(4) of the 1964 Act states that the question of fitness to be tried must be determined by a jury. Where the determination is made on arraignment,† then if the trial proceeds, the accused must be tried by a jury other than the one which determined that question.[22] Where the determination takes place later, it will be made either by a separate jury or by the jury before which the accused is being tried, as the court may direct.[23]

Appeal

Section 4(6) of the Criminal Procedure (Insanity) Act made it possible, for

---

†An arraignment occurs when the prisoner is called to the bar of the court by name. He is read the substance of the indictment and asked whether he pleads guilty or not guilty.

the first time, to appeal against a finding of disability in relation to the trial. This provision was superseded by section 15 of the Criminal Appeal Act 1968, which states that where a finding of disability in relation to the trial is returned, an appeal is available.

An appeal may be made on any ground which involves a question of fact alone; or with leave of the Court of Appeal, on any ground which involves a question of fact alone, or mixed law and fact, or on any other ground which appears to the Court of Appeal to be sufficient. No leave of the Court of Appeal is needed if the trial judge grants a certificate to the effect that the case warrants an appeal.

The criteria which the Court of Appeal must use to decide whether to allow an appeal are given in section 16 of the 1968 Act.

The magistrates' court

The powers provided by sections 14 and 26 of the Magistrates' Courts Act 1952 allow the court to obtain a medical report only after conviction or a finding of guilt. As a result, a magistrates' court cannot deal with the question of disability; it must wait to be determined at the Crown Court.[24] The magistrates' court can require the defendant to undergo a medical examination as a condition of bail,[25] but few defendants who may be under disability are likely to be suitable for the grant of bail.[26]

The Butler Committee has proposed that the magistrates' courts should be given jurisdiction to determine the issue of disability; that where there is doubt about the defendant's ability to consent to summary proceedings, his representative should be empowered to consent for him, with the promise that if the accused does recover and come to trial, the matter will be put to him personally; and that magistrates should be empowered to call, at any stage, for medical reports in the same form as is necessary for orders under section 60 of the Mental Health Act.[27]

Effect of a Finding of Unfit to Plead

According to the Criminal Procedure (Insanity) Act, if a defendant is found unfit to plead, the trial proceeds no further.[28] The court must make an order admitting the defendant to a hospital named by the Home Secretary,[29] and he must be detained in accordance with sections 60 and 65 of the Mental Health Act 1959 (under a hospital order with special restrictions on discharge, made without limit of time[30]).

Remit for Trial

If the person's mental condition subsequently improves, the Home Secretary (after consultation with the responsible medical officer) is empowered by section 5(4) of the Act to remit him for trial.

In a memorandum to the Butler Committee, the Home Office pointed out that there are practical difficulties in proceeding with the prosecution of a person who has been detained in hospital for a long time. Accordingly, the

Home Secretary's power to remit the patient for trial is sparingly used, generally only in cases where the patient's mental condition has improved rapidly, and the desirability of reaching a formal decision on his guilt is not counterbalanced by other considerations.[31] †

Observations and Proposals for Reform

In making a determination that the defendant is under a disability, the court's intent is that he should receive treatment at the earliest possible time. This saves the defendant from the stress of a court appearance; it is better for the dignity of the legal process; and it authorises detention in a therapeutic environment. Moreover, it is unjust to make a mentally disabled person the subject of a criminal trial if he is unable to comprehend the proceedings and contribute to his own defence. It would be unfair to convict such a person because, if he were capable, he might be able to exculpate himself. Mental disability may substantially diminish a defendant's capacity to testify, to recall exonerating circumstances or identify corroborative witnesses, to instruct his lawyer, and so forth. Similarly, he may be highly suggestible, even to the point of incriminating himself where he is not in fact guilty of the offence charged. The Confait case, which follows, illustrates this point.

In November 1972, Colin Lattimore, then aged 18, was found guilty of the manslaughter of Maxwell Confait on the grounds of diminished responsibility.*[32] He was made the subject of a hospital order, and sent to Rampton Special Hospital. The conviction was based almost solely on a confession he had allegedly made to the police.[33]

Mr. Lattimore complained that he had been hit by the police and frightened into making the confession.[33-35] The boy's father pointed out that his son had a mental age of eight; he was very suggestible and could easily have been made to confess without fully understanding the nature of his confession.

After Lattimore had been detained for two years and seven months in Rampton Hospital, his case was referred to the Court of Appeal by the Home Secretary under section 17(1)(a) of the Criminal Appeal Act 1968. The Court of Appeal heard evidence (which had been available at the original trial) which demonstrated that Mr Lattimore could not possibly have been at the scene of the crime.[33] Quashing the conviction, Lord Justice Scarmon said: "The admissions, in whatever circumstances they came to be made as

---

†Mr Paul Bacon, a solicitor, reported in *The Guardian*, November 11, 1976, that Mr Ian Adams was found unfit to stand trial for the murder of his great aunt. Mr Adams has spent seven years in Rampton Hospital. Mr Bacon claims to have submitted new evidence to the Home Office which proves that Mr Adams was innocent. He plans to apply to the High Court in London for an order of *mandamus*.

The Home Office accepts that Mr Adams is fit to plead but they are reluctant to remit the case for trial because of practical problems involving the length of time which has elapsed and because one of the defence witnesses has died.

*Two other younger youths were also convicted of offences arising out of the same events.

alleged, must be unreliable and the convictions, accordingly, must be unsafe and unsatisfactory."[35]

As a result of the case, Christopher Price, Labour MP for Lewisham West, introduced a ten-minute Rule Bill which provided that any statement made by a mentally handicapped person would not be admissible unless either a solicitor was present throughout the interview during which the statement was made, or the prosecution had satisfied the court that stringent requirements regarding the fairness of the interview and reliability of the statement had been fulfilled.[36] The Bill was not enacted, but the Home Office and Attorney General set up an inquiry into the case, headed by Sir Henry Fisher.[32]

The criminal process should, as far as possible, protect the mentally disordered defendant from being wrongly convicted; the adoption of legislation along the lines suggested by Christopher Price would be an appropriate step in this direction.* However, the inability of the accused to defend himself

---

*The *Judges' Rules on the Interrogation and Taking of Statements by Police*[37] do not make special provision for the mentally subnormal. Yet medical evidence suggests that "severe mental disability may make a person vulnerable to any sustained period of stress".[38] While it would be wrong to say that any statement by a mentally handicapped person is unreliable, there may be special cases where certain safeguards should be used to prevent the possibility of a forced confession. The case of Paul Hails[38 39] illustrates the problem. Mr Hails, a 23-year-old mentally handicapped labourer, was the first to confess to the murder of a 6-year-old boy, Gary Shields. For the first 12 hours of interrogation, Mr Hails refused to confess. Then he made a series of confession statements, denying and admitting in turn. He has since retracted his confession. Not long after, a 14-year-old boy, also mentally handicapped, confessed to the same murder; he also withdrew his confession. The court convicted Paul Hails and sent him to Rampton Hospital. Recently, a third person, Kenneth Woodhouse, confessed to the murder. The Court of Appeal therefore reversed Hails' conviction and he was released after spending more than one year in Rampton. Now the Department of Public Prosecutions is contemplating the prosecution of Mr Woodhouse. The Queen's Counsel who represented Mr Hails has told MIND that there is reason to believe that Mr Woodhouse's confession may also be unreliable.

It is noteworthy that on 21 July 1976, the Home Office issued to chief officers of police a circular of guidance on this subject (No. 109/1976). The circular draws attention to the need for special care in the interrogation of such persons. It says that the Home Secretary appreciates that it may be difficult for a police officer to decide whether a person who is to be interviewed is mentally handicapped. However, he considers it important that a police officer should take special care in putting questions and accepting the reliability of answers, if it appears to him that a person (whether a witness or a suspect) whom he intends to interview has a mental handicap which might affect his understanding of questions or make him especially open to suggestion.

On the question of the presence of a third party the circular points out that so far as mentally handicapped children are concerned, paragraph 4 of the administrative directions appended to the Judges' Rules already applies. In addition the circular says that the Home Secretary thinks it desirable that, so far as practicable, and where recognised as such by the police, a mentally handicapped adult (whether suspected of crime or not) should be interviewed only in the presence of a parent or other person in whose care, custody or control he is, or of some person who is not a police officer (for example, a social worker).

The circular goes on to say that any document arising from an interview with a mentally handicapped person of any age should be signed not only by the person who made the statement, but also by the parent or other person who was present during the interview. Since the reliability of any admission by the mentally handicapped person may even then be challenged, the circular advises the police that care must still be taken to verify the facts admitted and to obtain corroboration where possible.

properly should not prevent an investigation of the offence; he may in fact have committed the criminal act with which he is charged, and may therefore have to be confined for the protection of society. On the other hand, a simple showing that the defendant is mentally disordered at the time of the trial does not justify his compulsory confinement for an indefinite period of time, unless there is also proof that he committed an imprisonable offence. For some defendants, such as those suffering from certain forms of organic psychiatric illness or from severe subnormality, there is little or no chance that their mental capabilities will significantly improve; they become subject to potentially life-long involuntary confinement.[40]†

Under the Criminal Procedure (Insanity) Act, the court can determine that the defendant is unfit to plead without making a full finding of the facts. Moreover, if disability is found, the court *must* make a hospital order, coupled with a restriction order without limit of time. The defendant is therefore subject to confinement in hospital until the Home Secretary either remits the case for trial* – which very rarely occurs – or conditionally discharges the patient from hospital. In this regard, the Home Secretary must naturally assume that the patient committed the crime with which he was charged, and this may affect his estimation of when he can safely be released.

For example, MIND represented one patient in a local NHS hospital who was accused of killing his wife some 10 years ago. He was found unfit to stand trial and admitted to hospital indefinitely. For the last 4 years he has been working in the community; he claims never to have missed a day's work. His responsible medical officer feels that he is mentally fit to be released. The Home Secretary, however, has so far refused to grant a discharge, presumably due to the serious nature of the crime for which the person was charged, but never convicted.

Similarly, in the Confait case, the doctors at Rampton Hospital did not believe that Colin Lattimore could safely be released into the community; they had to assume that he committed manslaughter. When he was absolved of that crime by the Court of Appeal, the clinical assessment of

†In *Jackson v Indiana*, 406 U.S. 715 (1972), the United States Supreme Court reviewed an incompetency statute which was remarkably similar to the Criminal Procedure (Insanity) Act. The facts of the case illustrate the problems of a person found unfit to stand trial. The defendant – who was arrested for a petty theft – was a deaf mute with virtually no capacity to communicate. Two psychiatrists testified that he was unfit to stand trial and was unlikely ever to recover from this disability. Despite these dreary prospects, the lower court authorised his indefinite detention in hospital. The manifest injustice in Jackson's case, which the Supreme Court saw as a life sentence for a permanently incompetent defendant, led the Court unanimously to hold the statute unconstitutional, as violating both equal protection of the law and substantive due process.

*In a case reported to MIND by a consultant in a special hospital, the patient explained to the doctor that there was positive evidence that he did not in fact commit the crime he was charged with. The consultant kept him in hospital for two months and then received permission from the Home Office to remit him for trial. The patient was then found not guilty on the facts.

This is one of those rare instances where the power to remit the patient for trial was exercised. Yet if the defendant had been less articulate, or the consultant less vigilant, the patient could have been confined for many years in a high security hospital for a crime which he had not committed.

dangerousness became unreliable; for this reason many of his hospital records have been destroyed.*[41]

Given the severe consequences of a determination that the defendant is under a disability in relation to the trial, it is important that the facts of his case should be established by a court. It is often unjustifiable to confine an individual indefinitely if he has not committed the offence charged against him. He may, for example, be a mentally handicapped person living peaceably with his parents, and it would be tragically unjust to admit him to hospital on a charge which cannot be substantiated. Such a person is not liable to long term compulsory admission to hospital under the civil provisions of the Mental Health Act for two reasons: first, a mentally subnormal adult can under no circumstances be compulsorily admitted under section 26 of the Act; and second, mental disability alone is not a sufficient basis for compulsory detention. It must also be shown that the person is in need of hospital treatment and the detention is in the interests of the patient's health or safety or for the protection of others. The mere filing of criminal charges against a person should not be taken as grounds for affording him less protection against confinement in a mental institution than all others are given. Of course, if the person is actually dangerous, the observations of the Criminal Law Revision Committee, (3rd report, 1963) apply:[42]

"The possibility that the accused is innocent cannot be excluded, and if he is it is an injustice that he should be dealt with as a person unfit to plead; if he is insane and dangerous, he should be dealt with, if at all, under the provisions of the Mental Health Act 1959 which relate to non-criminals. It might even possibly happen that a crime might be falsely attributed to an insane person or a deaf mute with the object of getting him detained as unfit to plead."

Regardless of whether the person is guilty or innocent of the crime charged, he may feel that he deserves a court hearing on the facts. MIND has heard several complaints from patients who feel it is unjust that they are indefinitely confined without having ever been tried for the crime charged. This sense of grievance may in itself make them resist treatment.

A finding of facts is also important for the professionals who have care of the patients, since they will want as much information as possible about their alleged criminal behaviour. They may prefer to rely on a court determination rather than on the speculation and hearsay which is often found in a patient's hospital record.

Accordingly, MIND takes the view that the facts of the case must be inquired into publicly by the court, without undue delay. Incompetent defendants should sometimes be excused from trial, but the excuse should be only temporary; trial should be delayed only long enough to permit a disabled defendant to become more competent. At some point, regardless of whether

*The Home Office, however, has given instructions to preserve certain medical reports, at least for the time being, for the purposes of the Fisher Inquiry.

he has yet regained competence, the facts surrounding the criminal charge should be rigorously determined by the court under procedural rules which as far as possible redress the incapacities suffered by the particular defendant.[43]

MIND specifically endorses the following proposal made by the Butler Committee:[44] when the question is raised whether the defendant is under disability, it should be decided immediately. If disability is found but the medical evidence suggests that recovery is possible within a few months, the judge can adjourn the proceedings for a maximum of six months,† during which time the defendant will undergo treatment. The trial may be reconvened at any point during this period on medical evidence that the accused is either recovered, or on the other hand has not responded to treatment. At the adjourned proceedings, the question of disability will be re-opened. It may then be found that the defendant has become fit to stand trial. If he is found to be still under disability, a finding of facts will take place; the object of this is to enable the jury to return a verdict of not guilty where the evidence is not sufficient for a conviction. If the jury finds that the defendant actually committed the criminal act, he will not be found guilty, because his disability has made it impossible for him to contest his guilt fully. Instead, the Butler Committee recommended the verdict that "the defendant should be dealt with as a person under disability".

Disposal

As has already been stated, when a person is found unfit to stand trial, the court has no choice but to make an order for his admission to hospital, with special restrictions imposed without limit of time. On the other hand, once a conviction has been registered, the court has discretionary power under sections 60 and 65 of the Mental Health Act to make a hospital order with or without restrictions, for whatever period it considers necessary; it may also pass a non-custodial sentence such as a psychiatric probation order. It is anomalous that the court has considerable discretion in dealing with a convicted person, but has none in dealing with a person who has not even stood trial for the crime charged.

Accordingly, the present law should be changed to give the court wide discretion in the matter of disposal. The Butler Committee recommended[44] that the court should have the power to make any of the following social or medical orders:*

(a) an order for in-patient treatment in hospital with or without a restriction order
(b) an order for hospital out-patient treatment
(c) an order for forfeiture of any firearm, motor vehicle, etc., used in crime

---

†The adjournment should be for up to three months in the first place, with renewals of one month at a time, up to a maximum of six months.

*Notably, a penal disposal – prison, borstal, or a fine – is not included within the recommendations.

(d) a guardianship order

(e) any disqualification (e.g. from driving) normally open to the court to make on conviction

(f) discharge without any order.

The usual criteria for the making of orders under (a), (b) and (d) should be observed.

The wide discretion given to the courts in Butler's proposals reflects the Committee's feeling that hospital admission should not inevitably follow a finding of disability in relation to the trial. If the court is satisfied that some other arrangement can be made which serves the best interests of the individual and the public (such as his admission to a hostel or his return home), it is preferable that this should be done.

Accordingly, if disability is found, a social inquiry report should be obtained from either the local authority social services department or the probation and after care service, to enable the court to consider all possible alternatives to hospital admission.†

MIND endorses these recommendations. We offer the single modification that a hospital order made under (a) above, with or without restrictions, should have a limited duration, in proportion to the severity of the alleged offence. Indefinite confinements should be authorised only for life-carrying offences or, alternatively, those offences which qualify for the reviewable sentence proposed in Appendix 4 of the Butler Report. A more detailed account of MIND's recommendations on sections 60/65 of the Act is given in Chapter 5 of this report.*

†For an account of the related concept of least restrictive alternative and of the social inquiry report, see Volume I of this report (pp. 13-14 and 142-145).

*It might be useful now to draw attention to the triviality of some offences for which defendants are found unfit to plead and given a mandatory restriction order. In 1974, for example, disability was found in cases where the defendant was charged with such offences as shoplifting, minor thefts, handling stolen goods and minor fraud.[2] In these cases it might have been an advantage for the defendant to stand trial, even if he were convicted. The judge would at least have had the option of making a hospital order without restrictions, or a psychiatric probation order. Even if he had passed a sentence of imprisonment, it would have been minimal, and the defendant could thereafter have received treatment informally or under Part IV of the Act. Any of these options would have been more attractive than an unlimited restriction order, which must be made after a finding of unfitness to plead.

References and Notes

1. *Royal Commission on Capital Punishment,* 1953, HMSO, Cmnd. 8932, para. 219.
2. *Criminal Statistics in England and Wales for 1974,* HMSO, Cmnd. 6168.
3. Mental Health Act 1959, ss. 72, 73.
4. *Ibid.,* s. 72(2).
5. *Ibid.,* s. 72(3).
6. *Ibid.,* s. 76(1).
7. *Ibid.,* s. 76(2)(a).
8. *Ibid.,* s. 76(2)(b).
9. *Ibid.,* s. 76(3).
10. Letter from Michael Bellis, of Edward Oliver and Bellis, *The Times,* November 11, 1975.
11. *The Butler Report,* para. 10.3.
12. *Royal Commission on Capital Punishment,* reference 1, para. 233.
13. R v Podola [1960] 1 Q.B.325.
14. R v Robertson [1968] 3 All E.R.557.
15. Criminal Procedure (Insanity) Act 1964, s. 4(1).
16. J. C. Smith and B. Hogan, *Criminal Law,* 3rd ed., 1973, p.132; R v McCarthy [1966] 1 All E.R.447, discussed by A. R. Poole, "Standing mute and fitness to plead", *Crim. L. Rev.* (1966), p.6.
17. R v Podola, *op. cit.,* p. 330.
18. *The Butler Report,* para. 10.16.
19. Smith and Hogan, *op. cit.,* p. 133.
20. R v Webb [1969] 2 Q.B.278; [1969] 2 All E.R.626.
21. R v Burles [1970] 2 Q.B.191; [1970] 1 All E.R.642.
22. Criminal Procedure (Insanity) Act 1964, s. 4(4)(a).
23. *Ibid.,* s. 4(4)(b).
24. *The Butler Report,* para. 10.33. See also Boaks v Reece [1957] 1 Q.B.219.
25. Criminal Justice Act 1967, s. 21.
26. See generally, the Cobden Trust Report on "Bail or Custody".
27. *The Butler Report,* para. 10.35.
28. Criminal Procedure (Insanity) Act 1964, s. 4(5).
29. *Ibid.,* s. 5(1)(c).
30. *Ibid.,* 1st Schedule, "Effect of Orders for Admission to Hospital".
31. *The Butler Report,* para. 10.17.
32. *Hansard,* November 25, 1975, Written Answer No.40.
33. Leading article in *The Times,* October 18, 1975.
34. *New Psychiatry,* November 6, 1975 and January 16, 1975.
35. *The Guardian,* June 25, October 18 and October 31, 1975; *Sunday Times,* October 19, 1975; *Daily Mirror,* October 10, 1975.
36. *Hansard,* March 5, 1975, pp. 1486-88.
37. C. T. Latham and J. Richman (eds.) *Stone's Justices' Manual,* 106th ed., vol. 1, 1974, pp. 435-438.
38. Statement made to court in Hails' case by Dr. John Hawkins, *The Observer,* February 29, 1976.
39. *The Times,* May 7, 1976.
40. *The Butler Report,* para. 10.18.
41. Information obtained directly from Christopher Price, M.P., and reported in MIND Information Bulletin No. 14, February 1976.
42. *Criminal Law Revision Committee,* 3rd report, 1963, HMSO, Cmnd. 2149, para. 20.
43. Rough guidelines for procedural rules which may be adopted for this purpose are provided by Burt and Morris. "A proposal for the Abolition of the Incompetency Plea", *U. Chicago L. Rev.* vol. 40, 1972, p.72.
44. *The Butler Report,* Ch.10.

2. Hospital order without restrictions: Exposition of the present law

In pursuance of section 60 of the Mental Health Act 1959, a court may authorise a person's admission to, and detention in, a specified mental hospital, or place him under the guardianship of the social services department of a local authority, or a person approved by the authority.[1] Where an order is made under this section, the court cannot pass sentence of imprisonment, impose a fine or make a probation order in respect of the offence. However, it can make any other order within its powers[2] – for example, it can disqualify the person from driving, or order him to pay costs.

The following conditions must be fulfilled if a hospital or guardianship order is to be made. First, the person must have been convicted of an offence: in the Crown Court, an offence other than one for which the sentence is fixed;*[3] in a magistrates' court, an offence punishable on summary conviction† with imprisonment.

A magistrates' court may make a hospital or guardianship order without recording a conviction if satisfied (where the accused suffers from mental illness or severe subnormality) that he committed the act or made the omission charged.[4]‡ In 1973 the magistrates' courts made 758 hospital orders; 86 (11%) of these were made without a finding of guilt.[5] The corresponding figure for 1974 was 10%.[6]

Secondly, the court must be satisfied, on the written or oral evidence of two medical practitioners, that the offender is suffering from one or more of the

---

*It is the almost invariable practice of Parliament to fix a maximum but no minimum sentence, and to leave it to the judge or magistrate to set the sentence, which can vary from an absolute discharge to the statutory maximum. The only significant exception is murder, where the court must impose a sentence of life imprisonment under section 1(1) of the Murder (Abolition of Death Penalty) Act 1965. Notably, the Butler Report has suggested that there should not be a fixed life sentence for murder, and MIND agrees with this suggestion. The other offences for which the sentence is fixed by law are treason (Treason Act 1814, s. 1) and piracy with violence (Piracy Act 1837, s. 2).

†For procedural purposes crimes are classified as indictable and summary offences. Summary offences may be tried by courts having summary jurisdiction, and the trial is conducted by magistrates without a jury; but all proceedings on indictment take place before a jury and are brought before the Crown Court (Courts Act 1971, s. 6). When the Crown Court sits in the City of London it is known as the Central Criminal Court (s. 4(7)). Thus, for practical purposes, the difference between summary trial and trial on indictment is the presence or absence of a jury. In other respects the trial is similar. Generally speaking, an indictable offence is more serious than a summary offence.

‡The Butler Committee (para. 10.34) recommended the repeal of section 60(2) of the Mental Health Act, which authorises the magistrates' court to make a hospital order without recording a conviction. MIND supports this recommendation.

four specific forms of mental disorder (mental illness, psychopathic disorder, subnormality or severe subnormality), and that the mental disorder is of a nature or degree which warrants his detention in hospital for medical treatment.[7] The medical practitioners must specify and agree on the particular form of mental disorder† (although either of them may also describe him as suffering from another form[8]). It was noted in *Smith's* case[9] that if the two medical practitioners diagnosed the same form of mental disorder (e.g. mental illness), that would satisfy the requirements of section 60. It did not matter that one psychiatrist made a more specific diagnosis (e.g. paranoid schizophrenia), while the other only diagnosed mental illness.

Thirdly, the court must be of the opinion, considering all the circumstances, including the nature of the offence and the character and antecedents of the offender, and the other available methods of dealing with him, that the most suitable method of disposing of the case is a section 60 order.[10] There are no further standards to guide the courts in making hospital orders, and the concept of dangerousness to self or others is absent from the criteria for a section 60 order. In comparison, a civil admission for observation or treatment requires a showing that detention "is necessary in the interests of the patient's health or safety or for the protection of other persons".[11]

Finally, a hospital order under section 60 cannot be made unless the admission of the offender to the hospital specified in the order has been arranged; and he must be admitted to that hospital within 28 days from the date on which the hospital order is made.[12] In practice, this means that the court must be satisfied that the hospital specified in the order is willing to accept the offender. It may specify a special hospital (Broadmoor, Rampton, Moss Side or Park Lane) if the offender is thought to be dangerous; otherwise he will normally be admitted to an ordinary psychiatric hospital in his home area.

Similarly, the court cannot make a guardianship order under section 60 unless it is satisfied that the local authority is willing to receive the offender into guardianship.[13]

The Court of Appeal has jurisdiction under section 97(7) of the Criminal Justice Act 1967 to act upon new medical evidence, and make a section 60 order in substitution for another sentence.[14] Further, because a hospital or guardianship order is not considered more severe than imprisonment, section 4(2) of the Criminal Appeal Act 1966 allows the substitution of a section 60 order for a term of imprisonment.[15]

---

†Section 4 of the Mental Health Act defines the other three specific forms of mental disorder (psychopathic disorder, subnormality and severe subnormality), but not "mental illness". The term "mental disorder" is defined to include the four specific disorders "and any other disorder or disability of the mind". Notably, a person may be civilly admitted to hospital either informally or under sections 25, 29 or 136 of the Act, even if he is not suffering from one of the four specific forms of mental disorder, so long as he is considered to be suffering from " any other disorder or disability of the mind". This is not so in a civil admission for treatment under section 26, nor for a hospital order under section 60.

Medical evidence in hospital order cases

The medical evidence must be given by two medical practitioners, at least one of whom must be approved by an Area Health Authority for the purposes of section 28 of the Act as having special experience in the diagnosis or treatment of mental disorders.[16] The evidence of a medical practitioner may be in the form of a signed report, in which case the court may also require that he be called to give oral evidence.[17] Where the court has directed that a medical report be produced in evidence "otherwise than by or on behalf of the accused", a copy must be given to counsel or the solicitor who represents the accused.[18] If he is not legally represented* he must be informed of the substance of the report; where he is a child or young person, his parent or guardian must be so informed.[19] The Court of Appeal has also thought it advisable that the judge should hear evidence from the doctor who will be treating the offender.[20]

The accused may require that the medical practitioner be called to give oral evidence, and evidence to rebut that contained in the medical report may be called by or on behalf of the accused.[21]

Preference for a hospital order over a sentence of imprisonment

It is generally thought that where sufficient medical evidence is given to satisfy the criteria and procedures of the Mental Health Act and where it is consistent with public safety, the court should make a hospital order,[22] rather than sentencing the offender to imprisonment and relying on the Home Secretary to transfer him to hospital under section 72 of the Act.[23] The only exceptions are where:

(a) there is a particular need to mark the gravity of the offence with punishment. Thus, in extreme cases where the defendant has committed a particularly heinous crime, the court may impose a sentence of imprisonment even if there is sufficient medical evidence to warrant a hospital order;[24]

(b) the offender presents a danger to the public and a place cannot be found for him in a *secure* hospital;[25]

(c) the offender is not susceptible to psychiatric treatment.[26] Thus, it is unusual for a court to make a hospital order if the offender is suffering from a mental disorder for which there is no treatment available (for example, some psychopathic disorders) or the prospects of successful treatment are negligible.

---

*The Court of Appeal has said in R v Blackwood [1974] Cr.App.R. 170 that "when the court is considering the making of orders under section 60, and particularly under section 65, of the Mental Health Act, a defendant should be represented by counsel".

The effect of a hospital order

A hospital order made under section 60 is sufficient authority for a constable, a social worker or any other person directed by the court to convey the patient to the hospital specified in the order within a period of 28 days from the making of the order.[27] The order authorises the hospital managers to admit him to hospital at any time within that period, and thereafter detain him in accordance with the Mental Health Act.[28] (The National Health Service Reorganisation Act 1973, Schedule 4, para. 90 has designated Area Health Authorities as managers; under section 59 of the 1959 Act the Secretary of State for Social Services acts as the manager of the special hospitals.) The court may order that he be conveyed to a place of safety pending his admission to hospital within the 28-day period.[29] If the hospital specified is unable to receive the patient within this period, the Secretary of State for Social Services may direct his admission to another hospital.[30]

The effect of a hospital order is to place the person in hospital on a similar basis to a patient admitted for treatment under the civil provisions of section 26 of the Act.[31] However, if a patient is under a hospital order, the nearest relative cannot exercise the right provided in section 47 to order his discharge.[32] In addition, the age-limits laid down in sections 26 and 44 for the admission and detention of psychopathic and subnormal patients do not apply to patients detained under a hospital order.[33]

Patients admitted to hospital under section 60 may be detained for a period not exceeding one year. The authority for detention may be renewed for a further year, and thereafter for two years at a time. The renewal is made by the responsible medical officer: he must examine the patient within the two months before the day on which the authority for detention ceases. If it appears to him that "it is necessary in the interests of the patient's health or safety or for the protection of other persons that the patient should continue to be liable to be detained" he reports this to the managers. This has the effect of renewing the authority for detention.[34]†

In making a hospital order, the court is placing the patient in the hands of doctors, and is nominally foregoing the imposition of punishment. Therefore (unless the order is coupled with a restriction order under section 65), the court and the Home Office relinquish control over the patient; either the responsible medical officer, a Mental Health Review Tribunal or the hospital managers can discharge the patient at any time.

When a patient is admitted to hospital under a section 60 order, any previous application, hospital or guardianship order under which he is liable to be detained ceases,[36] unless it has been made with an order under section

†The Butler Report rightly points out that the criteria given in section 123 for Mental Health Review Tribunals to decide upon the discharge of a patient are different from those used by the RMO for renewal. Thus the RMO need not find that the person is suffering from a specified form of mental disorder in order to renew the authority for detention: the tribunal, if it finds no evidence of a mental disorder, *must* discharge the patient even if there is good evidence that he could pose a danger to society.[35]

65 restricting discharge.[37] If, however, the section 60 order is quashed on appeal, the original application or order will remain in full effect.[36]

A patient under a section 60 order, or his nearest relative, has the same right to apply to a Mental Health Review Tribunal as a patient admitted for treatment under section 26;* the tribunal has the same powers and follows the same procedures. This means that the patient may apply for a tribunal hearing within the six months following the making of the order. He may also apply at any time during each period of renewal. The nearest relative may apply to the tribunal up to twelve months after the making of the order, and in any subsequent period of twelve months.[38] The tribunal has the power to discharge the patient, but does not have any lesser powers – for example, to order a transfer to another hospital or to grant a conditional or delayed discharge.[39]

The effect of a guardianship order

A guardianship order under section 60 confers on the authority or person named as guardian the same powers as a guardianship application made and accepted under sections 33 and 34 of the Mental Health Act, except that the age-limits for psychopathic and subnormal patients do not apply, and the nearest relative has no power to discharge the patient from guardianship.[40]

Guardianship can legally require a person to accept the help or advice of a local authority (or a person named in the order) on a wide range of issues such as employment, residence, training and treatment. Once someone is accepted into guardianship, the local authority or person named as guardian has the power to exercise control over him as if he were under 14 years of age and the guardian were his father.[41]

Hospital or guardianship order made under the Children and Young Persons Act 1969

Section 1 of the Children and Young Persons Act 1969 provides that a Juvenile Court may make any of the following orders in respect of a child under the age of 17 years: (a) an order requiring the parent or guardian to take proper care and exercise proper control of the child or young person; (b) a supervision order; (c) a care order (other than an interim order); (d) a hospital order within the meaning of Part V of the Mental Health Act 1959; or (e) a guardianship order within the meaning of the 1959 Act.

The court may make any of these orders if satisfied that any of the conditions set out in section 1(2) of the 1969 Act is met† and that the child or

---

*A patient of less than 16 years of age may not apply to a Mental Health Review Tribunal.[38]

†One of the conditions set out in section 1(2) is that the child or young person is guilty of an offence, excluding homicide.

young person is in need of care or control which he is unlikely to receive unless such an order is made.

The Juvenile Court cannot make a hospital or guardianship order unless the conditions under section 60 of the 1959 Act are also satisfied. It may then make the order as if the child or young person had been convicted of an offence punishable on summary conviction by imprisonment.[42]

A court which makes a hospital or guardianship order cannot also pass sentence of imprisonment, impose a fine, or make a probation order, a supervision order or an order binding over the parents under sections 7(7)(a) and (b) of the 1969 Act. Subject to these restrictions the court may make any other order within its powers.[43]

Before proceeding to the next chapter, which makes some observations on hospital orders without restrictions, the reader may find it useful to refer to Table 3 in Chapter 4, which summarises the more important legal provisions that have just been outlined.

References and Notes

1. Mental Health Act 1959, s. 60(1).
2. *Ibid.*, s. 60(6).
3. In R v Morris [1951] 1 K.B. 394, the Court of Criminal Appeal affirmed the rule that where the punishment for a criminal offence is not laid down by statute, the judge may fix the period of imprisonment at his discretion.
4. Mental Health Act 1959, s. 60(2).
5. *Criminal Statistics in England and Wales for 1973*, HMSO, Cmnd. 5677, pp. 62-63.
6. *Criminal Statistics in England and Wales for 1974*, HMSO, Cmnd. 6168, pp. 60-61 and 70-71.
7. There are no age limits for subnormal or psychopathic patients as in section 26 of the Act.
8. Mental Health Act 1959, ss. 26(4), 60(5). See also N. Walker and S. McCabe, *Crime and Insanity in England,* vol. 2, 1973, pp. 82-85.
9. R v Nigel Gordon Smith, not reported. Judgement given July 30, 1974.
10. Mental Health Act 1959, s. 60(3).
11. Section 26(2)(b) of the Mental Health Act uses the words "it is necessary" while section 25(2)(b) uses the word "ought".
12. Mental Health Act 1959, s. 60(3).
13. *Ibid.*, s. 60(4).
14. R v Greenburg [1964] *Crim. L. Rev.* 236; R v Rafi [1967] *Crim. L. Rev.* 715; R v Farrel [1967] *Crim. L. Rev.* 185.
15. R v Bennett [1968] 2 All E.R. 753; 1 W.L.R. 988. See generally S. White, "Assessing the severity of sentence on appeal", *Modern L. Rev.,* vol. 36, 1973, p. 388.
16. Mental Health Act 1959, s. 62(1).
17. *Ibid.*, s. 62(2).
18. *Ibid.*, s. 62(3)(a).
19. *Ibid.*, s. 62(3)(b).
20. R. v Blackwood [1974] 59 Cr.App.R. 170.
21. Mental Health Act 1959, s. 62(3)(c).
22. R v Cox [1967] 52 Cr.App.R. 130. See also the commentary in *Crim. L. Rev.,* 1971, pp. 664-665; 1972, pp. 323-324; 1974, p. 438; P. Fallon, *Crown Court Practice: Sentence,* 1975, pp. 118-134.
23. R v James [1961] *Crim. L. Rev.* 842; R v Cox [1968] 1 All E.R. 386.

24. R v Morris [1961] 2 Q.B. 237; R v Higginbotham [1961] 45 Cr.App.R. 379; R v Gunnell [1966] 50 Cr.App.R. 242; R v Harvey and Ryan [1971] *Crim. L. Rev.* 644. See generally N. Walker and S. McCabe, *op cit.,* pp. 86-89; D. A. Thomas, *Principles of Sentencing,* 1970, ch. 7.
25. R v Higginbotham [1961] 3 All E.R. 616; R v Morris [1961] 2 All E.R. 672; R v Cook [1969] *Crim. L. Rev.* 98; R v Horan [1974] *Crim. L. Rev.* 438.
26. R v Gills [1967] *Crim. L. Rev.* 247; R v Woolland [1967] 51 Cr.App.R. 65; R v Carr, *The Guardian,* March 26, 1963; R v Nicholls, not reported. Judgment given April 16, 1973.
27. Mental Health Act 1959, s. 63(1)(a).
28. *Ibid.,* s. 63(1)(b).
29. *Ibid.,* s. 64(1).
30. *Ibid.,* s. 64(2).
31. *Ibid.,* s. 63(3).
32. *Ibid.,* s. 63(3)(a).
33. *Ibid.,* s. 63(3)(b).
34. *Ibid.,* s. 43.
35. *The Butler Report,* HMSO, Cmnd. 6244, 1975, paras. 14.18-14.19.
36. Mental Health Act 1959, s. 63(5).
37. *Ibid.,* s. 65(4).
38. *Ibid.,* s. 63(4).
39. L. Gostin, *A Human Condition,* vol. 1, pp. 62-64.
40. Mental Health Act 1959, ss. 63(2), 63(3).
41. *Ibid.,* s. 34(1).
42. Children and Young Persons Act 1969, s. 1; Mental Health Act 1959, s. 80(2) (". . . an offence punishable on summary conviction with imprisonment shall be construed without regard to any prohibition or restriction imposed by or under an enactment on the imprisonment of young offenders").
43. Mental Health Act 1959, s. 60(6); *The Guardian,* May 12, 1976.

3. Hospital orders without restrictions: Some observations and proposals for reform

Section 60 in the courts: Some illustrative case studies

Who tenders the psychiatric reports in evidence?

The medical evidence required under section 62 of the Act may be adduced by either party, or by the court itself.* The defence may refute the psychiatric reports obtained by the court or the prosecution, either through cross-examination or by tendering its own psychiatric evidence on behalf of the accused. This appears to offer the defence sufficient opportunity to submit evidence either in support of or against the making of a hospital order with or without restrictions.

Defence solicitors, however, may feel that a hospital order is a 'soft option' for their client. They may not know that the courts at present tend to make hospital orders subject to special restrictions without limit of time. They also may not be aware of the full effects of a restriction order† i.e. that the defendant may be admitted to a high-security institution such as Broadmoor, to be released only with the consent of the Home Secretary. Accordingly, they may request or agree to a psychiatric disposal without the full knowledge or consent of their client. Sometimes the defendant has never seen the psychiatric reports, and has had no opportunity to present evidence against the making of a section 60 order. Unfortunately, a client who is charged with a crime and who may also have social or psychiatric problems is in a vulnerable position and is often fully reliant on the knowledge, understanding and good faith of his lawyer.

---

*Medical evidence for the purposes of section 62 is normally obtained by remanding the defendant in custody for an examination by a prison psychiatrist. The Home Office Report on the Work of the Prison Department, 1974, p. 49, reported that 12,530 persons were remanded in custody for psychiatric investigation in 1974; in 1973 the figure was 12,542.
†The legal profession has at times misunderstood the true effects of a hospital order. For example, in *R. v Harvey and Ryan*[1] the court failed to distinguish between a hospital order with and without restrictions. It said that a hospital order allows the patient to claim the right of discharge if "cured". Of course, if the patient is subject to a restriction order, a tribunal cannot discharge him; at best it can only recommend discharge to the Home Secretary. The Home Office does not regard itself as legally obliged to accept this advice if the patient is 'cured', but still in its view presents a risk to the public.
Section 65 is sometimes misunderstood even by clinicians. For example, in *Evaluating Community Psychiatric Service*, edited by J. K. Wing and A. M. Hailey, section 65 is described as an "admission under court order with the proviso that only the court can discharge the order" (p.223). Of course, once a court makes a section 65 order only the Home Secretary can discharge it (except on appeal).

The following two case studies illustrate the point:

M's Case

A patient aged 25 was convicted of arson in which the damage caused amounted to less than £50. He was put on probation. During his probation he was found guilty of dangerous driving, for which the maximum prison sentence is two years. No injury was caused by his dangerous driving.

The patient and his parents did not want a hospital order, but preferred a prison sentence. If a hospital order was to be considered, they wanted the patient's Royal Navy psychiatrist to furnish one of the two necessary medical reports to the court. This psychiatrist, who had known him for several years, was the only doctor who knew him well. The Royal Navy psychiatrist was firmly opposed to the making of a hospital order with restrictions in this case.

But, contrary to the express wishes of M and his parents, the lawyer did not submit the Royal Navy psychiatrist's report. When speaking to the sentencing court, she said:

> "We have on our own initiative obtained medical reports which all appear to point to the conclusion that the accused is and has been ill for some time and is in need of medical treatment, and he accepts that. He would have preferred that an order should not have been made under section 65, but in view of the recommendations of the doctors, I think I would have been at great difficulty in attempting to persuade your Lordships to make any other order."

The patient was placed under a hospital order with restrictions and without limit of time. He has now been in a special hospital for more than three years, one year longer than the maximum prison sentence for dangerous driving.

DMF's Case[2]

The Divisional Court refused an application by Miss DMF, aged 28, at present detained in Rampton Hospital, for an order of *certiorari* to quash a hospital order made by the magistrates' court. She had been un-represented at the magistrates' court hearing, and the substance of the medical reports had not been disclosed to her (as required by s. 62(3)(b)). Nor did the justices acquaint her with her right to have medical practitioners present for cross-examination or to call evidence in rebuttal (s. 62(3)(d)). In spite of these inequities, the Divisional Court refused to quash the hospital order.

The defence has ample opportunity to submit its own psychiatric reports, without waiting for the court to take the initiative. In fact, in one case reported to MIND, the solicitor surveyed a wide range of psychiatric opinions and submitted only those that were opposed to the making of a hospital order.

In the following case, the solicitor appeared unaware of the procedural rights of his client.

Evans' Case[3]

After three years as an informal patient in a local NHS hospital, a young woman aged 20 set fire to a chair. The fire was immediately extinguished by a nurse. The patient was charged with arson. The RMO pressed the charge, because he had held from the beginning that the patient should be in a high-security hospital, but no such institution had been willing to receive her.

The patient's parents and solicitors contacted MIND's Rights Service because they were in a dilemma. They wanted a hospital order to be made, but feared that this would not occur because of the trivial nature of the offence. If no hospital order were made and the patient were conditionally discharged by the court, the RMO would refuse to re-admit her. The parents felt they could not have their child in the home, and the local social services department refused to accept any responsibility. Thus, if no hospital order were made, the patient would have nowhere to go.

The solicitor was not aware that he could tender psychiatric reports in evidence, so that during the trial no reports were presented to the court in support of a section 60 order. On the advice of MIND, counsel asked for a court adjournment in order to secure the two requisite reports. It was MIND's opinion, however, that a restriction order was unnecessary in this case, and that the parents wanted the courts to fill the gap left by the social services, because they felt unable to cope with their daughter.

When the hearing was re-convened, two medical reports were presented and Miss Evans was admitted to Rampton Special Hospital under a restriction order made without limit of time. The medical evidence presented to the court pointed out that she was "suffering from a personality disorder that is not susceptible to any known form of psychiatric treatment".

With this prognosis, Miss Evans at the age of 20 faces indefinite and long-term confinement in a maximum-security institution.

The court may have violated two important legal principals in *Evans'* case:

1. The Mental Health Act does not authorise the making of a hospital order unless the offender is suffering from a mental disorder which is susceptible to psychiatric treatment.[4] This principle has been reiterated by the Court of Appeal[5] and reinforced by the Butler Committee.[6] The medical evidence presented to the court clearly indicated that, although suffering from a personality disorder, Miss Evans would not benefit from treatment.

2. A court should not use the criminal law to correct the deficiencies in the health and social services. This principle was established by the Court of Appeal in the following case.

Clarke's Case[7]

Dawn Clarke had a long history of criminal convictions, mostly of the type which could be described as social nuisances. In 1970 she was convicted of unlawful possession of cannabis and was sent to Rampton Special Hospital.

After her discharge from Rampton by a Mental Health Review Tribunal, her behaviour was described as "eccentric and anti-social". She was admitted to a local hospital after taking an overdose of Anadin. She was subsequently discharged from that hospital but refused to leave because she had 'nowhere to go'.

When pressure was put on her to leave she called the police. While the police and the hospital employees were talking about her in the adjoining room, she smashed a flower pot on the floor, causing damage worth £1. She was charged with criminal damage.

She was interviewed by the prison psychiatrist, who diagnosed her as psychopathic but said no hospital could properly treat her. The court commented: "It is surprising that the diagnosis should have been made in those terms when Rampton's medical staff only about two months ago told the tribunal that treatment was necessary and that the appellant was making some progress."

The court also looked into the possibility of a probation order, but the Probation and After Care Service said they could not cope with Miss Clarke. The local social services also would not accept responsibility for her. On this evidence the trial court passed a sentence of 18 months' imprisonment.

The Court of Appeal reversed this decision and said:

"If the Courts become disposers of those who are socially inconvenient the road ahead would lead to restriction of liberty. It should be clearly understood that HM Judges stand on the road barring the way . . . .
The NHS and the social services cannot cope with a woman of this type who does not require treatment (so it is said) but who cannot live in the community without disturbing others . . . . This court has no intention of filling that gap by sending people to prison . . . . 'sentences should fit crimes' . . . . We ask ourselves, what was the appropriate sentence for breaking a flower pot? The answer is a fine of £2."

Examining the evidence that underlies the experts' judgment

If the two medical reports both state that a hospital order should be made, this virtually decides the issue; the courts have not often taken the initiative to safeguard the defendant's liberty by fully examining the evidence that underlies the experts' judgment. As the Court of Appeal said in *Smith's* case,[8] "only in most exceptional circumstances would it interfere with the clinical judgment of doctors."

The Court of Appeal should be more careful and discriminating when deciding whether to make a hospital order with restrictions. It was the Court of Appeal itself that set the standard in *Turner's* case: "Before a court can assess the value of a psychiatrist's opinion it has to know the facts upon which it was based."[9]

Psychiatric evidence is important to the court in deciding whether to make a hospital order with restrictions. Yet sections 60/65 require that other factors be considered which are outside the scope of medical expertise – for example, the nature of the offence, the antecedents of the offender, and other available methods of dealing with him. Even the need to protect the public requires the consideration of social factors which cannot be sufficiently assessed in a psychiatric interview. In fact, a social inquiry report by the probation service or local social services should be a legal prerequisite for the making of a hospital order.

Furthermore, not all doctors are sufficiently aware of the technicalities of the Mental Health Act to make the legal conclusion that a section 65 order should be made. In *Blackwood's* case,[10] the psychiatrist was asked whether an order "without limit of time" should be imposed. He did not fully understand the question, but nonetheless agreed that this was the appropriate order. Later, he said he had not realised that the Home Secretary would have to be consulted before the patient could be transferred or discharged; if he had understood he would never have agreed. On appeal, a conditional discharge for three years was substituted for the restriction order.

When the court is hearing and evaluating medical evidence, it should observe every propriety; the procedures laid down by the Mental Health Act and by ordinary concepts of criminal justice are no less important for the mentally abnormal offender than for all others charged with imprisonable offences.

Absence without leave

The principles by which a court should be guided in deciding whether to make a hospital order with restrictions were laid down in the cases of *Gardiner*[11] and *Toland*.[12] In *Gardiner's* case, the court took the view that "some courts do not fully appreciate the advisability in some cases of making a Restriction Order", and that "they should be made in all cases where it is thought that the protection of the public is required". Further, the court thought that "the safer course is to make a Restriction Order unlimited in point of time".

In *Gardiner's* case the Court of Appeal was reluctant to make a hospital order without restrictions, partly because of the provisions of section 40(3) of the Mental Health Act, which apply to unrestricted, but not to restricted, patients. Under section 40(3), if an unrestricted patient escapes and remains at liberty (or is otherwise absent without leave) for 28 days, he cannot be readmitted to the hospital, except on a voluntary basis or through the procedures for compulsory admission contained in Part IV of the Act.*

The Royal Commission on the Law Relating to Mental Illness and Mental Deficiency (the Percy Committee)[13] recommended that this provision be made for patients civilly admitted to hospital, presumably in the belief that

*The 28-day period is extended to six months in the case of a psychopathic or subnormal patient over the age of 21.

if a patient is able to remain at liberty for that amount of time, he no longer needs in-hospital treatment.* For some reason, The Third Schedule of the Act made section 40(3) applicable to patients detained under a hospital order without restrictions.

A patient who is subject to a hospital order has been convicted of an imprisonable offence, and it is improper that legal custody should be so easily lost if he absconds from hospital. Under these circumstances, the courts will naturally be reluctant to make a hospital order without restrictions, even if the offence is not serious enough to justify all the restrictive effects of a section 65 order. Accordingly, MIND recommends that the Government should repeal section 40(3) insofar as it applies to patients under hospital orders.

Compulsory after-care and supervision for the unrestricted patient

In *Gardiner's* case, the Court also expressed some concern that for patients under a hospital order without restrictions, after-care is available only on a voluntary basis. Indeed, medical practitioners in the special hospitals sometimes regard restriction orders as essential, so that the offender can be made subject to mandatory after-care and supervision.† In a talk to a local branch of the British Association of Social Workers, Dr James McKeith, consultant psychiatrist at Broadmoor, maintained that a restriction order made it easier for him to discharge a patient because it guaranteed more effective supervision for the offender in the community. Dr Patrick McGrath, physician superintendent at Broadmoor, has similarly stated that a restricted patient "does not have to become subject to section 25 or 26 to be re-admitted to the hospital. His conditional discharge can be revoked at any moment". Dr McGrath gave examples of cases in which this power of recall was, in his opinion, vital as a life-saving procedure – at the first sign of danger to self or others, the patient could be quickly recalled to hospital.[14] Although in some cases a section 65 order lasts too long and is over-restrictive (Dr McGrath pointed out that "conditional discharges are subject to such conditions by and large for the rest of their lives"), there is merit in what these Broadmoor consultants have said.

---

*N. Walker & S. McCabe, in *Crime and Insanity in England*, vol. 2, p.166 aptly comment: "The truth is that discharge by operation of the law [under section 40(3)] is a very crude and questionable safeguard . . . It dates from a time when the only other safeguard against the unscrupulous relative and the complacent doctor was the Justice of the Peace. Now that the patient – including a hospital order patient – can have recourse to a tribunal, is there a need for it? So far as hospital orders are concerned the rescue is by no means academic. No less than 78 of our men and 26 of our women gained their legal freedom in this way within twelve months of being committed to hospital".

†A restricted patient can be discharged by the Home Secretary subject to specific conditions. For example, the patient can be required to remain in a known residence or make regular visits to a local social worker or general practitioner. If he fails to comply with any of these conditions he can be recalled to hospital.

A substantial volume of evidence given to the Butler Committee suggested that after-care should be compulsory for all patients under hospital orders.[15] The Magistrates' Association, for example, thought that a conditional discharge should be arranged on a similar basis to the parole system for prisoners released on licence. The consultant forensic psychiatrists thought that unrestricted patients should be subject to the same compulsory after-care system as offenders under psychiatric probation orders.

There is also some evidence that after-care and supervision of the offender make a re-conviction less likely, and result in a more stable employment record.[16] This research goes hand in hand with the substantial body of professional literature, concerning both abnormal[17] and ordinary offenders,[18] which argues the case for community care as opposed to institutional treatment.

Although the Butler Committee was well informed of these arguments, it took the view that after-care should not be mandatory for unrestricted patients. Instead, it suggested[19] that hospitals should take advantage of the provisions of section 39 of the Mental Health Act, which provides that compulsory patients may be given leave of absence from the hospital. They are subject to recall at any time during the leave of absence, but the power to revoke the leave itself lapses after six months.

The Butler Committee was right to emphasise the existing authority of doctors to grant a leave of absence. Indeed, section 39 should be used much more often by the medical profession, both for hospital order patients and for those detained under Part IV of the Act. Nevertheless, leave of absence is limited to six months, and if during this period the patient has not returned to the hospital, the authority for his detention ceases. As a result, in actual practice section 39 is not often used by doctors to provide compulsory after-care and supervision. Finally, section 39 only allows the RMO to grant leave of absence. Therefore, in a case such as Patrick Mackay's (see *infra*), in which the patient was discharged by the *tribunal,* there is no provision for an interim device such as leave of absence.

Compulsory supervision and after-care are essential to the well-being of the individual and the protection of the public. The most efficient, most humane and least expensive way to protect society is to provide help for the offender in the community. It is important to alleviate the causes of dangerous behaviour and not merely to clamp on a lid of preventive detention. Accordingly, MIND recommends that a hospital order patient who is discharged (whether by the RMO, the hospital managers or the tribunal) be made subject to compulsory supervision and after-care, if the discharging authority feels that this is necessary.

It would be an unnecessary infringement of the privacy of the individual to subject him to compulsory supervision beyond a certain limited period. Unless he is under a life sentence or an unlimited restriction order (both of which should be imposed only for very serious offences), no offender is subject to supervision in the community for an unlimited period. For example, a person on parole may not be deprived of his liberty after his parole expires, and the average period is eight months; a psychiatric probation order cannot extend beyond three years.[20] We think it reasonable that an unrestricted patient should be liable to mandatory supervision for a maximum of one year, at the discretion of the discharging authority.

We must point out that the purpose of this recommendation is to encourage the courts to make hospital orders without restrictions in cases where some continuing supervision is required, but the full machinery of an unlimited restriction order is not necessary; and to encourage the medical profession to rely more on community support in appropriate cases (for example, local social services or the Probation and After Care Service).

Patrick Mackay – a case in point

Patrick Mackay was, at the age of 23, made the subject of a hospital order without restrictions and was admitted to Moss Side Special Hospital. This meant that he could be unconditionally discharged either by his RMO or by a tribunal. After his release in 1971, he committed three murders.

It happened that Mr Mackay was discharged by a tribunal against the advice of the RMO. This caused a bitter outcry from the media, with several commentators calling for the abolition of tribunals in hospital order cases. Of course, errors of judgment must sometimes occur when persons are discharged from high-security hospitals. In the cases of Graham Young, Peter Cook, Terence Iliffe and Ian Dunlop (all of whom committed serious crimes after being released or transferred from Broadmoor Hospital on the recommendations of hospital doctors) it was the Broadmoor doctors who made the misjudgments; in Mackay's case it was a Mental Health Review Tribunal sitting at Moss Side Hospital. The tribunal decided to override the RMO in the Mackay case, knowning full well that doctors seldom discharge patients at Moss Side (of course, they do make favourable recommendations to tribunals). In fact, in 1971 not one hospital order patient was discharged from Moss Side on the authority of hospital doctors. Conversely, the doctors at Broadmoor assume most of the responsibility for the discharge of hospital order patients (86.5% in 1971).[21] It was not therefore surprising that they (and not the tribunals) made the incorrect decisions in the cases of Young, Cook, Iliffe and Dunlop. The aggregate discharge rates are roughly the same in all of the special hospitals; it is just that in some hospitals the doctors take the risks, while in others the tribunals do so.

In Mackay's case, neither Moss Side Hospital nor the local social services department knew where he was living, who he was associating with, what treatment (if any) he was receiving, whether he was ever re-admitted to hospital (he was, in fact, re-admitted twice under s. 136 of the Act, and the receiving hospital was unaware of his previous record), or whether he was acting in a dangerous or bizarre manner. Several deaths resulted before all this information came to light.

Patrick Mackay was an unrestricted patient. He was therefore under no obligation to accept after-care as a condition of discharge; in fact, he refused to accept any help from local social services. Moreover, since he was discharged by a tribunal, the provisions of s. 39 of the Mental Health Act, which allow the RMO to make a trial leave of absence for six months, did not apply.*

If the recommendation which MIND is now making had then been in effect, the tribunal could have released Mr Mackay subject to certain conditions – for example, he might have had to remain in a known residence, visit social services periodically and attend an adult training course. Had he failed to comply with these conditions at any time within one year after his discharge from Moss Side, he could have been recalled.

The management of violent, or potentially violent, abnormal offenders

Section 60(3) of the Mental Health Act states that a hospital order "shall not be made under this section unless the court is satisfied that arrangements have been made for the admission of the offender to that hospital specified in the order ... and for his admission thereto within a period of twenty-eight days ...." This puts the judge in an unfamiliar position as regards his sentencing powers. He cannot make a hospital order unless a consultant at a psychiatric hospital is willing to receive the patient, and in the case of a special (secure) hospital he must also obtain the approval of the Department of Health and Social Security (DHSS).[22] There have been many cases in which doctors or the DHSS have refused to make a bed available for the offender;[23] hence, although the judge has heard the requisite medical evidence, he cannot make a hospital order. The courts' frustration in this situation was succinctly expressed by Mr Justice Mais in the case of *Brazil:*[24] "I find it hard to understand how it is that an order of this court is apparently incapable of being carried out".[25]

The courts have made every attempt to impose their judgments upon hospital authorities, but often to no avail. In the cases of *Brazil*[25] and *Arant*[26] the judges made stern verbal admonitions to the appropriate officials; in *Nicholls'* case[27] Lord Justice Edmund Davies became "very disturbed about

---

*The case of Patrick Mackay is fully described in T. Clark and J. Penycate, *Psychopath*, 1976. John's case, which follows, also illustrates the importance of a conditional discharge.

A public hearing of an MHRT took place at Broadmoor Hospital on 19th October, 1976. John was convicted of arson in 1969 and admitted to borstal. In 1972 he was transferred to Broadmoor.

The tribunal members were of opinion that John did not present a sufficient risk to the public to justify his detention in a special hospital. But they felt that it would be far preferable to transfer him to a less secure setting, than to discharge him outright or, at a minimum, to provide him with after-care and supervision in the community.

The tribunal members heard that no local NHS hospital would accept John, but there was a possibility that he would be accepted by a regional secure unit when it was complete in three months' time.

The tribunal members expressed regret that they did not have the power to discharge him conditionally. They said they had no choice but to order his immediate release. Thus, after seven years in maximum security institutions, he packed his bags and left the hospital. He is under no obligation to accept any help or support from social services.

this situation" and adjourned the case for the third time in order for the "Secretary of State to give further consideration to the matter". In the strongest statement of judicial consternation yet made, Lord Justice Lawton, in *R. v Officer* (discussed on p. 48 *infra*)[28] said:

> "From time to time in the past decade judges had been put in the position of having to sentence to prison for life, persons who clearly ought to have gone to a mental hospital. Judges took the judicial oath of office to do justice by all men. When they had had in the past to send persons to prison because no beds were available in a secure hospital, their judicial consciences were strained almost to breaking point. It is hoped that in such cases, that kind of problem will never arise again."

In *Marsden's* case,[29] the court found that there was no vacancy in any hospital within the region where Quarter Sessions happened to be. Accordingly, it concluded that a section 60 order may be made for admission to a hospital in any part of the country where a vacancy exists.

There are several reasons why hospital authorities and the DHSS have, on occasion, resisted a court's request to make a bed available in a psychiatric hospital; they are discussed below. In some instances they involve genuine differences of clinical opinion, and in others administrative difficulties.

No bed available in a secure hospital

There is no adequate provision for the group of mentally abnormal offenders whose needs fall between the services offered by the special and the local hospitals. These offenders, because of their violent propensities, require extra security which is not provided by the local psychiatric hospitals; but they do not require the degree of security provided in special hospitals.[30] This situation results in disputes between the courts, the special hospitals and the local hospitals as to which hospital should receive them.

Where the disputes cannot be resolved, the offenders may be given sentences of imprisonment. (Often a life sentence is chosen, because its flexible, indeterminate nature allows the authorities to release the offender at an early stage or to detain him indefinitely, as they deem fit.)* One hopes that the Home Secretary would thereafter transfer the offender from prison to a psychiatric hospital; but if the disputes continue, he will remain in prison even though he is in need of psychiatric care. The Government has accepted the Butler Committee's recommendation that regional secure units should be provided,[31] but these will not be in full operation for some time.[32] The courts appear hopeful that the establishment of regional secure

---

* MIND is involved with one case where a mentally disordered person was convicted of an offence which involved the taking of a small sum of money from a woman in an underground station. No physical injury resulted. The judge proposed to make a hospital order, and a consultant in the local psychiatric hospital provisionally agreed to this. The judge then announced his intention to make a restriction order, and the doctor withdrew his offer of a bed in the hospital. The judge then proceeded to pass a life sentence. The case is now on appeal.

units will go a long way toward solving their problems.[27, 32-34] MIND, however, has significant reservations in this area (see Chapter 8 *infra*).

In several cases, the Court of Appeal has said that, before making a hospital order with restrictions, a Crown Court should ascertain which hospital will receive the offender, and ensure that the hospital has facilities for keeping him in safe custody.[35] Here clinical disputes may develop: the medical practitioner giving evidence before the court may consider that the offender requires a high security hospital, while the DHSS and the special hospital consultants disagree with this opinion and refuse to make a bed available. These disagreements are exacerbated by the fact that the special hospitals are severely over-crowded; hence the DHSS may be reluctant to find a vacancy unless the candidate absolutely requires treatment in a high-security establishment, both in his own interests and for the protection of the public.[27 34] If secure accommodation is not available, the court may pass a sentence of imprisonment even though a local hospital is prepared to accept the offender.

The following two cases illustrate the problem.

Farrell's Case[36]
Cameron Farrell pleaded guilty at the Birmingham Crown Court to a charge of burglary. Dr William Canning, of the Midlands Centre for Forensic Psychiatry, described Mr Farrell as a dangerous psychopath and recommended that he be sent to a special hospital under a restriction order without limit of time. The DHSS refused to make a bed available, saying that "the treatment required could be given in a less secure hospital". It told the court that the special hospitals were "overcrowded and in some cases, understaffed and subject to very great strain". If the overcrowding were increased, the quality of treatment would suffer and security would be weakened.

Ryan's Case[37]
Barnard Ryan, aged 18, was convicted on a charge of causing criminal damage by fire. No local hospital would have him. The DHSS also refused to make a bed available in a special hospital. The senior medical officer at the remand centre criticised the Department for making its judgment without ever seeing the patient. "Not only is it clinically impossible but I regard it as highly offensive to the doctors involved."

Judge Robin David at the Chester Crown Court adjourned the case and asked for the Department's co-operation. "It is crystal clear from the medical reports that he is severely mentally ill. He may die and there is no suggestion of his being committed to prison. The problem is that he needs to be treated in a maximum security hospital. This is supported by the independent views of two doctors involved. But the Department, who control admissions to the three such hospitals have decided from reports, but without examination of the patient that they cannot provide a place. The situation is scandalous."

The problem is sometimes caused by the lack of co-ordination and communication between the courts and the DHSS. The case of Ian Officer[28] is the most recent and the clearest example. The Court of Appeal said that in this case,

> "the judge was placed in a position in which no judge should ever be placed by the Department. He had before him reports of two consultant psychiatrists of outstanding experience. Both were agreed that the appellant should be detained in a secure hospital and there could not have been a clearer case for a patient to go to a secure hospital but, because no doctor from Broadmoor had examined him and there was no intimation by the Department that a bed was available, Mr. Justice Willis had no alternative but to send the appellant to life imprisonment."

The court explained that quite possibly the Department had never been alerted to the situation because communications passed between doctors without anybody in the Department realising what was going on. The court had met that situation before, and felt that something ought to be done at an administrative level to ensure that it never happened again. In the end the Department was notified, and it made a bed available for the appellant in Broadmoor.

No bed available in a local hospital

Sometimes the roles are reversed: the medical pratitioners who report to the court do not feel that the offender needs treatment under secure conditions, but nevertheless, no local NHS hospital is willing to accept him as a patient. In *Suchodolski's* case[38] the Liverpool Crown Court reported that four doctors had said he should be treated under non-secure conditions. Yet no local hospital was prepared to take him, because they considered their security inadequate. In the case of Samuel Twigger,[39] the Central Criminal Court was forced to sentence the defendant to life imprisonment after four mental hospitals had refused to accept him. Finally, in Margaret Smith's case,[40] the Shrewsbury Crown Court was forced to sentence her to nine months' imprisonment for stealing 36 pence, after psychiatrists in local hospitals had refused to take her because of the effect they thought she would have on other patients in an open ward.

Anthony Ledger's Case[41]
Ledger has spent $2\frac{1}{2}$ years in and out of prisons and mental hospitals. His offences have been relatively trivial: stealing a toy, stealing a bag of coal, taking a free ride on the railways, and booking in at a boarding house without any money. Recently, he committed a minor assault on a policeman.

The Crown Court heard evidence that Mr. Ledger is mentally disordered and in need of treatment. Special hospital consultants agree that he needs long-term institutional care, but not in a maximum security hospital. Local doctors also refuse to accept him because he might be too disruptive for an open-door institution. The prison doctor made the following statement to the court: "The realities are that the National Health Service mental hospitals will not now accept responsibility for such cases as Mr Ledger. Having abandoned all forms of security control they can now claim that they have no facilities for the treatment of patients with aspects of dangerousness . . . . The prison medical service will therefore be compelled to face the task that should more properly be the responsibility of others."

The court felt that it had no choice but to pass a sentence of imprisonment for 18 months.

Recently there has been a spate of cases in which the consultant in a local hospital has agreed to accept the offender as a patient, but the nursing staff, represented by the Confederation of Health Service Employees (COHSE) and other health service unions, have refused. What is worrying here is that the refusal was based not upon an individual consideration of the particular offender, but upon the general policy that no restricted patient should ever be admitted. One example was reported in the *Health and Social Services Journal*:[42] "COHSE branches at Oakwood Mental Hospital in Maidstone, Kent have passed a resolution which bans from hospital any patient sent by the courts under sections 65 or 71 [restricted patients] of the 1959 Mental Health Act." Similarly, the *Sunday Telegraph*[43] reported: "Nursing members of COHSE at John Conolly Hospital, have reached an agreement with Birmingham Area Health Authority that violent patients should not be admitted."

R v Brazil[24] was the first important case to elicit a strong and unified response from COHSE. The case is worth relating in full:

On October 3, 1975, at Bristol Crown Court Mr Justice Mais made orders under sections 60/65 of the Mental Health Act directing that John Brazil (aged 41) should enter Glenside Hospital, Bristol for psychiatric treatment. Brazil had pleaded guilty to manslaughter (under diminished responsibility) of his wife. As required under the Act, the consent of the doctor who would be treating him there was obtained, and this was never withdrawn.

Union members at Glenside Hospital threatened strike action if Brazil was admitted, and the case was referred back to the judge on October 30. As Brazil would have been allowed to go free on October 31 (28 days after the order was made) if he had not by then been transferred to the hospital, the judge passed the life sentence, which he described as "wholly inappropriate".

The Regional Union Chairman of COHSE was quoted as saying: "We are not trying to undermine the authority of the courts, but we are thinking of our members. What is being suggested is that this man be put on a ward where at night there may be only one member of staff on duty who is untrained and a slip of a seven stone girl at that."

At the resumed hearing, a consultant psychiatrist told the judge that Brazil was suffering from a morbid psychotic jealousy, but was not a danger to anybody except himself. In passing the life sentence, the judge said: "I find it very difficult to understand how it is that medical opinion has been overturned by those who are nursing and have not had the experience and skill of the doctors . . . I am told that no-one on the staff has had access to the doctor's report on Mr Brazil, nor has anyone approached the consultant psychiatrist. It is extremely difficult to understand how it comes about that this threatened action has taken place when they are unaware of the treatment which he requires."[25] (Workers at Glenside denied that they had no access to medical reports. They said that the consultant psychiatrist had circulated copies of his court report to nursing staff.)[44]

On November 1, 1975 a second hospital refused to accept Mr Brazil, and on November 4 a third hospital did the same.[45]

On November 24, 1975 Mr Justice Mais revoked the life sentence and substituted a hospital order with restrictions to St. Lawrence's Hospital, Bodmin. Mr Brazil remains in St. Lawrence's Hospital (September 1976) and his doctor reports that he has been a "model patient".[46]

Immediately after the conclusion of the *Brazil* case, the Union's National Executive decided as follows:[47]

"That nurses should be able to choose whether they want to work with, or near, abnormal offenders in mental hospitals if they consider safety and security provisions are not adequate. . . . This decision will continue until the union is satisfied that the level of the treatment facilities do not expose nursing staff to unacceptable degrees of bodily danger."

Since the publicity given to the *Brazil* case, and no doubt as a consequence of the trade union activities, the press have reported a myriad of cases in which hospital staff refused would-be patients from the courts.[48] The DHSS, in an attempt to reduce the anxieties of hospital staff, recently issued a circular on the management of violent or potentially violent patients.[49] It gave some guidance on how to recognise behaviour patterns that suggest a patient presents some degree of special risk.

The Department said that special-risk patients require more supervision, which must be taken into account in the staffing of the wards they are in. The prevention of violence requires a knowledge and understanding of these individual patients on the part of the staff, and a quiet surveillance of those factors that may precede a period of disturbed behaviour. Signs such as increasing emotional instability, changes in normal habits, anxiety, depression or bizarre behaviour ought to alert nurses, who should bring these factors to the notice of the medical staff. The Department's main advice is that where physical intervention is thought necessary, the degree of force used should be the minimum required to control the violence, and should be applied in a manner calculated to calm rather than provoke further aggression.[50]

On March 15, 1976, COHSE instructed its 165,000 members to ignore the Ministry's guidelines on the management of violent patients. The Union felt that it should have been consulted in the preparation of the health circular; it also felt that the guidelines were not specific enough to be of any help to the nurses on the wards. COHSE set up its own working party to suggest guidelines which may be more useful and more favourable to its members.[32]

Consultation and multi-disciplinary assessment

The nurses in psychiatric hospitals, by the nature of their profession, take primary responsibility for the day-to-day care of patients. They remain with patients in a sheltered environment for long periods, sometimes without the full support and understanding of the managers and psychiatric staff of the hospital. On occasion, they are not even consulted about decisions concerning the admission, management and care of potentially violent patients; yet these decisions may affect the nurses more than any other members of the hospital staff. For example, in *Brazil's* case the consultant psychiatrist told the court that he would make a bed available in his hospital before he had even consulted the nursing staff who would care for him; it was simply taken for granted that they would agree. Similarly, when preparing the circular on the management of violent patients, the Ministry did not consult COHSE, which represents most of the 43,000 nurses in psychiatric hospitals.*

Psychiatric nurses feel a special sense of responsibility in the care of violent patients. Younger nurses have been trained to work on open wards, where a premium is placed on freedom of choice and movement for all patients. The introduction of a particularly disturbed or potentially violent patient may result in a closed-door situation. The nursing staff may have to spend a disproportionate amount of time and energy in supervising this one patient; this may have an adverse effect on other patients (for example, certain restrictions may have to be placed on their freedom of movement), and may make the nurse's job more difficult.

Nurses in local psychiatric hospitals ask why they should take the risks involved in working with potentially violent patients when the nurses in special hospitals are paid and trained to do this.[51] They also point out that the special hospitals have a higher staff/patient ratio and tighter physical security, which makes the supervision and control of violent patients much easier. Finally, it is worth noting that local hospital nurses belong to a health service union, while special hospital nurses are represented by the Prison Officers' Association.

On the other hand, it should be pointed out that nursing is a profession, and part of the essence of a profession is that the defence of its status and interests cannot properly be separated from the maintenance of its standards of performance. In seeking, at a Departmental and hospital level, to obtain more support and a fair share of resources, the nursing staff should not

*The DHSS did, however, consult with the Royal College of Nursing.

deprive patients of their basic right to treatment.† The staff in a local hospital must keep in mind that if they refuse to take a patient from the courts, he may be sent to prison or to a special hospital such as Broadmoor. It is a failure of the overall provision of the National Health Service when a patient for whom no bed is available locally is placed in a special hospital (with all the stigma and deprivation of liberty that are entailed), although he does not need the maximum security provided by the special hospitals.[55] Furthermore, he takes a scarce bed within the special hospital which could otherwise be used for a more appropriate case.

The psychiatric consultants at some local hospitals have also been reluctant to accept offenders from the courts. This sometimes arises from genuine differences of clinical opinion; the doctors who present the evidence to the court may feel that the disorder is susceptible to treatment in a local psychiatric hospital, while the local consultant feels that he cannot help that particular person. Some may also refuse for less particular reasons. For example, a psychiatrist may feel that the presence of a potentially dangerous patient in his hospital may cause concern in the local community. It should be part of his job to reduce such concern, but it may take only one act of violence by a patient to convince the community that all mental patients are dangerous. Thus, the availability of jobs, housing and other forms of support for the mentally disordered in the community may suffer. The consultant may therefore decide that it is not worth the risk to accept patients from the courts.

Although these reasons are understandable, the same overriding principles apply. A local hospital should not close its doors to people in need because there is some small chance that they may cause a disturbance or become violent. Of course there are some abnormal offenders who absolutely require a high-security environment, but if a court of law is prepared on the basis of medical and other evidence to send the offender to a non-secure hospital, that hospital should be prepared to take the risk, unless there is a genuine difference of opinion in the particular case. If, after accepting the offender, the local hospital finds that it cannot cope with him it seems clear that the DHSS should be sympathetic and make every effort to transfer him to a

---

†Nurses have attempted to assert their own rights to the disadvantage of the rights of patients in other contexts as well. When a magistrates' court convicted Mr Griffiths, a nurse at Broadmoor, of assaulting Mr Pountney, a patient, the nursing staff of the hospital went on strike. Patients and relatives maintained that as a result, post was not delivered to the patients, no visiting was allowed, most of the industrial therapy was halted, and so forth.

In April, 1976 delegates of the Royal College of Nursing reported that members of Health Service trade unions were using restrictive practices to block the education and training of mentally handicapped patients.[52]

And in May, 1976 the psychiatric nurses at Brookwood hospital in Surrey threatened industrial action unless the staff/patient ratio was increased. They warned that new admissions would have to be turned away.[53] Similarly, the nurses at Normansfield Hospital, Middlesex threatened to go on strike if a certain consultant psychiatrist were reinstated.[54]

MIND maintains that disputes which develop between the management and staff of psychiatric hospitals should not, if possible, be resolved by methods which affect the quality of the care and treatment of patients.

special hospital. There should also be some improvement when regional secure units are established but, as the Department has said:[56]

"It must be recognised that the units should not be expected to deal with all patients who might cause difficulties in local hospitals . . . either by their behaviour or occasional absconding. Experience suggests that most forms of difficult and disturbed behaviour can be contained by a high level of staff observation and supervision, combined with the use of locked rooms on occasion and for limited periods. Local hospitals are expected to deal with patients who occasionally exhibit difficult behaviour and violence, and only when a patient is recurrently so difficult and dangerous that his treatment entails security measures continuously . . . should his case be regarded as beyond the resources of a local unit."

The role of the Area Health Authority as hospital managers

In a non-psychiatric hospital each bed is in the control of a consultant and in practice he makes the decision as to whether that bed shall be occupied by a patient – for whom he then accepts full clinical responsibility. Psychiatric hospitals are now commonly following these arrangements. In the normal course of events the consultant psychiatrist decides whether to accept patients, and the hospital managers routinely ratify his decisions.

This practice appears inconsistent with the statutory duties laid upon the Area Health Authority (AHA), as hospital managers, to receive and detain patients – for example, section 63 of the Mental Health Act exclusively authorises "the managers" to admit offender-patients to hospital.*

The consultant has no statutory right to admit a patient to hospital without the authority of the managers.[57] It is, moreover, possible to conclude that a consultant ought not to be regarded (from a legal point of view) as an appropriate delegate or agent for the AHA in respect of admission. For cases clearly arise when a medical report required by section 62 of the 1959 Act is furnished by a consultant working at the relevant hospital:[58] it would not be proper for the self-same consultant to exercise, on behalf of the managers, the right of reception or admission that is expressly vested in them – and not in a medical practitioner. (Any medical duty that the consultant may owe to a patient arises from his position as the servant of the Regional Health Authority (RHA) that employs him, although his services may have to be rendered within the particular AHA where he is contractually required to perform his duties.) Similarly, it does not appear that any officer of the AHA, other than those specifically delegated by the Authority as "managers", can have any independent right or duty in relation to the admission of patients.

Thus the AHA, as hospital managers, has exclusive authority to admit patients to psychiatric hospitals. Moreover, its authority may be exercised with wide discretion, i.e. it is under no explicit obligation to accept a mental-

---

*See also sections 29(3)(b), 30(1) and 30(2) of the 1959 Act, where it is only when the managers receive a recommendation, application or report that the authority to detain a patient is established. (But cf. sections 43(3) and 43(5), which appear to leave the managers with the right to reject the opinion expressed in a report from the RMO.)

ly disordered person into hospital. For example, sections 25 and 26 of the 1959 Act say only that a patient "may" be admitted to a hospital, and the word "application" for admission, which is used throughout the Act, implies a discretion to refuse admission. This impression is confirmed both by section 60(3), which is quoted on page 45 *supra,* and by the *Report of the Royal Commission on the Law Relating to Mental Illness and Mental Deficiency,* which is discussed on pages 45-46 of Volume 1 of this report.

But, the discretion given to AHAs to admit patients to psychiatric hospitals is not without limits. Under section 2(2) of the National Health Service Reorganisation Act 1973, the Secretary of State for Social Services is required to provide services "to such an extent as he considers necessary to meet all reasonable requirements". This basic duty is (or should be) transferred or delegated to RHAs and, through them, to AHAs.[59] The scope of the duty imposed upon the AHA is no wider than the flexible duty laid upon the Secretary of State by section 2(2).

Moreover, under section 57 of the National Health Service Act 1946, the Secretary of State is given power to secure the performance of a duty in any case where he is "of opinion . . . that any [AHA] have failed to carry out any function . . . imposed on them." Accordingly, the Secretary of State is empowered to compel an AHA to admit a patient if he holds that a refusal to admit amounted to a failure to provide a reasonable service.

Proposal for reform

The Department of Health and Social Security should issue a circular to all AHAs instructing them in their duties under the Mental Health Act, together with a statement that they will be held accountable for failure to carry out their duties properly under the Act. The AHAs would be expected to formulate reasonable standards for the admission of patients, which should be expressed by reference to specified maximum numbers, to minimum conditions of care and treatment, and to the specific psychiatric condition of the prospective patient (irrespective of his legal status under the Mental Health Act).

The following procedures should be used in any case where the court feels, after hearing the appropriate medical evidence, that an offender should be admitted to an NHS hospital. The hospital should send two or more representatives of its professional staff (e.g. medical, nursing, social work) to examine him and review his psychiatric and social history. A full report should then be sent to the appropriate AHA and to the court. The AHA would itself decide whether to admit the patient, in accordance with the standards it set for all admissions to hospital in its area. (It should, of course, have the opportunity to discuss the case with the hospital staff or other professionals. Moreover, it should be authorised to see the prospective patient and make an independent assessment of the situation.) If the AHA refused to accept the offender it should set out the reasons for this decision in writing to the Secretary of State and to the sentencing court.

Where the Secretary of State held that the decision was made without reasonable ground or in bad faith, he should direct the AHA under section 57 to admit the offender to the hospital.

An alternative proposal
To our knowledge, the Secretary of State has never used his powers under section 57 of the 1946 Act in this way. His unwillingness to intervene is well exemplified by the decision recorded in paragraph 143 of the Report of the Committee of Enquiry in South Ockendon Hospital:

"In March 1969 the HMC with the approval of the RHB banned all admissions . . . . This drastic action was supported by the Secretary of State".

More recently, the DHSS has severely criticised local hospitals for their *carte blanche* policies of refusing to admit offender-patients from the courts. Yet spokesmen for the Department have publicly stated that they accept no responsibility for these policies – they allege that it is purely a matter for the hospitals involved.

The reluctance of the Department to interfere with the decisions of Area Health Authorities may be attributable to the realities of 'medical politics'. The Secretary of State must maintain the co-operation and good will of all professionals in the National Health Service, and therefore he may not wish to question their clinical and administrative judgments regarding admission to hospital. Accordingly, the Department may wish to consider the following alternative proposal. The sentencing court could be empowered (by repealing section 60(3) of the 1959 Act, and making the appropriate amendment) to compel an AHA to admit an offender-patient to hospital. The court would not supplant its judgment for that of the AHA; however, it could override the decision not to admit an offender if it were made without reasonable ground or in bad faith.

The case of the special hospitals
The Area Health Authorities only have jurisdiction over National Health Service hospitals. The 'managers' in relation to special hospitals means the Department of Health and Social Security. Accordingly, the foregoing proposals are not strictly relevant to the situation in the four special hospitals. We should reiterate, however, that under section 2(2) of the 1973 Act, the Secretary of State for Social Services is under an obligation to provide services to meet all reasonable requirements. It is true that he can use a considerable amount of discretion in performing this duty but, in our view, not unfettered discretion. Accordingly, if the DHSS, as managers of the special hospitals, makes a wholly unreasonable decision not to accept a patient, it may properly be the basis of an order of *mandamus*.* We do not foresee that

Mandamus is defined by the *Osborn Concise Law Dictionary*, 5th ed., as follows: "A high prerogative writ which issued in the King's name from the High Court of Justice on application to the King's Bench Division, to some person or body to compel the performances of a public duty, where no other effective means of redress was available. It has been replaced by an order of *mandamus*. The procedure is that an application for leave to apply for an order is made *ex parte* to a Divisional Court of the Queen's Bench Division. If leave is given to apply for an order, the application is made by notice of motion to the Divisional Court, which must be served on all parties affected (see Ord. 59).

An action of *mandamus* lies to command the defendant to fulfil any duty in which the plaintiff is personally interested. It was created by the Common Law Procedure Act, 1854, s. 68, as being an additional common law remedy in the nature of specific performance (see Ord. 53)."

this will occur very frequently because the Department has been diligent in exercising its duties as hospital managers, but the option is one that can be explored.

Moreover, if our alternative proposal is accepted, it would be sensible to empower the sentencing court to override wholly unreasonable decisions made by the managers of special hospitals as well as local NHS hospitals.

A postscript

A draft copy of this chapter was released to the press before the date of publication.[60] As a result, we received many letters concerning similar cases in which the courts were forced to imprison mentally disordered offenders. We have been overwhelmed by the sheer number of unreported cases in which this occurs. Concern has been voiced by relatives, social workers, probation officers and the courts. We were informed of the following case by a probation officer who contacted us at the behest of a judge at the Kingston Crown Court. The judge was apparently making a determined effort to find some kind of social help for a woman who was badly in need of a home and proper care.

Jean's case
Jean was charged with reckless damage, and brought before the Kingston Crown Court. The court referred to the alleged offence as "quite minor". In fact, she had only been accused of damaging some flowers in a flower bed. The case was given to the jury, who returned a verdict of guilty to the charge of reckless damage.

The court was faced with the following dilemma in sentencing her. She had no criminal record. However, over the years she had been in the local psychiatric hospital under various emergency orders. She is considered by the local hospital and by local social services to be highly disruptive. As a result, neither one of them is prepared to care for her.

The consultant in the local psychiatric hospital prepared a report for the court. He said: "So far as her mental state is concerned, she is no longer disturbed. I am of the opinion that she is merely feigning the symptoms of mental disorder." Accordingly, he stated his intention not to receive her back into his hospital. Anomalously, he further stated that she was a proper candidate for a special hospital.

The judge was very concerned because Jean had nowhere to live. He did not therefore feel that it was proper simply to discharge her.

MIND informed the court of the very similar case of *Dawn Clarke* (see p.p. 39-40 *supra*) decided by the Court of Appeal. If the judge were to accept the guidance in that case, he would have no choice but to pass a non-custodial sentence. In the meantime, MIND is actively trying to find hostel accommodation for Jean.

Jean's case illustrates a problem which MIND is quite concerned about. Medical practitioners often feel that they should have the right to choose whom they will treat (one should note that other professionals, such as probation officers, do not have a corresponding right); and the nurses' unions assert that their members should not be required to deal with difficult or troublesome patients.

An easy option for professionals is to refer the case to a criminal court on an occasion when the client has caused some minor damage.

We firmly support the ruling of the Court of Appeal in *Clarke's* case. We do not feel that a court, whose task it is to mete out criminal justice, should respond to the invitation to make social judgments. The responsibility for homeless or troubled people lies with care-giving professionals. They have sufficient powers under the civil law to intervene in any medical or social crisis.

The Southampton Crown Court followed the decision in *Clarke's* case when it fined Suzanne Cornwell £10, and released her from custody on October 7 1976.[61] Miss Cornwell has a chronological age of 18, but a mental age of eight.* She was charged in connection with the theft of a bottle containing a few coins, and remanded in custody to Holloway Prison. On a previous remand to Holloway, Miss Cornwell was forcibly tattooed by other prisoners. When the judge set Miss Cornwell free he said:

"This is an abysmal state of affairs. Whatever happens I am not going to send her back to Holloway or Borstal. I am horrified that a mountain of civil servants and administrators cannot find her a hospital bed. The failure lies squarely on the Department of Health and Social Security. The fact that I cannot place this girl anywhere is not the fault of this court."

*Directly after *Cornwell's* case [62] was decided, the Bedford Crown Court was faced with a man aged 19, with a mental age of ten. No place in a special hospital could be found, so he was sentenced to four years' imprisonment.

References and Notes

1. R v Harvey and Ryan [1971] *Crim. L. Rev. 664.*
2. R v King's Lynn Justices, Ex parte Fysh, *Times Law Report,* November 20, 1963.
3. *The Guardian,* May 12, 1976.
4. Mental Health Act 1959, s. 60(1)(a).
5. R v Gills [1967] *Crim. L. Rev.* 247; R v Woolland [1967] 51 Cr.App.R. 65; R v Carr, *The Guardian,* March 26, 1963; R v Nicholls, not reported. Judgment given April 16, 1973.
6. *The Butler Report,* Chapter 5.
7. R v Clarke [1975] 61 Cr.App.R. 320.
8. R v Nigel Gordon Smith, not reported. Judgment given July 30, 1974. See also, R. J. Walker and M. G. Walker, *The English Legal System,* 3rd ed., 1972, pp. 523–525.
9. R v Turner (Court of Appeal), *The Times,* October 23, 1974.
10. R v Blackwood [1974] 59 Cr. App.R. 170.
11. R v Gardiner [1967] 1 All E. R. 895; 1 W. L. R. 464.
12. R v Toland [1974] 58 Cr.App.R. 453; *Crim. L.R.* 196.
13. *The Royal Commission on the Law Relating to Mental Illness and Mental Deficiency* (the Percy Report), HMSO, Cmnd. 169, paras. 478–482.

14. P. G. McGrath, "The mentally abnormal offender", *Medico-Legal Journal,* vol. 41, 1973, p.4.
15. *The Butler Report,* paras. 8.1-8.7.
16. N. Walker and S. McCabe, *Crime and Insanity in England,* vol. 2, 1973, pp. 186-193; Payne, McCabe and Walker, "Predicting offender-patients' reconvictions", *Brit. J. Psychiat.,* 1974, pp. 60ff and 125.
17. See generally L. Gostin, *A Human Condition,* vol. 1, pp. 13-14.
18. L. Blom-Cooper (ed.), *Progress in Penal Reform,* 1974, p. viii.
19. *The Butler Report,* para. 8.4.
20. Powers of Criminal Courts Act 1973, s. 2(1).
21. *The Butler Report,* p.291.
22. National Health Service Reorganisation Act 1973, s. 40.
23. See for example, R v X (an infant) (Court of Appeal), *Times Law Report,* July 21, 1969; R v Witt, not reported. Judgment given December 16, 1974.
24. *The Times,* October 29, 1975.
25. *Ibid.,* October 31, 1975.
26. *Ibid.,* December 6, 1975.
27. R v Frank Nicholls, not reported. Judgment given April 16, 1973.
28. *Times Law Report,* February 20, 1976.
29. R v Marsden [1968] 2 All E.R. 341.
30. *The Butler Report,* para. 1.4.
31. DHSS, *Priorities for Health and Personal Social Services in England, A Consultative Document,* HMSO, 1976, para. 8.19.
32. *The Times,* March 15, 1976.
33. R v Parker, Griffiths and Rainbird, not reported. Judgment given March 21, 1975; R v McFarlane [1975] 60 Cr.App.R.320; R v Smith, *The Guardian,* January 14, 1976.
34. R v McFarlane [1975] 60 Cr.App.R.320.
35. R v Morris [1961] 2 All E.R. 672; R v Higginbotham [1961] 3 All E.R. 616, at p.620; R v Cox [1968] 1 All E.R. 386.
36. *The Times, The Guardian* and *The Daily Mail,* January 30, 1976.
37. *The Guardian,* June 15, 1975.
38. *The Times,* December 9, 1975.
39. *The Times,* February 7, 1976.
40. *The Guardian,* January 14, 1976.
41. *Ibid.,* June 5 and 23, 1976.
42. *Health and Social Services Journal,* October 1975.
43. *The Sunday Telegraph,* February 8, 1976.
44. *The Observer,* November 2, 1975.
45. *The Times,* November 4, 1975.
46. *The Times,* November 25, 1975.
47. See generally, *The Times,* October 29, 1975 and November 25, 1975; *The Daily Telegraph,* October 29, 1975.
48. *The Times,* December 3, 6 and 9, 1975; January 8 and 30, 1976; February 7, 1976. *The Guardian,* June 5, 15 and 23, 1976. See generally, *The Observer,* July 4 and 11, 1976.
49. HC(76)11, March 1976.
50. See also, NAMH Consultative Document, *Guidelines for the Care of Patients who Exhibit Violent Behaviour in Mental Illness and Mental Subnormality Hospitals.*
51. P. Norton and A. Norton, "Some patients are special", *World Medicine,* October 9, 1974, p.31 (Broadmoor's nursing staff receive a lead payment of £321 a year.)
52. *The Daily Telegraph,* April 8, 1976.
53. *The Evening Standard,* May 4, 1976.
54. *The Guardian,* May 8, 1976.
55. Department of Health and Social Security, *Regional Security Units Design Guidelines,* July 1975, para. 3.1.
56. *Ibid.,* para. 2.2.

57. The North West Thames Regional Health Authority obtained the opinion of counsel on the role of the AHA in respect of hospital admissions. Sir Geoffrey Howe concluded that the consultant has no statutory right to admit a patient, except with the authority of the AHA. The opinion was given on December 2, 1974.
58. Under section 28(3) of the Mental Health Act 1959, one of the two medical recommendations required for compulsory admission may be given by a practitioner on the staff of the receiving hospital.
59. National Health Service Reorganisation Act 1973, ss. 7(1) and 7(2); National Health Service Functions (Directions to Authorities) Regulations, S.I. 1974 No.24, regs. 3 and 5(1).
60. *The Observer*, June 27, 1976.
61. *The Daily Telegraph*, September 23, 1976; *The Guardian*, October 7, 1976.
62. *The Times*, October 11, 1976.

4. Hospital orders with restrictions: Exposition of the present law

When a hospital order* is made by a Crown Court and it considers, having regard to the nature of the offence, the antecedents of the offender and the risk of his committing further offences if set at large, that it is necessary for the protection of the public, the court may also make an order under section 65 of the Act restricting his discharge from hospital. The restriction order may be either without limit of time or for a specified period.[1] If it is for a fixed term, once that term expires or otherwise ceases to have effect, the patient will still be detained under a hospital order without restrictions.[2]

As Table 1 illustrates, the use of fixed periods for restriction orders was at first fairly common. In 1961, for example, 44% of all restriction orders were made for fixed periods. But later the proportion steadily declined, so that in 1966 it was only 20%. In 1967, in *R v Gardiner*,[3] Lord Parker (then Lord Chief Justice) said:

"... since in most cases the prognosis cannot be certain, the safer course is to make any restriction order unlimited in point of time. The only exception is where the doctors are able to assert confidently that recovery will take place within a fixed period when the restriction order can properly be limited to that period."

Directly after *Gardiner's* case, the proportion of restriction orders made for fixed periods dropped to approximately 10%. By 1971 only 13 of the 232 restriction orders (6%) were for fixed periods;[4] in 1973 the proportion dropped to 3.7%, and in 1974 to only 1%.

The Butler Report has gone further and recommended that the statutory authorisation for making a restriction order of limited duration should be removed from the Mental Health Act. Instead, the Committee recommended that regular reports on patients under restriction orders should be made to the Home Office by their doctors.[5]

Power of magistrates' courts to commit to Crown Courts for restriction orders

A magistrates' court does not have the power to make a restriction order under section 65; however, if the accused is 14 years of age or older and is convicted of an offence punishable on summary conviction with imprisonment, the magistrates' court may, if it thinks necessary and if the conditions under section 60(1) are fulfilled, either commit the offender in custody to be dealt

---

*A restriction order under section 65 cannot be made unless a hospital order under section 60 is also made; no restriction order can be made when a guardianship order is made.

Table 1
The Use of Restriction Orders From 1961 to 1974*

Year	Total Number of Hospital Orders	Total Number of Restriction Orders	Restriction Orders as Percentage of Total	Percentage of Restriction Orders with Time Limit	Percentage of Restriction Orders involving Special Hospitals
1961	1059	154	14.6	44.2	33.1
1962	1131	138	12.2	39.1	50.0
1963	1247	159	12.8	40.3	47.2
1964	1378	185	13.4	21.6	47.6
1965	1317	196	14.9	17.8	42.4
1966	1438	180	12.5	20.0	54.4
1967†	1436	271	18.9	11.0	47.6
1968	1403	255	18.1	10.2	53.3
1969	1430	256	17.9	7.1	50.1
1973‡	1212	262	21.6	3.7	56.3
1974	948	194	20.4	1.0	68.3

*Source: *The Criminal Statistics for England and Wales.* The numbers of committals to special hospitals without restriction orders were supplied by the Department of Health and Social Security. The figures for 1961-1969 were compiled by N. Walker and S. McCabe in *Crime and Insanity in England,* vol. 2, 1973, p. 96. We thank the authors and Edinburgh University Press for their permission to use the figures here.

†The practice direction in *Gardiner's* case was issued early in 1967.

‡The figures for the years 1970-1972 are omitted.

with by the Crown Court,[6] or order that he be admitted to a specified hospital (under a restriction order without limit of time[7]) until the case can be disposed of by the Crown Court,[8]† In these instance, however, the Crown Court

†A person who is committed in custody to the Crown Court under section 67 may then be subject to the provisions of section 73(2)(b). Thus, on the recommendations of two medical practitioners, the Home Secretary may direct that the person be transferred to a hospital. This transfer direction *must* be coupled with a restriction order. (See "Removal to hospital of persons committed in custody for trial", p.18 *supra,* and Appendix 3). Under section 76(1), any such transfer direction will cease to have effect when the person's case is disposed of by the Crown Court, but without prejudice to any power of the Crown Court to make a hospital order or other order under Part V of the Mental Health Act. If, however, the Crown Court decides that it is impracticable or inappropriate to bring that person before the Court for sentencing, it may make a hospital order (with or without restrictions) in his absence. The Court must be satisfied on the evidence of two medical practitioners (complying with section 62(1) of the Act) that the person is suffering from mental illness or severe subnormality (*not* psychopathy or subnormality) of a nature or degree which warrants detention in hospital for medical treatment.

is not obliged to make a hospital order, let alone a restriction order; it may deal with the offender in any of the ways open to the magistrates' court.[9] Thus from 1964 to 1968, 204 people were committed to Quarter Sessions (now the Crown Court) with a view to making a restriction order. Only three-quarters were given hospital orders with restrictions; most of the remainder were given hospital orders without restrictions and 4% were imprisoned, fined, put on probation or discharged.[10]

A section 65 restriction order cannot be made unless at least one of the medical practitioners who gives evidence in pursuance of section 60 has given evidence orally before the court.[11] The practitioner who gives oral evidence need not be the one who has special experience in the diagnosis or treatment of mental disorders.

Effects of restriction orders

A person admitted to hospital with special restrictions under section 65 is not subject to the provisions of Part IV of the Act relating to the duration, renewal and expiration of the authority for the compulsory detention of patients.[12] This means that neither the responsible medical officer nor the hospital managers have the power to grant a leave of absence, a transfer to another hospital or a discharge without the consent of the Home Secretary.[13] In 1960 the Ministry of Health issued this statement of explanation:

> "The initiative in seeking the Home Secretary's consent to discharge lies with the RMO and the managers, and they should not hesitate to seek consent when they consider the patient's condition warrants it. The Home Secretary may sometimes think it necessary in view of his special responsibility for the protection of the public, to refuse or postpone consent to discharge, but he will rely on the hospital authorities to bring cases to his notice."[14]

The Ministry also pointed out that it is the duty of the RMO continually to review the suitability for discharge of all restricted patients, in the same way as for all other patients. In addition, Parliament was given an undertaking during the passage of the 1959 Act that formal reports on restricted patients would be made not less frequently than the reports made on other patients in pursuance of section 43.[15] The Butler Committee seemed to feel that this undertaking has not always been fulfilled, and therefore re-stated that it is advisable that the RMO should make regular reports to the Home Office on all restricted patients.[16]

No restricted patient may apply to a Mental Health Review Tribunal; nor may his nearest relative.[17] The Home Secretary, however, may at any time refer his case to a tribunal for its advice.[18] The patient can make a written request that his case be referred to a tribunal not sooner than one year after the relevant hospital order is made and once in any subsequent two-year period.[19] The Home Secretary must refer the case to the tribunal within two months of receiving the request.[18] Restricted patients who are recalled from a conditional discharge have the additional right to request a reference to a tribunal between 6 and 12 months after the date of recall.[20]

The tribunal has no power over a restricted patient, and no authority to discharge him. It may only *advise* the Home Secretary in the exercise of his powers. (The advice is given in secret; neither the patient nor the public will be informed of the decision the tribunal has reached.) The decision on whether to accept the advice remains exclusively with the Home Secretary. Furthermore, if he rejects the tribunal's recommendation, he need not give his reasons.

Tribunals can make the following specific kinds of recommendation to the Home Office in respect of restricted patients: discharge; transfer to a local mental hospital; removal of the restriction order; advancement within the present hospital; transfer to another special hospital; trial leave of absence; repatriation; and review or reference to the tribunal within 12 months.

The Home Secretary may at any time discharge a restricted patient from hospital, either absolutely or subject to conditions.[21] As Table 2 shows, 92% of his discharges in 1974 were conditional. With a conditional discharge, he may at any time during the continuance of the restriction order recall the patient by warrant to a hospital specified in the warrant;* the patient will then be detained as if the original restriction order were still in effect.[22] In 1974, 25 people (6 of them female) were recalled to hospital. These represented 10% of the restricted patients received into hospital in that year; 17 were recalled to local hospitals and 8 to special hospitals.[23]

A restriction order will continue in force for the natural life of the patient unless: the order was made for a fixed period which has since lapsed[24] (this occurred in 38 cases in 1974 – see Table 2); the Home Secretary has absolutely discharged the person from hospital[18] (15 cases in 1974); or the Home Secretary is satisfied that a restriction order is no longer required for the protection of the public and directs that the patient shall cease to be subject to special restrictions[25] (26 cases in 1974). Dr Patrick McGrath, Physician Superintendent at Broadmoor, has pointed out that most restriction orders last for the rest of the patients' lives.[26]

For the convenience of the reader, Table 3 gives in chart form a summary of the differences between hospital orders with and without restrictions.

---

*The Butler Committee recommended (para. 14.31) that the Home Secretary should also be given the authority to recall a discharged restricted patient to "a place of safety" for a period of up to 72 hours. "A place of safety" is defined in section 135(6) of the Mental Health Act. In practice, a police station has frequently been used as a place of safety for detentions under the authority of section 136. The Butler Committee, however, envisages that a "place of safety" will normally be a regional secure unit, when these are established, but until then the hospital of a local remand prison or a remand centre should be used.

Table 2
Discharges and Disposals From Hospital of Persons Subject to Special Restrictions Under the Mental Health Act 1959†

Discharge or disposal	Special Hospital		Ordinary Hospital		Totals for All Hospitals	
	M	F	M	F	M	F
On expiry of special restrictions						
Discharged by hospital authorities	—	—	4	—	4	—
Remained as liable to be detained	15	1	14	—	29	1
Remained as informal patient	—	—	4	—	4	—
On termination by the Secretary of State of special restrictions						
Remained as liable to be detained	1	1	22	2	23	3
Discharged by warrant of the Secretary of State						
Absolutely	3	—	11	1	14	1
Conditionally	37	6	119	14	156	20
Discharged with the consent of the Secretary of State						
Left hospital	—	—	12	2	12	2
Remained as informal patient	—	—	3	—	3	—
Remitted to prison to resume sentence	2	1	10	—	12	1
Remitted to prison to stand trial	1	—	3	—	4	—
s. 73 patients dealt with by the Courts	1	—	8	1	9	1
Made subject to a further order	1	—	3	—	4	—
Released on licence	—	—	4	—	4	—
Died	8	1	12	2	20	3
Other disposal	4	—	2	—	6	—
Total	73	10	231	22	304	32

†Reproduced from *Criminal Statistics for England and Wales for 1974,* Cmnd. 6168, p. 242.

Table 3
Comparison of effects of hospital orders made with and without restriction orders on discharge.
Unless otherwise stated, the legislation referred to is the Mental Health Act 1959.

Hospital order made without restrictions on discharge	*Hospital order made with restrictions on discharge*
Enabling legislation	
s. 60(1) Empowers the court on conviction of an offence punishable with imprisonment, to make a hospital order, except where the offence carries a sentence fixed by law (e.g. murder).	s. 65(1) Empowers the Crown Court to make an order restricting discharge in conjunction with a hospital order if the Court is of opinion that such measures are necessary for the protection of the public. The restriction order may be made with or without limit of time.
(2) Empowers magistrates' courts to make a hospital order without conviction, if satisfied that the defendant did the act or made the omission charged.	s. 67(1) Magistrates' courts cannot themselves make a restriction order, but may remit the case for the Crown Court to do so.
	(3) Where a case is referred under s. 67(1) the Crown Court may either make a hospital order (with or without restrictions on discharge) or pass any other sentence available to the magistrates' courts.

65

Specification of illness

s. 60(1) Two medical practitioners must satisfy the court that the offender is suffering from mental illness, psychopathic disorder, subnormality or severe subnormality, of a nature or degree which warrants detention in a hospital for medical treatment; and that a hospital order is the most suitable method of disposal considering the character and antecedents of the offender.

s. 62(1) States that at least one of the medical practitioners giving evidence must be a practitioner approved by the Secretary of State as having special experience in the diagnosis or treatment of mental disorders.

s. 65(2) Before a restriction order is made, one medical practitioner must give oral evidence before the court (though this need not be the practitioner approved as having special experience in the diagnosis or treatment of mental disorders).

Admission to hospital

s. 63(1) The patient must be admitted to hospital within 28 days of the making of the order; he may be conveyed there by a constable, a social worker or any other person specified by the court. A hospital order is sufficient authority for the hospital managers to detain the patient.

s. 64(1) Authorises the conveyance of the patient to "a place of safety" (generally a police station, but it may be a mental hospital) pending his admission to hospital within the 28-day period referred to in s. 63(1).

As with hospital orders without restrictions on discharge.

Location of hospital

s. 60(1)	The hospital is specified by the court.
(3)	The court must be satisfied that arrangements have been made for admission to the hospital specified in the order.
s. 64(2)	The Secretary of State for Social Services may direct the patient to another hospital if the hospital specified in the order is unable to accept him.

As with hospital orders without restrictions on discharge.

Duration of authority to detain

s. 43(1) and 3rd Schedule	Initially for one year.

s. 65(1) A restriction order may be made for a period fixed by the court, or without limit of time.

Renewal of authority to detain

s. 43(2) and 3rd Schedule	Authority to detain may be renewed (a) for a further period of one year in the first instance, and then (b) for a further period of two years and so on for periods of not more than two years at a time, provided that:
(3)	within the period of two months ending on the day on which authority to detain would cease, the RMO examines the patient and concludes that further detention is necessary in the interests of the patient's health or safety or for the protection of the public. If the RMO so decides, he shall furnish to the hospital managers a report to that effect.
(5)	This shall renew the authority to detain.

s. 65(5) If the order is made for a fixed period and ceases to have effect while the hospital order is still in force, then the hospital order has the same effect as if it had just been made (see s. 43(2) opposite).

Transfer to a different hospital

s. 41(1) and 3rd Schedule	Under circumstances prescribed, and regulations made by the Secretary of State for Social Services, the patient may be transferred to another hospital (or into guardianship).	3rd Schedule	Transfer is only possible with the consent of the Home Secretary; no transfer into guardianship is permitted.

Reclassification of illness

s. 38(1) and 3rd Schedule	If the RMO reports to the hospital managers that the patient is suffering from an illness other than that specified in the order, the order shall have effect as if the reclassified illness were specified.	3rd Schedule	No provisions on reclassification apply.
s. 123(3)	A Mental Health Review Tribunal may reclassify.		As with hospital orders without restrictions on discharge, except that the tribunal may only *recommend* reclassification.

Leave of absence

s. 39(1)	The RMO may grant a leave of absence with or without conditions. Leave may be for:	s. 65(3) (c) (i) and 3rd Schedule	Leave of absence may be granted only with the consent of the Home Secretary, who has the power of recall.
(2)	an indefinite or a specified period;		
(3)	the RMO may direct that the patient remain in the custody of:		
	an officer on the staff of the hospital, or any other person authorised in writing by the hospital managers.	(c)	The Home Secretary or the RMO has the power to recall a patient who is granted a leave of absence under section 39.
(4)	The RMO may recall the patient at any time if he feels it to be in the interests of his health or safety or for the protection of others.	(d)	The Home Secretary has the power of recall at any time during the continuance of the restriction order.
(5)	If the patient is on leave of absence for a period of 6 months without recall, after that period he shall no longer be subject to recall, and ceases to be liable to be detained.		

Absence without leave

s.40 — If a patient is absent from the hospital without permission, he may be taken back into custody, except:

(3)(a) after 6 months' absence (in the case of a psychopathic or subnormal patient aged 21 or over) or;

(b) in any other case, after 28 days' absence.

s. 65(3)(a) and 3rd Schedule — The patient may be taken back into custody at any time, at the instigation of the Home Secretary.

Mental Health Review Tribunals

Who can apply and when

s. 38(2) — If the patient is reclassified (see above) and is aged 16 or over, the patient or the nearest relative may apply for a hearing within 28 days of reclassification.

s. 65(3)(b) and 3rd Schedule — No application may be made either by the patient or the nearest relative.

s. 43(6) — If the patient is aged 16 or over and a report is furnished under s. 43 for renewal of detention, he may apply for a hearing during the period of the renewal.

s. 66(6) — The Home Secretary may *refer* any case for *advice only* at any time; and a written request from a patient for him to do so (in accordance with the provisions of subsection 7) must be referred for a hearing within 2 months.

s. 57 — The Secretary of State for Social Services may request a hearing at any time.

(7) — One year must expire before the patient can make a request for referral under (6) above; and thereafter the patient may request once during each period during which he could have made an application if he were not subject to a restriction order (i.e. on the expiration of the second period of 12 months of detention, and every two years thereafter).

s. 63(4) (a) The patient may apply within the first 6 months of the making of the order (see above) or on attaining 16 years, whichever is the later.

(b) The nearest relative may apply within the first 12 months of detention, and within any subsequent period of 12 months.

(8) — If the patient has been conditionally discharged and then recalled, he may request a hearing between 6 and 12 months after the date of recall.

s. 123(1) The Tribunal must discharge the patient if satisfied that: he is not then suffering from mental illness, psychopathic disorder, subnormality or severe subnormality; or it is not necessary in the interests of the patient's health or safety, or for the protection of the public to detain him further; or where application is made under s. 44(3) (that the patient is classified as psychopathic and has attained 25 years of age and is likely to act in a dangerous manner if released) and the Tribunal is of opinion that the patient is not likely to act in a dangerous manner.

(3) The Tribunal may recommend that the patient be reclassified.

s. 66(6) The Tribunal may advise the Home Secretary that the patient should be discharged, transferred to another hospital, advanced within the present hospital, given trial leave of absence, that the restrictions on discharge should be removed, that the patient should be repatriated, or that his case should be reviewed or referred for another hearing within 12 months.

Discharge from hospital

s. 43(6)	The hospital managers may discharge.
s. 47 and 3rd Schedule	The RMO or the hospital managers may discharge.
s. 47(4) and 3rd Schedule, and para. 88, 4th Schedule. NHS Reorganisation Act 1973 and NHS Regulations, s. 1, 1973, No. 1286.	The powers conferred on the hospital managers by section 47 may be exercised by any three or more members of the authority or by three or more members of a committee of the authority or body authorised by the authority.
s. 123(1)	The Mental Health Review Tribunal may discharge.
s. 66(1)	If the Home Secretary is satisfied that it is not necessary in the public interest, he may direct that the restriction order shall cease to have effect; and where he so directs, the patient will then be subject to the provisions of s. 65(5) and will be treated as if admitted under a hospital order made on the date on which the restrictions on discharge ceased to have effect.
(2)	The Home Secretary may discharge absolutely or subject to conditions (when the patient is subject to recall at any time until the order lapses).
s. 47 and 3rd Schedule	With the consent of the Home Secretary, the RMO or hospital managers may discharge.

71

References and Notes

1. Mental Health Act 1959, s. 65(1).
2. *Ibid.*, s. 65(5).
3. R v Gardiner [1967] 1 All E.R.895; 1 W.L.R.464; *Crim L. Rev.* 231.
4. *The Aarvold Report,* Cmnd. 5191, January 1973, para. 7.
5. *The Butler Report,* p. 194.
6. Mental Health Act 1959, s. 67(1).
7. In accordance with section 68(2), an order under section 68(1) of the Mental Health Act has (until the case is disposed of by the Crown Court) the same effect as a hospital order with special restrictions made without limit of time, except that the references to the 28-day period are omitted. In practice this means, *inter alia,* that the hospital specified in the order must be willing to admit the patient.
8. Mental Health Act 1959, s. 68(1).
9. *Ibid.*, s. 67(3).
10. N. Walker and S. McCabe, *Crime and Insanity in England,* vol. 2, 1973, p. 89.
11. Mental Health Act 1959, s. 65(2).
12. *Ibid.*, s. 65(3)(a).
13. *Ibid.*, s. 65(3)(c).
14. "Memorandum on Parts I, IV to VII and IX of the Act" 1960, para. 167.
15. *Ibid.*, para. 166.
16. *The Butler Report,* para. 14.25.
17. Mental Health Act 1959, s. 65(3)(b).
18. *Ibid.*, s. 66(6).
19. *Ibid.*, ss. 66(7) and 43(6).
20. *Ibid.*, s. 66(8).
21. *Ibid.*, s. 66(2).
22. *Ibid.*, ss. 66(3), 65(3)(d) and 39.
23. *Criminal Statistics in England and Wales for the Year 1974,* Cmnd. 6168, pp.240-241.
24. Mental Health Act 1959, s. 66(4).
25. *Ibid.*, s. 66(1).
26. P. G. McGrath, "The mentally abnormal offender", *Medico-Legal Journal,* vol. 41, 1973, p. 4.

5. Restriction orders – observations, analysis and proposals for reform

In analysing the law relating to mentally abnormal offenders, it is important to examine whether they are treated differently from other people in a similar position solely because they have been diagnosed as mentally disordered. The two groups compared in this chapter are those detained in prison as 'ordinary' offenders and those detained in hospital as 'abnormal' offenders. In comparing the two groups, the nature of the crime committed must be taken into account. Later, it will be necessary to determine whether the evidence justifies any difference in treatment between the two groups.

Comparison between the abnormal offender subject to a restriction order and the ordinary offender subject to a life sentence

Apart from the restriction order, the life sentence* is the only truly indefinite sentence in English law.[1] The Home Secretary may release a person serving a sentence of life imprisonment at any time[2] (if recommended to do so by the Parole Board, and subject to consultation with the Lord Chief Justice and the trial judge if available). Figures supplied by the Home Office show that the average length of detention under a life sentence is nine years,[3] while the average period under a restriction order is somewhat less (the precise figures are given later in this chapter). Yet in both cases, the disposal may be considered as "truly one for the duration of natural life in that the convicted person remains under supervision and is subject to recall".[4] Also, in both cases it is possible for a prisoner or patient to be detained for the rest of his natural life, and in both cases this has on occasion happened.

Thus, so far as release is concerned, an abnormal offender subject to an unlimited restriction order is in much the same position as a person sentenced to life imprisonment.[5] Accordingly, in the case of abnormal offenders convicted of life-carrying offences, we think it proper that judges should make restriction orders without limit of time if they believe it to be in the best interests of the offender. However, unlimited restriction orders are sometimes made for non-life-carrying (sometimes even non-violent or trivial) offences; in such cases, MIND has serious reservations concerning the power of courts to impose an indefinite sentence which may result in prolonged detention in a high-security institution.

Comparison between the abnormal offender subject to a restriction order and the ordinary offender subject to a fixed sentence

The ordinary offender usually receives a finite sentence related to the

*Detention at Her Majesty's Pleasure is similar in effect to a life sentence.

severity of the offence, and for each category of offence (other than life-carrying offences) Parliament has placed limits beyond which he cannot be detained. If the Executive keeps the offender in custody beyond his finite sentence, the detention is illegal and he may be freed through the remedy of *habeas corpus.*[6]

The system of parole adds a small element of indeterminacy to the usual prison sentence. Parole may be defined as:

> "the discharge of prisoners from custody in advance of their expected date of release, provided they agree to abide by certain conditions, so that they may serve some portion of their sentences under supervision in the community, but subject to recall for misconduct".[7]

A prisoner is entitled to be considered for parole after serving one-third of his sentence; he is entitled to unconditional release with remission after serving two-thirds of his sentence. A person released on parole is said to be 'on licence'. During the currency of his licence he is subject to recall for breach of any of its conditions. It will last, however, only until the date when he would be entitled to unconditional release with remission, i.e. after two-thirds of his finite sentence.[8] After that, any further detention in prison must result from a fresh conviction by a criminal court; detention in a mental hospital can only result if the procedures under Part IV of the Mental Health Act are followed.

In contrast, the period of legal custody for the abnormal offender is wholly indefinite and bears no clear relation to the severity of his offence. If the detention persists beyond the maximum possible prison sentence for the particular category of offence, there is no legal redress. When the restricted patient is discharged on licence, the conditions of discharge will not expire after some finite period. He is subject to supervision and may be recalled to hospital at any time during the duration of the restriction order (often for life) – no formal procedures are necessary and no reasons need be given.

Tables A and B† indicate the types of offence for which offender-patients have been detained. The broad categories shown encompass a wide diversity of criminal behaviour, ranging from the serious (involving bodily harm to a person) to the relatively trivial (involving minor property damage or negligible harm to a person). For example, Walker and McCabe[9] classified the harmfulness of the sexual offences committed by a sample of 161 abnormal offenders (including restricted and unrestricted patients). Of these cases, 70% involved either minor shock or no effect on the victim, or trivial incidents; 21% involved indecent exposure; and only 9% involved serious bodily harm or some violence to the person.

The authors reported that acquisitive offences (robbery, theft, fraud, and breaking and entering for gain) represented by far the highest proportion of cases. Some of these involved serious violent behaviour, but the authors suggested that more often they were petty affairs that involved food, small sums of money, or minor saleable items.[10]

---

†Tables A-F are shown at the end of this chapter.

Despite the diversity of criminal behaviour covered by the various categories of offence shown in Tables A and B, a substantial proportion of the restricted patients were convicted for serious offences. In 1974, 48% of all restriction orders to special and other hospitals were made in cases that involved homicide, attempted homicide or other violent offences against the person (Table A). The corresponding figure for *residents of special hospitals only* on 31 December, 1975 was 52% (Table B). These crimes would often have led to long fixed sentences or indefinite (e.g. life) sentences; hence a restriction order cannot be described as more severe.*

These tables also show that the abnormal offender need not be a seriously violent person; he may have been convicted of a relatively trivial offence, such as fraud and forgery, criminal damage, vagrancy and street offences, or other non-indictable offences. The Criminal Statistics give a more detailed breakdown of the broad categories shown in Tables A and B. Restriction orders are on occasion made for social offences such as frequenting, prostitution, disorderly behaviour, shoplifting, drunkenness, indecent exposure and misuse of drugs. Many of these involve no substantial harm to another person, and therefore do not justify the severe effects of a restriction order.

Walker and McCabe reported one case in which a 17-year-old mentally handicapped boy was given a restriction order. His offences involved homosexual acts with consenting adults – usually for money – and one or two petty thefts. In another case, a 19-year-old mentally handicapped boy was given a restriction order after being found guilty of sexual intercourse with a mentally handicapped girl not much below the age of consent. Walker and McCabe classified 17 sexual offences in their sample as 'trivial'. In one case, a mentally handicapped man in his thirties had been paying boys for mutual masturbation. When they increased their charges, he found himself in debt and went to the police for their advice. In another case, a depressed man of 23 had placed his hand on the leg of a 12-year-old girl sitting beside him on a bus.[11]

Similarly, D. A. Thomas[5] reported cases where restriction orders were made for malicious damage to a shop window, obstructing a railway carriage and petty larceny.

Dr Henry Rollin reviewed 127 abnormal offenders admitted to Horton Hospital in 1961 and 1962 (16% of these were subject to restriction orders). In the following cases, it was difficult to see the need for a hospital order: one person was charged with stealing a box of tomatoes from Covent Garden Market, and another with the theft of a bottle of milk; another was charged with fraud involving a sum of £70.00. There were 51 offences against the public order, mainly for 'being a suspected person', 'wandering abroad', or 'begging'. There were five sexual offences, all involving indecent exposure. Dr

---

*One should point out, however, that even where convicted of these two categories of offences, offenders may be treated more leniently under the penal law than under the Mental Health Act. The figures discussed later in this Chapter show that even for these serious offences, ordinary offenders are often given non-custodial or short-term fixed prison sentences. But restricted patients tend to spend many years in hospital after conviction for the same type of offence.

Rollin also reviewed some cases in which the offences were more serious. He concluded that "the range of offences are indistinguishable from that of offences committed by a comparable sample of mentally normal offenders."[12]

The Butler Committee made this observation about the excessive use of restriction orders by the judiciary:

> "The making of a restriction order has potentially serious consequences for the defendant because of the special procedural steps, involving the Home Secretary, taken to establish that he is fit to be discharged, and . . . because of his liability to remain subject to supervisory conditions. (In 1974 the average period of detention under a section 65 order was $4\frac{1}{2}$ years. Detention could last for life.) For this reason . . . restriction orders should not be made unless they are fully justified. Evidence given to us by the Home Office has indicated the possibility that these orders are imposed in numbers of cases where their severity is not appropriate. . . . Some courts have evidently imposed restrictions on, for example, the petty recidivist because of the virtual certainty that he will persist in similar offences in the future. In our view, this is not the sort of case in which a section 65 order should be imposed."[13]

The Percy Committee recommended that a restriction order should be made only as a result of a 'serious' offence.[14] Unfortunately, this recommendation was not enacted by Parliament; instead, the Mental Health Act authorised the judiciary to make restriction orders as a result of any imprisonable offence, including non-violent or trivial offences. MIND's view is that unlimited restriction orders should be made only after a conviction for specified serious offences. (Specific proposals are made at the end of this chapter.)

MIND also knows of a number of other cases where restriction orders did not appear appropriate. The cases of Evans and 'M' have already been cited in Chapter 3. Miss Evans, while an informal patient in a local hospital, set fire to a chair; only nominal damage was caused. She was convicted of arson and admitted to Rampton Special Hospital under a restriction order without limit of time. Two medical practitioners said she was suffering from a mental disorder that was not susceptible to treatment. This meant she might have to spend many years as a restricted patient in a secure hospital. Her lawyers told MIND that by contrast, she would probably have received a non-custodial sentence if she had been dealt with as an ordinary offender.

M was a top recruit in the Royal Navy who was given an unlimited restriction order for dangerous driving (although no harm was actually done). The question was raised whether he was attempting to run his girl-friend over, but this was not proved at the trial. The girl-friend, in fact, did not even know that he was in the vicinity at the time. M has now been in Broadmoor for more than three years – one year longer than the maximum prison sentence for dangerous driving.

Smith's case[15] is another good example. In 1974, Nigel Gordon Smith was convicted of fraud for entering into a 'forecasting venture': he invited people to put up money in return for offers of inspired forecasts concerning horse races, and made extravagant claims of past success. As a result, he made a total profit of £2,580, but £2,250 was recovered. The loss to the 'punting' public was £330. The court noted that "this was not a new kind of fraud, and compared with others of the same kind, it was not at all serious."

Nigel Smith has no history of mental illness and no criminal record.

The court gave the opinion that Mr Smith was not a violent person, but added that "section 65 does not refer to violence". The court heard evidence from several psychiatrists:

"Some doctors conceded that nothing more than out-patient treatment was required; others have been of the opinion that the applicant should be treated as an in-patient in a National Health Mental Hospital. One doctor – a Dr Loucas – who is on the staff at Broadmoor Hospital, right from the beginning took the view that this applicant should be dealt with in a secure hospital."

Mr Smith was first considered dangerous as a result of his psychiatric interview. He told the psychiatrist that he had acted violently while at school, and on one occasion had attempted to strangle his mother.* Both Nigel and his mother told MIND that they did not believe at the time that this statement would be taken seriously. The Court of Appeal made investigations and concluded that the account of past violence he had given the doctor was not true. Nevertheless, the psychiatrist felt this was a delusion which could potentially cause Mr Smith to act dangerously.

On November 30, 1973, the court ordered that Mr Smith should be detained in Broadmoor Hospital under a restriction order, made without limit of time; he is still (November, 1976) detained in Broadmoor, and there is no indication that he will be transferred or discharged in the near future.

In *McFarlane's* case (1975)[16] the Court of Appeal uncharacteristically went out of its way to refer to the injustice Nigel Smith had suffered. The Court described Smith as a "petty fraudsman" who had no history of violence, saying that "special hospitals should not be cluttered up with cases of his sort". Indeed, the court stated that the criteria for admission to special hospitals found in section 40 of the National Health Service Reorganisation Act 1973† had not been properly met.

The apparent injustice in *Smith's* case, which should be of particular concern to lawyers, is the statutory effect of an unlimited restriction order. If Nigel Smith had been dealt with as a 'normal' offender, he would have received a non-custodial sentence or perhaps a very short prison sentence (he had no criminal record). Instead, he was diagnosed as mentally ill and dealt with as an 'abnormal' offender.

*Mr Smith told MIND that he was under stress while the psychiatrist interviewed him in prison; he had been the victim of a homosexual attack in prison the day before.

†Under section 40 of the National Health Service Reorganisation Act 1973, a person should not be admitted to a special hospital unless the secretary of State for Social Services is of opinion that he requires treatment under conditions of special security on account of his dangerous, violent or criminal propensities.

He was 24 years old when he entered Broadmoor; he has been detained for three years, and he remains liable to detention (at the discretion of the Home Secretary) for an indefinite period. When he is released he will undoubtedly be on licence; and the licence will not expire, except by direction of the Home Secretary. He may quite conceivably remain under legal custody or legal control (i.e. under mandatory supervision in the community and liable to recall for breach of conditions of discharge) for the rest of his life.

It is argued that the Home Secretary, and the psychiatric consultants who advise him, exercise their power wisely and make every effort to discharge all offender-patients as quickly as possible: in fact, there is a severe shortage of beds in the special hospitals and for this reason alone, doctors do not wish to keep patients any longer than is necessary. It is also true that the conditions of discharge placed on restricted patients are reasonably calculated to help them cope in the community. Yet if a person like Nigel Smith has been convicted only of a non-violent offence, it is hard to justify the imposition of potentially life-long control on the grounds that it will be exercised in good faith and for benign purposes. Restricted patients are sometimes discharged fairly quickly from hospital, but the Butler Report highlighted the undoubted fact that doctors are very cautious about recommending the release of abnormal offenders.[17] This is understandable, given the pressures upon them to protect the public from even the possibility of violent behaviour: if a patient is released from a special hospital and subsequently harms himself or others, the doctor is shown to have made an error of judgment, and he may be subject to unfair criticism by the Government, the media and the public. But if the patient is confined until there can be a virtual guarantee that he will not re-convict, the doctor is fully protected. He has no way of knowing whether he is detaining a non-violent individual, but there will be no outcry from the public (except, perhaps, from a few relatives and friends*).

Of course, the ultimate decision on whether to discharge a restricted patient is left to the unfettered discretion of a Government Minister, who is an elected Member of Parliament. He is under enormous political pressure to confine the offender, perhaps longer than is justified by the nature and severity of the offence.† This is especially so since the public has been out-

---

*It may be of some interest to the reader that Nigel Smith's mother printed a very defamatory statement against the staff at Broadmoor. She did so with the express desire that the individuals involved would sue her for libel. She was convinced that she could prove the truth of her statement in open court. No member of staff has pursued the issue.

†In its evidence to the Butler Committee, the National Council for Civil Liberties was emphatic on this matter:
"The Home Secretary cannot claim to be a psychiatric expert. He is a politician and subject to popular pressures which may not always reflect the best interests of the detained individual. The N.C.C.L. believe that no elected politician should have the power to prevent the release of an individual originally detained by judicial authority."
The *Broadmoor Chronicle* written by the patients at the special hospital, graphically described the feelings of the patients: "Are we to pay for the sins of Graham Young?"

raged by cases such as those of Graham Young, Patrick Mackay and Ian Dunlop. In fact, in 1972, the year when Graham Young's case was disclosed, the number of discharges made by the Home Secretary dropped by 30% (see Table C, shown at the end of this chapter).

On the other hand, when an ordinary offender is discharged after serving a fixed sentence and subsequently re-offends, no one can be blamed. The decision on discharge (within predictable limits) was taken by the trial judge at the time of sentencing, and neither the prison officials nor the Home Secretary have discretionary authority to keep the offender in preventive detention after the expiry of his sentence.

Some statistical observations

Longitudinal studies have been made in the United States[18] and the Scandinavian countries[19] which suggest that abnormal offenders are confined for longer periods than ordinary offenders convicted of the same crimes. Although there have been no comparable studies in this country, there is some statistical support for the belief that this also happens here.

Restricted patients in special and local hospitals are detained for an average of $4\frac{1}{2}$ years.[13] In the case of special hospitals only, the figure is approximately $5\frac{1}{2}$-8 years.*

These periods of detention are considerably longer than those customary for ordinary offenders, regardless of the types of offence considered.† One notes, for example, that consistently more restriction orders are made for the offences of manslaughter, wounding or other act endangering life, and for arson, than for any other particular offence.‡ The most frequent prison sentence for conviction of any of these three offences is 2-3 years[22] (see Table 1), which means that with good behaviour an ordinary offender can be assured of release with remission in 16-24 months.

Table 1 compares the prison sentences given to ordinary offenders for the three particular offences under consideration, with the actual length of detention of residents of special hospitals.

---

*Of patients who left Broadmoor during 1974 and 1975, the average length of stay was 5 years and 7 months for discharged patients, and 6 years and 3 months for patients transferred to local NHS hospitals.[20] (Most of these patients were transferred to local NHS hospitals, where they continued to be detained for indefinite periods.) In Walker and McCabe's survey[21], 60% of all restricted male patients in the special hospitals had not yet been discharged after 8 years of detention.

†The offence of murder cannot be included in this analysis, since the sentence is fixed by law. The average length of detention for a life sentence is 9 years.[3]

‡In each of the last three years, a consistent 48-49% of all restriction orders were made for one of these three offences. See *Criminal Statistics in England and Wales* for 1973 (Cmnd. 5677), 1974 (Cmnd. 6168) and 1975 (Cmnd. 6566).

The most significant difference between the two groups of offenders is that 47% of the 'abnormal' group in special hospitals have been detained for 5 years or more, while only 14% of the sentenced prisoners are in this position. Furthermore, the sentenced prisoners, with good behaviour, will be released with remission after two-thirds of the actual sentences shown in the table.

The bar graph on page 81 visually illustrates the marked propensity for the abnormal offender to be detained in a special hospital much longer than ordinary offenders in prison. The figures used are taken from Table 1.

Table 1

Sentence without remission* Number of years detained†	Percentage of total population (to the nearest 1%)	
	Special hospital patients	Sentenced prisoners
1 or less	5	14
1-2	15	26
2-3	14	29
3-4	12	9
4-5	9	8
5-7	15	6
7-10	12	3
Over 10 (including life sentences)	20	5

*Sentences passed by the Crown Courts in 1974 for the offences of manslaughter, wounding or other act endangering life and arson.
Source: Criminal Statistics in England and Wales for 1974, Cmnd. 6168, pp.206-215.

†Number of years detained in the special hospitals as mid-1974.
Source: unpublished information received from the Department of Health and Social Security. The raw data are shown in Table E at the end of this chapter.
Note:
   A similar comparison of the actual lengths of detention of the prison and special hospital populations is shown in Table D at the end of this chapter.

Table 2 shows the number of long-stay patients in the special hospitals in mid-1974. One patient in every five had been detained for 10 years or more (and continued to be detained). Nearly 6% had been detained for 20 years or more. Fifty-two people had been detained for 30 years or more, 14 of them for 40 years or more and 3 for more than 50 years.[23] The comparable prison statistics for similar offences against the person show that prisoners released after serving life sentences had typically spent 8 to 10 years in jail and only a few over 13 years (see Table 3). Currently, the longest surviving prisoner has been in jail for 24 years.[24]

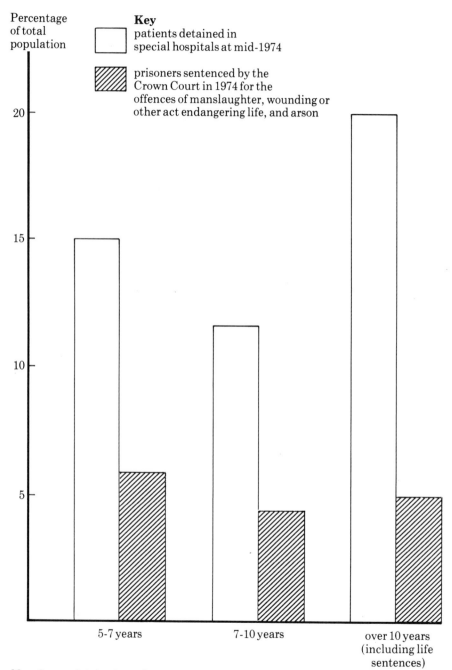

Percentage
of total
population

Key

□ patients detained in
special hospitals at mid-1974

▨ prisoners sentenced by the
Crown Court in 1974 for the
offences of manslaughter, wounding or
other act endangering life, and arson

20

15

10

5

5-7 years   7-10 years   over 10 years
(including life
sentences)

No. of years detained or prison sentence received

Table 2*
Long-stay residents of special hospitals in mid-1974: number of years detained

Number of years	Over 4	Over 5	Over 7	Over 10	Over 15	Over 20	Over 30	Over 40
Hospital								
Broadmoor (846 patients)								
Number	435	364	264	166	75	51	19	3
Percentage of total	51.4%	43.0%	31.2%	19.6%	8.9%	6.0%	2.2%	0.4%
Rampton (1,061 patients)								
Number	625	526	366	249	133	77	31	11
Percentage of total	59.0%	49.6%	34.5%	23.5%	12.5%	7.3%	2.9%	1.0%
Moss Side (428 patients)								
Number	231	192	111	52	24	10	2	—
Percentage of total	54.0%	44.9%	25.9%	12.1%	5.6%	2.3%	0.5%	
All special hospitals (2,335 patients)								
Number	1,291	1,082	741	467	232	138	52	14
Percentage of total	55.3%	46.3%	31.7%	20.0%	9.9%	5.9%	2.2%	0.5%

*Compiled from unpublished information received from the Department of Health and Social Security. (The raw data are given in Table E, shown at the end of this chapter.)
Note: the numbers and percentages are cumulative.

Table 3*
Persons under life sentences who were recommended for release on parole in 1974.

Number of complete years served	3	5	6	7	8	9	10	11	12	13	14	15	18
Number of prisoners	1	1	2	2	7	11	5	1	5	3	1	1	2

*Source: Report of the Parole Board for 1974, p. 2.

The great disparity between the detentions of abnormal and ordinary offenders is probably not due to any difference in the 'criminality' or 'dangerousness' of the two groups of offenders: the evidence suggests that abnormal and ordinary offenders as a whole have similar criminal records[25] and re-conviction rates. Rather, the reason given for the prolonged detention of the abnormal offender is usually the patient's need for treatment. In the following pages, we explore, *inter alia*, the soundness of this thinking.

The 'therapy' label

One reason often given for treating abnormal and normal offenders differently is that the former are receiving 'therapy', while the latter are receiving 'punishment'. This traditional assumption has caused the lawyer to stop at the hospital door, and not really apply his mind to the comparative effects of a restriction order and a prison sentence.

Members of the legal profession argue that the partly indeterminate nature of the criminal justice system, notably the parole and juvenile legislation, is based upon the insupportable concept of the 'rehabilitative ideal'.[26] The most important arguments are these:

(1) There is no empirical evidence that treatment in prison can reduce the reconviction rate or otherwise rehabilitate the offender. Even pro gressive institutions such as Grendon Underwood* cannot claim a marked success rate.[27]

(2) The success of the treatment offered in a prison may largely depend upon the inmate's voluntary compliance. His compliance is unlikely to be genuine where his release date is to some extent dependent on his cooperation and response to treatment.[28]

*Grendon Underwood, situated in Buckinghamshire, was opened in 1962 for selected convicted prisoners who are thought to need psychiatric observation or treatment. Grendon does not accept inmates direct from the courts, but receives them from prisons and borstals at the direction of the Prison Department and upon preliminary investigation by medical officers at those establishments. The prisoners must be willing to undergo psychiatric observation and treatment.

Research conducted under the auspices of the Home Office produced no significant evidence that reconviction rates are lowered by the psychiatric treatment given at Grendon.[27]

(3) The concept of rehabilitation legitimises too much. It can lead to longer confinement and to physical treatment against the offender's wishes. If reform is regarded as one of the purposes of prison, more powers may be taken over the inmate's life than his offence can justify.[29]

With some modifications, these and other arguments could also be applied to abnormal offenders. Yet the legal profession has blindly accepted the concept of indefinite confinement for the mentally disordered.

J. E. Hall Williams states, without explanation, that definite sentences are preferred in the English law, with the sole exception of cases concerning the mentally disordered and children.[30] Similarly, Rupert Cross, Professor of Law at the University of Oxford, offers this unquestioning observation:[31]

"Although there is, no doubt, a large class of mentally ill offenders who would rather be in a prison than a mental hospital, if only on account of their horror of being thought 'nuts', I do not think that anyone would wish to quarrel with the development to which I have referred [unlimited restriction orders]."

The courts also use the therapy label to avoid a detailed consideration of the comparative effects of a hospital order and a prison sentence. In *Bennett's case*,[32] the Court of Appeal held that a restriction order without limit of time is no more severe than a prison sentence of whatever length.* Lord Justice Widgery said:

"In our judgment, a hospital order, which is a remedial order designed to treat and cure the appellant, cannot be regarded as more severe than a sentence of imprisonment, even though in certain events the hospital order may involve detention of the appellant for a longer period of time."

It is true that a mentally disordered person should be 'treated' in hospital and not 'punished' in prison; its very truth makes it more obvious that although a hospital has an essentially caring role, compulsory attendance is often just as much a deprivation of liberty as a prison sentence.[33] This is especially true when one compares a special hospital with an open prison. Broadmoor, for example, though humanely run, must necessarily be as restrictive as a prison.

In fact, there are legitimate reasons why some patients in special hospitals may prefer to be in a prison: †

(1) As has already been pointed out, an abnormal offender may be detained longer than the maximum prison sentence for the crime of which he is

---

The Butler Report (para 13.23) recommended that the Court of Appeal should not be empowered to substitute a hospital order for a term of imprisonment without the offender's consent. MIND agrees with this proposal.

†In *Civil Liberty*, vol. 39, no. 6, 1973, the National Council for Civil Liberties writes: "Broadmoor, it is claimed, is a hospital, yet the conditions are such that detainees often ask the NCCL if we can help get them transferred back to prison."

convicted; moreover, he can never look forward to a date when he is certain to be released.

(2) The patient is categorised as both 'mentally abnormal' and 'criminal'; these two categories together carry a much more malevolent stigma than they do separately. This dual stigma may reduce the patient's prospects of obtaining housing and employment when released.

(3) The abnormal offender must accept treatment against his wishes.‡ There are no apparent limits to the types of treatment that may be imposed; these may include surgical, chemical, electrical or aversive therapies which are often repulsive to members of the public. The abnormal offender may be tacitly compelled to cooperate in receiving such treatment, even though the law is silent on this issue, because his release date is directly linked to his response to treatment. By comparison, the trial judge sets a maximum period of detention for most ordinary offenders, so they can refuse a coerced 'cure'.

Professor Glanville Williams, Q.C., offers a more thoughtful explanation of the differences between the treatments of ordinary and abnormal offenders. He believes it unjust that an offender who was originally imprisoned for a fixed term should remain liable to detention in hospital after his prison sentence has expired.[34] When MIND asked him whether he would extend this objection to abnormal offenders initially sentenced under sections 60/65 of the Mental Health Act, he replied:[35]

"I agree that if a person gets a prison sentence that is that; he should not be liable to detention afterwards except under civil commitment. But if he goes to hospital at the outset, the judge cannot foresee the length of detention that will be necessary. If you agree that section 65 is necessary for some people who have committed offences and who are sent to hospital under section 60, then it is again true that the judge cannot foresee the length of detention that will be necessary or the length of time that special restrictions will be needed. To argue otherwise is to confuse the hospital disposal with penal disposal. *The restriction order is not intended as a punishment, and cannot be governed by penal considerations.*" (Italics added.)

Here, Professor Williams is apparently distinguishing between two groups of abnormal offenders: those classified as abnormal when sentenced, and those classified as abnormal during the course of their sentences. This distinction is based upon the fortuitous circumstance of whether the mental disorder

---

‡Although in practice abnormal offenders are often required to accept treatment without their consent, the legal position is not clear on this point. See for example *A Human Condition*, vol. 1, pp. 121-124; J. Jacob, "The right of the mental patient to his psychosis," *Mod. L. Rev.*, vol. 39, Jan. 1976, p.17; *The Butler Report*, paras. 3.50-3.62; DHSS, *A Review of the Mental Health Act 1959*, HMSO, 1976, paras. 8.20-37.

develops before or after sentencing – or, even worse, when it is detected.* If an offender is classified as abnormal when sentenced, he may be detained under a *restriction order without limit of time.* If he is classified as abnormal while serving his sentence, he may not be detained after the expiry of his sentence except by a hospital order *without restrictions* (see Chapter 6 *infra*), and Professor Williams suggests that he should not be liable to detention at all. This important difference is apparently based upon the label given: either 'punishment' or 'therapy'. (A prisoner who is transferred to hospital is still being 'punished' as part of his prison sentence; he should not therefore be liable to detention after the expiry of that sentence. But a restricted patient is being 'treated', and therefore no time limits should be placed on his detention under the restriction order.)

It is also interesting to note that if an offender develops a mental disorder *after* he has served his prison sentence, he cannot be detained in hospital unless fresh proceedings are brought under the civil provisions of Part IV of the Mental Health Act. Once his prison sentence has expired, he is simply an ex-offender and has the same right to liberty as any other citizen. Thus, a person is treated differently under the law, depending on when he is classified as mentally disordered – at the time of sentencing, while serving a sentence, or after serving a sentence.

When Professor Williams and others say that "the restriction order is not intended as a punishment, and cannot be governed by penal considerations", they suggest that it is made for the purpose of treatment. Yet it is a hospital order which authorises detention for the purpose of therapy. The accompanying restriction order merely takes the decision on discharge from the doctor, and places it with the Home Secretary. The restriction order also labels the patient as dangerous. It therefore makes it more likely that he will be detained longer, and less likely that he will be accepted by the community when discharged.

A restriction order is made purely for *custodial* purposes; here the Home Secretary's first duty is to protect the public, and he is not legally obliged to discharge a potentially dangerous offender, even if he no longer suffers from a definable mental disorder. The case of *Frederick Michell* provides a good example of this.[36]

Mr Michell was admitted to Warlingham Park Hospital under a restriction order in 1970. In 1973 Dr C. McDonald, his responsible medical officer, felt that Mr Michell was no longer suffering from a definable mental disorder and asked the Home Secretary for his consent to discharge him. This was refused.

*Nigel Walker in his classic text *Crime and Punishment in Britain,* (rev. ed. 1968, pp. 264, 282-283), observes that an offender's abnormality may remain unrecognised until after sentencing:
"Sometimes his disorder is one that might have been diagnosed had he received a psychiatric examination earlier. He may be enjoying a remission of his symptoms when he is arrested and tried; there are cases in which the commission of the offence itself seems to produce a temporary improvement. Other prisoners may develop the first signs of mental illness during their sentence."

In February 1974 Mr Michell was transferred to Broadmoor Special Hospital (against the advice of Dr McDonald). Recently Dr Loucas, consultant psychiatrist at Broadmoor, concluded that Mr Michell was not mentally ill, and also asked the Home Secretary for permission to discharge him. The Croydon Social Services Department agreed to accept responsibility for Mr Michell in the community.

Despite the opinions of these two doctors and the local social services department, the Home Secretary has again refused to permit his discharge. (This is somewhat surprising, since Mr Michell is 70 years of age and dependent on crutches.)

We make no suggestion that Mr Michell should be exonerated for his crime. What this case-study should suggest, however, is that the restriction order was made very much for custodial, not for therapeutic reasons.

Psychiatrists in local hospitals have argued effectively that a restriction order is in fact anti-therapeutic; it ties the hands of the doctor, who cannot grant a leave of absence, a transfer or a discharge without the consent of the Home Secretary.

The decision in *Gardiner's* case,[37] where Lord Parker criticised the courts for "the alarming number of cases" in which hospital orders had been made without restrictions, attracted a good deal of comment from the psychiatric profession. Dr W. A. Heaton-Ward said in a letter to *The Times*:[38]

"In my experience, a restriction order is quite inappropriate in the case of a mentally subnormal patient admitted to an open psychiatric hospital which is trying to fulfil a therapeutic, rather than a merely custodial role. A patient subject to a restriction order cannot be allowed out of the hospital alone or accompanied for any reason without the prior permission of the Secretary of State. A normal programme of rehabilitation is, therefore, impossible."

Dr W. Woolen and Dr P. Graham Woolf, consultant psychiatrists at Darenth Park Hospital, Dartford, Kent, similarly stated:[39]

"Home Office approval for even trivial and routine decisions interferes gravely with the treatment of restriction order patients. Sometimes they cause interference with the treatment of other patients. Restricted patients cannot, without approval, go to a shop on Saturday. In the case of restricted patients in a ward of 40 or 50, if nurses decide to take them for a walk on a fine day, they have to remain within the hospital grounds. . . . It is important in the treatment and training of all patients that they should take part in local community activities."

Psychiatrists expressed further concern about restriction orders after the following incident. A local hospital received an official summons to send a restricted patient to the Court of Appeal. The hospital sent him, but was later admonished by the Home Office for not obtaining approval. One doctor asked sarcastically: "What happens if a restricted patient needs an urgent operation and he has to be sent to another hospital where there are the facilities? Are we to wait while permission is obtained?"[39]*

Psychiatrists in local hospitals have been reluctant to accept restricted patients (see for example the *Brazil* case in Chapter 3 *supra*). This is partly because hospitals commonly have inadequate security arrangements, but it is also because contemporary ideas on proper psychiatric treatment, which emphasise the importance of the patient's freedom and contact with the community, are incompatible with the terms of a restriction order. Dr Henry Rollin considers it unfair ever to admit a restricted patient to a local hospital.[41]

"Firstly, it is unfair to the public because of the lack of security which obtains. Secondly, it is unfair to the hospital because of the double standard of treatment expected of it in relation to those patients with restriction orders and those without. Lastly, it is unfair to the patient himself who is on a restriction order. He, understandably, may harbour a sense of grievance because he is subjected to a different standard of treatment, which indeed might incite him to abscond."

The argument that a restriction order is meant for treatment is most strongly refuted by the statistics on special hospitals presented earlier in this chapter. No psychiatrist would maintain that after 20, 30 or sometimes 50 years in a secure hospital, the offender's confinement is continued for treatment. There is, in fact, evidence that rehabilitation cannot take place if the offender is detained for long periods in a custodial setting.[42] The point was illustrated by Dr Richard Fox, consultant psychiatrist at Severalls Hospital, in a letter to *The Guardian*:[43]

"Courts, all too often, impose this section 65 restriction without limit of time which can mean interminable correspondence with the Home Office, the passing of the right moment for taking the next step in rehabilitation and the steady, institutional deterioration of the patient while administrative decisions are awaited from way up the network. . . . One is therefore left with a man who has partially or completely recovered, with or without maintenance medication, and who sits round the institution for weeks, months or years watching others coming and going, and becoming thoroughly demoralised as a result."

Similarly, the Hospital Advisory Service Report on Broadmoor points out that the medical staff can influence, but do not decide, the time of a patient's discharge. Accordingly, a patient's discharge may be delayed long past his recovery from mental disorder, for political rather than medical reasons.[44]

If treatment is still unsuccessful after some reasonable period of time, one must conclude that the detention is merely custodial. Hence it should be

---

*Shortly after that incident, the Home Office stated that consent may be assumed when patients detained under section 74 (and presumably under section 65) are to appear before the Court of Appeal, or need to be removed to another hospital for emergency medical treatment.[40]

governed by penal considerations – that is, its length should be roughly proportional to the gravity of the offence. The following two case studies illustrate some of the issues involved:

Robert's case[45]

On 8th June, 1966 at the Highgate Magistrates' Court, Robert was convicted of indecent assault on a male person and committed to Middlesex Quarter Sessions for sentence. (He was also convicted of a common assault, sentence for which was adjourned *sine die*.) When he appeared there on July 8, 1966 he was diagnosed by two medical practitioners as suffering from psychopathic disorder and the court authorised his detention in Broadmoor under section 60 of the Mental Health Act, with special restrictions for an unlimited period under section 65.

Robert had one previous conviction on September 13, 1965 for store-breaking with intent to commit a felony. He was conditionally discharged for 12 months. He had previously sought voluntary psychiatric help concerning his sexual problems.

In the summer of 1971, while still in Broadmoor Hospital, Robert was one of 12 patients who were to take part in an apparently experimental treatment programme of sex hormone implants. (In the event, only five patients actually went through with the treatment.) The treatment is designed to curb abnormal sexual desires in the sexual offender, who either takes an anti-male hormone drug, Androcur, in pill form every day, or has it implanted in pellet form in his buttocks or abdomen. Robert had an implant into his abdomen every three months for nearly two years. He was shown pornographic films of young boys every six weeks to test whether he was still sexually aroused.

As part of the treatment, Robert had an operation on his breast to prevent it from becoming enlarged. The operation, however, was done only on the right breast. The left breast, shortly after, became quite pronounced and began to hurt. It continued to grow until it became as large as a woman's breast. Robert was subject to extreme ridicule from other patients and some members of staff. Three of the patients, including Robert, eventually had to have an operation to remove the enlarged breast. The other two patients still suffer from one larger breast. One patient who received the mastectomy lost part of the skin and a nipple when the dressing from the operation was removed.

Robert and the two other patients now claim to suffer from the following injuries. The left breast is concave as a result of the major surgery upon it. There is nerve damage such that they have no feeling for a radius of three to four inches all around. Occasional deep aching pains occur in the left breast, and there is visible scarring under and to the side of the left nipple. The right breast is slightly enlarged.

The Department of Health and Social Security has been contacted.

They assert that the patients gave an informed consent to the treatment programme and that the treatment itself is well established. On the other hand, Robert claims that he was told that if he accepted the treatment and it was successful, he would be released within two years. His mother points out that "naturally, a person in his situation who is always looking for mercy to help him get out of that confinement, could hardly refuse to agree." She further alleges that the hospital had not sought her permission before embarking on the treatment. Moreover, she states that the reason the doctors give for his continued detention, and for the hormone treatment, is that he still has homosexual relations with fellow patients. She asks why this is necessary, since homosexual relations with consenting adults in private is now legal.*

At 8.30 pm on April 7, 1974, a fellow patient attacked Robert with a kitchen knife with intent to murder him. Robert was admitted to hospital with very serious injuries, including a severely cut throat and eleven stab wounds. He lost a massive amount of blood and there was great concern for his life. He is now badly scarred on the abdomen and throat.

Robert has recently been transferred to Park Lane (a special hospital in Maghull, Lancs.) where he still remains. MIND will represent him at a tribunal hearing which is to take place soon.

Robert's case illustrates several points: he has been detained under maximum security conditions for 10 years now, and there is no indication that he will be released in the near future. This is the equivalent of a 15-year prison sentence, and it resulted from an offence where he caused no actual physical injury. Further, since he went to hospital instead of prison, the medical authorities were able to impose upon him an apparently experimental treatment programme which has had tragic consequences.

Robert was given a hospital order as a result of two medical opinions that he suffered from a psychopathic disorder. The Butler Committee wrote at length on this subject,[46] and made the following three observations. (a) Psychiatrists disagree on the meaning of the term psychopathic disorder and over its diagnosis in particular cases. Some would limit it to a narrow group of dangerously anti-social individuals, but others extend it to cover inadequates of all descriptions, including those with sexual disorders. (b) The concept of 'psychopathic disorder' is itself intractable, and the behaviour of those diagnosed as psychopathic overlaps with that of other ordinary offenders. (c) The labelling of people as psychopaths has proved stigmatic, harmful and indelible. For this reason, Scotland and Northern Ireland have never introduced the term into their legislation.

Accordingly, the Butler Committee recommended an amendment to section 60 of the Mental Health Act to make clear the primary responsibility of the prison system for dealing with dangerous anti-social offenders. In

---

*MIND is advising Robert on his course of legal action. Domestic legal remedies may be sought. If unsuccessful, his case may well constitute cruel and degrading treatment under the European Convention.

particular, they suggest that sexual deviation alone should not be grounds for admission to hospital.

This is not to say that offenders who suffer from personality disorders cannot sometimes benefit from treatment. They should certainly be allowed to *choose* treatment as an alternative to prison. It is not desirable, however, for a judge to make a hospital order without the offender's consent. Moreover, even if the offender chooses hospital instead of prison, he should not face the prospect of unlimited detention, regardless of the severity of his offence. For if the release date is in the hands of the professional who provides treatment, it is unrealistic to believe that the patient can give an uncoerced and informed consent to the treatment programme.

Ford's case[47]

A trial judge passed a sentence of 27 months for the offence of dishonesty. This was especially severe for the particular offence: the court's reasoning was that the defendant, an alcoholic, had failed to cooperate on previous occasions. The lengthy sentence was made 'in his best interests' in the hope that he would be able to receive treatment in prison. The Court of Appeal reduced the sentence to 12 months. It said that a wrong principle had been applied; the trial court should not increase a sentence in order to include a curative element. This principle was re-affirmed by the Court of Appeal on two later occasions.[48]

Some inherent effects of indeterminate sentences

With determinate detention, the length of the sentence is decided by the trial judge, but with indeterminate detention it is decided by the Home Secretary and his advisers while the offender is in the institution. This difference lies at the heart of the controversy over indeterminate sentencing, for both the abnormal and the ordinary offender.*

It is argued that at the time of sentencing there is no way of knowing how long the offender will take to recover and can safely be released.[49] If the decision on discharge is taken while he is in the institution, more information will be available on treatment and housing in the community, job prospects, his mental condition and his family situation. Further, the offender's attitudes and behaviour in the institution can be taken into account.

It is therefore argued that those who have day-to-day responsibility for the offender are in a better position than the trial judge to advise on his release.

*The parole system, which embodies a method of selective release, is a clear example of partial indeterminate sentencing; hence it has been the chief focus of this controversy in relation to ordinary offenders. Even taking account of the parole system, the trial judge can set certain limits on the length of detention, and with good behaviour, one can usually predict the approximate date of discharge. But the trial judge has virtually no influence over the release date of a restricted patient, except in the unlikely event that the section 65 order is made for a limited period of time.

The trial judge has the function of sentencing the offender according to his past criminal behaviour and the gravity of his current offence. Sentences should generally reflect the principles of justice and equality – that is, the judge should treat the offender before him as equal with other similarly situated offenders.[50] In contrast, the Home Secretary has a special duty to protect the public. He must use the information provided by his advisers to assess the potential danger to the public if the offender is released. Thus predictive considerations (although they undoubtedly enter into all sentencing decisions, no matter by whom or when they are made) play a greater role in indeterminate than in fixed sentencing.

Members of the legal profession in Britain and abroad† are increasingly sceptical about indeterminate sentencing.[29] This is partly because recent studies have demonstrated that dangerousness is difficult to predict[51] (notably, it is difficult to predict from an inmate's behaviour in the institution whether he is likely to re-offend once discharged)[52] and that the effectiveness of treatment in reducing recidivism is open to serious question.[26] [27] In the case of the abnormal offender, it has already been pointed out (see pp.6-8 *supra*) that there is often no relationship between his mental disorder and his criminal behaviour. Lawyers and psychiatrists agree that a person may be 'cured' of his mental disorder but still be disposed to commit crime. The doctor has a duty to treat people, and in our haste to find a prophet, we also unfairly expect him to make predictions which are often unrelated to his medical expertise.

Perhaps the most important reason why the trial judge should set the maximum length of detention is that the defendant can appeal against his decisions, but there is apparently little redress against the decisions of the Home Secretary. Some of the cases already cited illustrate this point. In *Ford's* case[47] the trial court passed a sentence of 27 months for a relatively trivial offence, in order to 'cure' the offender of alcoholism; the Court of Appeal reduced it to 12 months. In *Clarke's* case,[53] the trial judge passed a prison sentence of 18 months when a disturbed person broke a flower pot in a hospital; the Court of Appeal reduced this to a fine of £2.

Any sentence passed by the trial judge can be reversed on appeal if it is based on an improper legal principle. In these cases the Court of Appeal felt that the offenders should not be detained for long periods for trivial offences. It made this decision although the defendants in both cases had long histories of criminal behaviour, and were likely to re-offend. In these circumstances it might have been difficult for the Home Secretary to discharge them.

Moreover, defendants are generally represented by counsel at the time of judicial sentencing, but not while serving an indeterminate sentence. Counsel can help the offender to appeal against the judge's sentence if he feels it to be unjust; it is far more difficult to challenge an ongoing sentence whose duration has not yet been determined.

---

†The law of Denmark, until recently, authorised indeterminate sentencing. The Danish people, in fact, were at one time enthusiastic about the 'progressive' concept of indeterminacy. However, the country, in light of experience, has now discontinued its use.

On the other hand, the Home Secretary is apparently unfettered in his decisions on the discharge or transfer of restricted patients.* He is under no obligation to accept the advice of a tribunal or RMO. What is more, he need not follow any legal criteria when making his decision, and he does not have to give reasons. MIND has received many inquiries and criticisms from professionals and Members of Parliament about the unassailable nature of the Home Secretary's decisions, and the secrecy that surrounds them. These issues are explored in detail in Chapter 12 *infra.*

The concept of dangerousness

A final argument used to justify indeterminate sentencing for the abnormal offender is that he presents a grave danger to the community. The Home Secretary must take ultimate responsibility for the protection of the public, and should therefore have the power to detain the abnormal offender until reasonably confident that he will not re-offend.

It is argued that abnormal offenders who have committed even relatively minor offences may be a danger to the public.[54] A Broadmoor consultant gave this example to MIND. One of his patients was given an unlimited restriction order as a result of a conviction for stealing a cabbage worth four pence. The consultant justified this on the grounds that the offender had a history of disturbed behaviour; the current offence, although trivial, merely triggered a response which should have been made earlier.

In *Evans'* case (see Chapter 3), a young woman set fire to a chair in a local mental hospital. No significant damage was caused. She was convicted of arson and was admitted to Rampton Special Hospital under a restriction order. The restriction order was not based on the current offence, but on a past history of troublesome behaviour.

The case of *Janet Gill*[55] provides another example. Miss Gill, aged 22, was given an unlimited restriction order and sent to Rampton Hospital after she had confessed to damaging a typewriter at Derby Hospital. Deputy Circuit Judge Lowe said at the Derby Crown Court: "The offence is trivial. But you are suffering from a psychopathic disorder and are violent sometimes."

It is true that people like Janet Gill may be a nuisance to society if released. She may even present a greater danger than her past behaviour would indicate. But society takes a civilised risk every time it releases an offender from custody. The more important question is this: is it proper to detain these offenders longer than ordinary offenders with comparable criminal records? MIND knows of several cases where the difference between the treatment of ordinary and abnormal offenders is striking. In *Long's* case,[56] a

---

*In theory the Home Secretary is accountable to Parliament for all his decisions. It is felt, however, that this constitutional principle does not afford a sufficient practical safeguard for the individual. The only proper method of holding the Minister accountable is to give the aggrieved individual or his representative full information, and the express right to challenge his decisions in court on points of law.

19-year-old boy was convicted for setting fire to the gymnasium in his old school. He also asked the judge to consider another offence of setting fire to the school tuck shop. Repairs cost about £30,000. Mr Long was dealt with as an ordinary offender, and received a short prison sentence. After 6 months he was released, even though he presented a possible risk to the public. When one looks at this case from Evans' vantage point, it appears anomalous.

The reader will recall Robert's case, presented earlier in this chapter. He has been detained in a special hospital for 10 years as a result of an indecent assault on a boy. Robert's mother found it hard to understand the difference between the treatment of her son, and of the offender in a case she read about in *The Times*.[57] A police constable was convicted of five charges of assault, gross indecency and indecent assault of five boys, aged 13 to 16. He was dealt with as an ordinary offender and conditionally discharged. He is now being reinstated into the police force.

One must remember that when an ordinary offender has served his finite prison sentence, he must be discharged. Moreover, he cannot be recalled to prison unless he is on parole. He may be quite as dangerous to the public as a mentally disordered patient convicted of a comparable offence.[51] Yet, despite our reservations, we allow the ordinary offender to go free because the system of criminal justice is based upon that principle. This point was dramatically illustrated in an article in *The Times*[58] on the prisoners from the 'C' wing at Parkhurst Prison. This wing is intended for men who are considered dangerous psychopaths and others who are unmanageable in the normal prison regime. These prisoners are serving finite sentences and will have to be released, even though it is thought very possible that they will offend again.

Abnormal offenders as a group are apparently no more dangerous than other confined populations:

(1) We have explored in some depth (pp.6-8 *supra*) the established concept that there is a significant overlap between the prison and special hospital populations. Conservative estimates state that anywhere between one-tenth and one-third of the prison population could be clinically diagnosed as mentally abnormal.

(2) The indicators of possible future dangerous behaviour are similar for abnormal and ordinary offenders. The most useful are the number of previous convictions and the severity and type of the most recent offence.[59] On the other hand, diagnoses and other clinical information are not particularly important factors.[60]

(3) The Home Office Statistical Department compared the reconviction rates of 334 abnormal offenders discharged from mental hospitals in 1971, and 2,796 prisoners sentenced to 18 months' imprisonment or less who were also discharged in 1971. A two-year follow-up showed that the ex-prisoners had a higher reconviction rate (54%) than the ex-patients (32%).[61]

The concept of dangerousness as a rationale for the indefinite detention of abnormal offenders was well summarised by the special hospital psychologists in their evidence to the Butler Committee:

"The mentally abnormal offender is, in effect, subject to an indeterminate sentence in the special hospitals and he can be kept indefinitely for as long as it is considered that he is potentially dangerous. Yet, the concept of potential dangerousness is not invoked for mentally normal offenders who, with the exception of those who have been sentenced to life imprisonment, must be released when their determinate sentence expires.... The justification for this would seem to be that a mentally ill violent offender is more likely to re-offend than a mentally normal one. Although it would seem common sense that a mentally ill offender's behaviour is less predictable than a mentally normal one, there is no evidence, as far as we are aware, to have established this. On the contrary, such evidence as there is, suggests that dangerous behaviour is as likely to recur in normal as in abnormal people. Releasing the mentally normal offender is therefore just as likely to be a hazard to public safety as the discharge of a mentally abnormal one."

Butler's view

The Committee on Mentally Abnormal Offenders recommends that the facility for making restriction orders of limited duration should be removed from the Mental Health Act 1959. As a safeguard against abuse, the Committee proposes that regular reports on restricted patients should be made to the Home Office by the RMO.[62]

MIND considers this proposal inadequate, since it fails to address the underlying causes of abuse discussed in this report. By the nature of his office, the Home Secretary must observe strict standards for the protection of the public. The Butler Committee itself recognises that any indeterminate power creates the danger that the detention may be longer than is strictly necessary. Regular reports from the RMO may help the Home Secretary to carry out his functions, but they cannot be regarded as an adequate safeguard of the patient's liberty.

Moreover, an undertaking was given to Parliament during the passage of the 1959 Act to do exactly what the Butler Committee is now proposing – that is, to arrange for regular reports; and this undertaking has also been reinforced by a Ministry publication (see p. 62 supra).

But the cases and statistics reported in this chapter (and indeed in the Butler Report itself) on the inordinately long periods for which restricted patients are often detained, have occurred despite the undertaking to submit regular reports to the Home Office. There is no evidence that this pattern will be reversed as a result of the Butler Committee's reiteration of the need for these reports.

Proposals for reform

When a mentally disordered person has been convicted of a criminal offence, society is justified in protecting itself by holding him in custody for a period proportional to the gravity of his offence. During that period, society should do all that it can to rehabilitate him by offering treatment in a psychiatric hospital. Whenever possible, this treatment should be given on a voluntary basis. Society should not, however, use a label as a justification for holding the offender for indefinite periods, because we cannot change the character of a compulsory measure merely by calling it 'treatment'. Hence MIND makes the following proposals:

(1) *Restriction orders of unlimited duration*
The trial judge should be authorised (but not compelled) to make an unlimited restriction order only if the defendant is convicted of clearly specified offences which involve serious violence against person or property.

There are alternative ways in which Parliament could specify the types of offence which would qualify for an unlimited restriction order: either any life-carrying offence, or any offence which qualifies for the indeterminate reviewable prison sentence suggested in Appendix 4 of the Butler Report.*

(2) *Restriction orders of limited duration*
The trial judge should be authorised to make a restriction order of limited duration for any imprisonable offence. It would be made for a maximum period (decided in each case by the trial judge), but no minimum would be named. The trial judge, in determining the length of a restriction order, should apply the same principles used for ordinary offenders – for example, the length of the sentence should be proportional to the gravity of the offence.

(3) *Therapeutic detention*
After a restriction order has expired, treatment should be available on a voluntary basis. If the offender refuses to accept informal confinement to receive treatment, and is still unfit to be released, he could be detained only through civil procedures with appropriate safeguards.

---

*The Butler Committee proposed an indeterminate prison sentence for dangerous offenders who have a history of mental disorder, but cannot be dealt with under the Mental Health Act. Imposition of the sentence is restricted to those convicted of offences which caused or might have caused grave harm to others. These offences are listed in Appendix 4 of the Butler Report. Schedule A of Appendix 4 lists certain life-carrying offences, any of which would qualify for an indeterminate sentence. Schedule B lists certain non life-carrying offences. A person convicted of a Schedule B offence would only qualify for an indeterminate sentence if there had already been a conviction of a Schedule A offence (The Butler Report, paras 4. 39-4. 43).

(4) Alternative proposal

Section 60/65 patients could be detained on a similar basis to section 72/74 patients. Thus, if the restriction order were made for a finite period as suggested above, at the end of that period (with remission) the patient would continue to be liable to detention under a hospital order without restrictions. If the restriction order were not made for a finite period, the hospital order would automatically lapse after the expiry of the maximum sentence for the particular offence.

The essential difference between the alternative and the main proposal is that, with the latter, hospital authorities would not have to initiate civil procedures when a restriction order lapsed.

References and Notes

1. R. Cross, *Punishment, Prison and the Public*, Hamlyn Lectures (23rd series), 1971, p. 22; J. E. Hall Williams, "Alternatives to definite sentences", *Law Quarterly Rev.*, vol. 80, 1964, p. 41.
2. Criminal Justice Act 1967, s.61.
3. *Report of the Parole Board for 1974*, para. 8; *Report of the Parole Board for 1973*, para. 24.
4. J. E. Hall Williams, *op cit.*, pp. 46-47.
5. D. A. Thomas, *Principles of Sentencing*, 1973. (Thomas compared restriction orders with life sentences, saying that they were both indefinite preventive measures for certain categories of mental disorder, p.127.) See also *Crim. L. Rev.* [1971], pp.664-65.
6. Re Wring [1966] 1 W.L.R. 138.
7. *Report of the Parole Board for 1968*, para. 5.
8. R. Cross, *op cit.*, pp. 90-91.
9. N. Walker and S. McCabe, *Crime and Insanity in England*, vol. 2, 1973, pp. 131, 152, 177, 193.
10. *Ibid.*, p. 129.
11. *Ibid.*, pp. 93-95, 130.
12. H. Rollin, *The Mentally Abnormal Offender and the Law*, 1969, pp. 60-61.
13. *The Butler Report*, paras. 7.23 and 14.24.
14. *The Report of the Royal Commission on the Law Relating to Mental Illness and Mental Deficiency*, HMSO, Cmnd. 169, 1954-1957, para. 519.
15. R v Nigel Gordon Smith, not reported. Judgment given July 30, 1974. MIND is representing Mr Smith before the European Commission on Human Rights, Application No. 6870/75.
16. R v McFarlane [1975] 60 Cr. App.R. 320, p. 324.
17. *The Butler Report*, paras.4.11–4.16.
18. H. Steadman and J. Cocozza, *Careers of the Criminally Insane*, 1974; McGarry, "The fate of psychotic offenders referred for trial", *Amer. J. Psychiat.*, vol. 127, 1971, p. 1181; McGarry and Bendt, "Criminal vs. civil commitment of psychotic offenders: a seven-year follow-up", *Amer. J. Psychiat.*, vol. 125, 1969, p. 1387. See generally Dershowitz, "Indeterminate confinement: letting the therapy fit the crime", *U. Pa. L. Rev.*, vol. 123, Dec. 1974, pp. 297, 303.
19. L. Knight, "Butler: a secure future", *New Psychiatry*, Nov. 20, 1975, pp. 12-14.
20. David Owen, then Minister of State at the Department of Health and Social Security, replying to a Parliamentary Question by Keith Speed, M.P., in early 1976.
21. N. Walker and S. McCabe, *op cit.*, p. 172.
22. See *Criminal Statistics in England and Wales* for the years 1973 (Cmnd. 5677), 1974 (Cmnd. 6168) and 1975 (Cmnd. 6566). See also N. Walker, *Crime and Punishment in Britain*, 2nd ed., 1968, pp. 225-31.

23. NCCL, *The Rights of the Mentally Abnormal Offender: Evidence to the Butler Committee*, Oct. 1973, p. 1.
24. *The Times*, Sept. 14, 1976.
25. N. Walker and S. McCabe, *op cit.*, p. 124.
26. F. Allen, *The Borderland of Criminal Justice*, 1964.
27. M. Newton, "Reconviction after treatment at Grendon", Home Office CP Report, Series B, No. 1, 1971, reported in *The Prison Service Journal*, July 1972, pp. 12-13; *The Butler Report*, paras. 5.43 – 5.57; E. McLean, "Prison and humanity", *The Lancet*, March 1975, p. 507. See also L. Blom-Cooper (Ed.), *Progress in Penal Reform*, 1974, p. viii.
28. N. Morris, *The Future of Imprisonment*, 1974; G. Holland, *Fundamentals of Psychotherapy*, 1965, p. 36; R. White, *The Abnormal Personality*, 3rd ed., 1964, pp. 343-350.
29. R. G. Hood, "Some fundamental dilemmas of the English parole system and a suggestion for an alternative structure", in D. A. Thomas (Ed.), *Parole: Its Implications for the Criminal Justice and Penal Systems*, Cropwood Conference, December 1973; L. Blom-Cooper, reference 27, p.174; J. Mitford, *Kind and Usual Punishment*, 1973.
30. J. E. Hall Williams, "Alternatives to definite sentences", *Law Quarterly Rev.*, vol. 80, 1964, p. 41. See also B. Hoggett, "What is wrong with the Mental Health Act?", *Crim. L. Rev.*, Dec. 1975, pp. 677, 681.
31. R. Cross, *op cit.*, p. 136.
32. R v Bennett [1968] 1 W.L.R. 988; 2 All E.R. 753; 52 Cr.App.R. 514.
33. Letter to *The Times* from Dr Melitta Schmideberg, International President of the Association for the Psychiatric Treatment of Offenders, March 13, 1976.
34. Dissent from the Butler recommendation on transfer of offenders from prison to hospital by Professor Glanville Williams (text accompanying footnote 16, p.45 of *The Butler Report*).
35. Letter dated November 9, 1975, to the author from Professor Glanville Williams.
36. Mr Michell supplied the facts of his case in correspondence. It has been summarised in *Community Care*, July 31, 1974 and March 10, 1976.
37. R v Gardiner [1967] *Crim. L. Rev.* p. 231.
38. *The Times*, February 1, 1967.
39. *The Times*, "Doctors urge changes in mental case rules: restriction orders affect treatment", February 20, 1967.
40. H. Rollin, *op cit.*, p. 84.
41. *Ibid.*, p. 85. See also Dr James MacKeith's letter to *The Lancet*, November 15, 1975, p. 986: "Among other possible results, the universal application of section 65 restrictions in addition to section 60 orders could increase the regrettable reluctance of area psychiatric services to treat the mentally disordered offender. His nuisance value and criminal propensities alone already deter hospitals from providing appropriate containment and treatment."
42. M. Frankel, *Criminal Sentences*, 1973, p. 93.
43. *The Guardian*, March 21, 1975.
44. National Health Service Hospital Advisory Service, *Report on Broadmoor Hospital*, February 1975, para. 203.
45. The facts of Robert's case were extracted from the following sources: (a) statements by the patients involved; (b) *The Sunday Times*, July 7, 1974; (c) correspondence and papers relating to Robert's tribunal hearing, given to MIND by the National Council for Civil Liberties.
46. *The Butler Report*, chapter 5. See also *The Report of the Royal Commission on the Law Relating to Mental Illness and Mental Deficiency*, 1954-1957, Cmnd. 169, paras. 333-358.
47. R v Ford [1969] 53 Cr.App.R. 551.
48. R v Ashdown, *The Times Law Report*, November 1, 1973; R v Moylan [1969] 53 Cr.App.R. 590.
49. R v Gardiner, reference 37; *The Butler Report*, para. 14.25; N. Walker and S. McCabe, *op cit.*, pp. 90-92.
50. J. C. Smith and B. Hogan, *Criminal Law*, 3rd ed., 1973, pp. 9-11.
51. See generally *The Butler Report*, paras. 4.11 – 4.16; L. Gostin, *A Human Condition*, vol. 1, pp. 39-42; F. Simon, *Prediction Methods in Criminology*, Home Office Research Studies No. 7, 1971.

52. N. Morris, "The future of imprisonment", "Prison as coerced care" and "Rehabilitating the rehabilitative ideal", *The Cooley Lectures,* University of Michigan, 1974; Dean and Dugan, "Problems in parole prediction: A historical analysis", *Social Problems,* vol. 15, 1968, p. 450.
53. R v Clarke [1975] 61 Cr.App.R. 320.
54. British Psychol. Association, "Memorandum of evidence to the Butler Committee on the law relating to the mentally abnormal offender", *Bull. Br. Psychol. Soc.,* vol. 26, 1973, pp. 331-342; H. Rollin, *op cit.;* H. Prins, *Criminal Behaviour,* 1973, pp. 151-165.
55. *The Sun,* June 3, 1976.
56. *The Hampstead and Highgate Express,* June 4, 1976.
57. *The Times,* June 7, 1976.
58. *Ibid.,* March 2, 1976.
59. N. Walker, W. Hammond and D. Steer, *Crim. L. Rev.,* 1967, pp. 465-472.
60. Payne, McCabe and Walker, "Predicting offender-patients' reconvictions", *Brit. J. Psychiat.,* vol. 125, 1974, p. 60.
61. *The Butler Report,* p. 57, footnote 2.
62. *Ibid.,* para. 14.25.

Table A*
Hospital admissions of persons subject to special restrictions under the Mental Health Act 1959

Type of hospital and offence for which detained	Total		Subject to restriction order under s.65		Found unfit to plead or not guilty by reason of insanity		Transferred under s. 72/74		Transferred under s. 73		Recalled to hospital		Transferred To special hospital from other hospital		Transferred From special hospital to other hospital	
	M	F	M	F	M	F	M	F	M	F	M	F	M	F	M	F
Special hospitals																
Homicide and attempted homicide	37	6	29	4	2	1	3	–	1	–	2	1	3	–	–	–
Other offences of violence against the person	43	7	32	6	4	1	5	–	1	–	1	–	3	1	–	–
Sexual offences	16	–	15	–	–	–	1	–	–	–	–	–	1	–	–	–
Burglary	7	–	6	–	–	–	1	–	–	–	–	–	1	1	–	–
Robbery	7	–	5	–	–	–	1	–	–	–	1	–	–	–	–	–
Theft and handling stolen goods	5	–	3	–	1	–	1	–	–	–	–	–	–	–	–	–
Fraud and forgery	1	–	1	–	–	–	–	–	–	–	–	1	–	1	–	–
Criminal damage	29	8	23	7	4	–	1	–	–	–	1	1	1	–	–	–
Other indictable offences	1	–	1	–	–	–	–	–	–	–	1	–	–	–	–	–
Vagrancy and street offences	–	1	–	1	–	–	–	–	–	–	–	–	–	–	–	–
Other non-indictable offences	2	1	1	–	–	–	1	–	–	–	–	1	–	–	–	–
Total for special hospitals	148	23	116	18	11	2	14	–	2	–	5	3	9	3	–	–

Other hospitals	M	F	M	F	M	F	M	F	M	F	M	F	M	F	M	F
Homicide and attempted homicide	9	1	6	—	1	1	—	—	1	—	1	—	1	1	25	8
Other offences of violence against the person	31	7	16	1	2	3	2	1	4	—	7	2	2	1	18	4
Sexual offences	21	—	15	—	2	—	2	—	—	—	2	—	2	—	10	—
Burglary	19	—	5	—	2	—	9	—	1	—	2	—	2	—	6	—
Robbery	2	—	—	—	—	—	1	—	—	—	1	—	—	—	1	—
Theft and handling stolen goods	6	1	2	—	2	1	2	—	—	—	—	—	1	—	2	1
Fraud and forgery	4	1	2	—	1	1	1	—	1	—	—	—	—	—	—	—
Criminal damage	20	2	13	1	1	1	4	—	—	—	1	—	1	1	8	1
Other indictable offences	2	—	—	—	—	—	1	—	1	1	—	1	—	—	1	—
Vagrancy and street offences	1	—	1	—	—	—	—	—	—	—	—	—	—	—	—	—
Other non-indictable offences	4	2	—	—	—	—	3	—	1	—	—	—	—	—	2	—
Total for other hospitals	119	14	60	2	11	7	25	1	9	1	14	3	9	3	73	14
Total for all hospitals	267	37	176	20	22	9	39	1	11	1	19	6	9	3	73	14

*Reproduced from the *Criminal Statistics in England and Wales for 1974*, Cmnd. 6168, pp. 240-241. Besides the 40 persons transferred under s. 72/74, a further four were detained under s. 72 without restrictions on discharge. Of the restriction orders, 194 were without limit of time, one was for five years and one was for one year.

Table B*
Offences and legal status of patients in special hospitals on December 31, 1975.

Legal status of patient	Section 60 orders	Section 60 orders with Section 65 restrictions	Section 71, 72 and 73 orders	Other Acts (i.e. Criminal Procedure (Insanity) Act 1964 and pre-1959 Acts)	Total
Crimes					
Homicide or attempted homicide	11	265	67	126	469
Offences of violence against the person	80	248	21	38	387
Sexual offences	54	176	14	17	261
Robbery, burglary, theft, handling stolen goods	69	78	8	9	164
Criminal damage	30	87	3	6	126
Other offences	39	124	5	8	176
Offences not known	4	1	–	–	5
Total	287	979	118	204	1,588

*Source: Parliamentary Answer by Dr David Owen, Tuesday April 6, 1976 (PQ1656/1975/6).

Table C*
Restricted patients discharged with the consent of the Home Secretary from
1970 to 1974

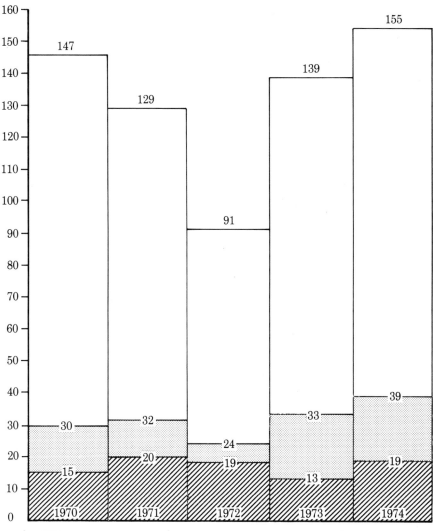

KEY: ☐ Patients who had been detained under the Mental Health Act, ss. 60, 65.
▒ Patients who had been detained under the Mental Health Act, ss. 72, 74.
▨ Patients who had been detained under Schedule 1 and s.3 of the Criminal
Procedure (Insanity) Act 1964.

*Source: Unpublished figures obtained directly from the Department of Health and
Social Security.

Note: the case of Graham Young was disclosed in 1972.

Table D
Length of detention: Comparison of prison and special hospital population

Years detained	Percentage of total population (to the nearest 1%)	
	Special hospital patients*	Prisoners in Prison Department†
1 or less	5	76
1-2	15	14
2-3	14	4
3-4	12	2
4-7	24	2
7-10	12	1
Over 10 (including life sentences):	20	1
10-15	10	
15-20	4	
20-30	4	
30-40	2	
40-51	1	

*Residents of special hospitals in mid-1974. The figures were provided by the Department of Health and Social Security, which has informed MIND that the numbers have not significantly changed since mid-1974. For the raw data from which this table was drawn up, see Table E, which follows.

†Sentenced prisoners in Prison Department establishments on 31 March, 1976 who had on that date been held for the various periods in question from the date of their sentence. The table disregards remanded prisoners, time spent on remand in custody, prisoners recalled from parole and life-sentence prisoners returned to custody on revocation of licence. *Source:* Letter from Dr Shirley Summerskill, Minister of State at the Home Office, to Eric Moonman, MP, c/o MIND, August 10, 1976.

*Table E**

Residents of special hospitals at mid-1974: Number of years detained

Hospital	Newly Admitted	Number of years													
		1	2	3	4	5	6	7	8	9	10-15	15-20	20-30	30-40	40-51
Broadmoor	51	133	118	109	71	63	37	43	24	31	91	24	32	16	3
(M)	(44)	(111)	(102)	(91)	(64)	(53)	(33)	(38)	(22)	(27)	(80)	(22)	(23)	(9)	(1)
(F)	(7)	(22)	(16)	(18)	(7)	(10)	(4)	(5)	(2)	(4)	(11)	(2)	(9)	(7)	(2)
Rampton	40	136	133	127	99	83	77	40	47	30	116	56	46	20	11
(M)	(29)	(97)	(104)	(109)	(81)	(71)	(59)	(30)	(42)	(26)	(77)	(39)	(30)	(13)	(5)
(F)	(11)	(39)	(29)	(18)	(18)	(12)	(18)	(10)	(5)	(4)	(39)	(17)	(16)	(7)	(6)
Moss Side	19	70	71	37	39	34	47	19	17	23	28	14	8	2	–
(M)	(10)	(48)	(48)	(33)	(34)	(31)	(37)	(15)	(16)	(19)	(21)	(10)	(6)	(1)	–
(F)	(9)	(22)	(23)	(4)	(5)	(3)	(10)	(4)	(1)	(4)	(7)	(4)	(2)	(1)	–
Total in all special hospitals (2,335)	110	339	322	273	209	180	161	102	88	84	235	94	86	38	14
(M)	(83)	(256)	(254)	(233)	(179)	(155)	(129)	(83)	(80)	(72)	(178)	(71)	(59)	(23)	(6)
(F)	(27)	(83)	(68)	(40)	(30)	(25)	(32)	(19)	(8)	(12)	(57)	(23)	(27)	(15)	(8)

*Source: unpublished information received from the Department of Health and Social Security.

Table F*
Patients who left special hospitals in 1973

Length of stay in years	All ages		Age groups					
	Numbers	Percentage of total discharged (excluding deaths)	15-19	20-24	25-34	35-44	45-54	55 and over
Under 1	24	8.1	4	9	8	–	3	–
1-2	50	16.8	10	11	9	15	3	2
2-3	40	13.5	2	6	15	10	5	2
3-5	67	22.6	4	15	24	13	9	2
5-10	61	20.5	–	6	27	21	5	2
10 or more	55	18.5	–	–	13	14	15	13
Total number of discharges and departures	297		20	47	96	73	40	21
Deaths	16		2	5	4	2	2	1
All leavers	313		22	52	100	75	42	22

*Source: unpublished statistics received from the Department of Health and Social Security.

Part II
Transfers

6. Transfer to hospital of persons serving sentences of imprisonment

Exposition of the present law

Criteria

Section 72 of the Mental Health Act authorises the Home Secretary to transfer a person serving a sentence of imprisonment to a local NHS hospital or a special hospital. The Home Secretary must be satisfied, by reports from at least two medical practitioners, that the person is suffering from mental illness, psychopathic disorder, subnormality or severe subnormality[1] of a nature or degree which warrants his detention in a hospital for medical treatment.[2] The Home Secretary must also consider, having regard to the public interest and all the circumstances, that it is expedient to make a transfer direction.[3] If the specified hospital does not receive the person within 14 days after the transfer direction is made, it ceases to have effect.[4]

Medical evidence

At least one of the medical practitioners who give evidence to the court must be approved for the purposes of section 28 of the Act by an Area Health Authority as having special experience in the diagnosis or treatment of mental disorders.[5] Further, the person must be described by each medical practitioner as suffering from the same form or forms of mental disorder.[6]

Effect

A transfer direction has the same effect as a hospital order. The Home Secretary can make the direction either with [7] or without [8] special restrictions on discharge. If it is made without restrictions (section 72), the person ceases to be subject to his prison sentence; hence he may be unconditionally discharged by his RMO, the hospital managers or a Mental Health Review Tribunal. But few transfers are effected without restrictions, and in these cases the prison sentence generally does not have long to run. In 1974 only four transfer directions were made without restrictions (there were four in 1973 and fifteen in 1972). This represented 9% of all the transfer directions made in 1974 (the figures were 7% in 1973 and 19% in 1972).[9]

A prisoner who is transferred to hospital with restrictions (sections 72/74) is subject to the provisions of section 65.[7] Thus he cannot be discharged, transferred to another hospital, or given leave of absence without the Home Secretary's consent. It must be remembered, however, that he is still subject to his prison sentence, and will not necessarily be discharged into the community even if the doctor feels it to be clinically appropriate. If the RMO notifies the Home Secretary that the offender no longer requires treatment for mental disorder, the Home Secretary has two options:

If the offender would have been eligible for release on parole or with remission, the Home Secretary can discharge him;[10] or the Home Secretary can direct that he be remitted to prison to serve the remainder of his sentence.[11]

When the Home Secretary exercises either option, the transfer direction ceases to have effect, and the prisoner is treated like any ordinary offender.

If the offender is still in hospital when the full term of his sentence expires, the restrictions cease to have effect; but he remains detained as if he had been admitted on that date in pursuance of a hospital order without restrictions.[12]

Mental Health Review Tribunals

A prisoner who is transferred to hospital without restrictions is detained in hospital as if he had been admitted under a hospital order on the date of his transfer.[8] Accordingly, he is eligible to apply for a tribunal at any time within the first six months after his transfer.[13]* He may also apply once during every period of renewal[14] (a year after the date of his transfer, the authority for his detention may be renewed for a further period of one year; thereafter it may be renewed for periods of two years at a time). As with every patient under a hospital order without restrictions, the tribunal can discharge him unconditionally.

The prisoner who is transferred to hospital with restrictions has no right to *apply* for a tribunal, although he can have his case *referred* to a tribunal by the Home Secretary. The patient is not entitled to ask for a referral to a tribunal until one year after the date of the transfer. Thereafter, he may make the request once in each period during which he could have made an application if he were not subject to a restriction order (that is, after the second period of twelve months in hospital, and every two years thereafter). A written request by a patient must be referred to a tribunal for a hearing within two months. As with every restricted patient, the tribunal has no right of discharge, but can only make a recommendation to the Home Secretary.

Of course, if the offender is still detained in hospital after the full term of his sentence has expired, the restriction order lapses, and he has the same right to apply for a tribunal as any other patient under a hospital order. He can therefore apply at any time within the first six months after his sentence has expired, and once during every period of renewal.

Finally, for the purposes of the Mental Health Act, the expiration of a person's sentence refers to the *full period* during which he would have been detained in prison (without remission) if the transfer direction had not been given. Further, any period during which he may be absent from the hospital without leave is not treated as part of his sentence.[15]

*A patient cannot apply to a tribunal until he is 16 years old.

Observations and proposals for reform

The guiding principle in this report is that once an offender has been detained for a period proportional to the gravity of his offence, he should not be detained further, except through civil procedures. (If treatment is the reason given for continued detention in hospital, then he should be subject to a civil "admission for treatment" under section 26 of the Act.) The principle is especially clear in the context of an ordinary offender who has been sentenced to a fixed term of imprisonment; when that term expires, he should have the same rights and freedoms as any other ex-offender. There is no apparent justification for distinguishing a person who is nearing the end of a penal term from all other citizens liable to detention in hospital due to mental disorder.†

Yet several cases are known where prisoners nearing the end of a sentence have been transferred to hospital. As a result they have been detained long after they would have been released from prison. The following case illustrates the problem.

A firm of solicitors is receiving instructions from a Broadmoor patient. The patient was given a 3-year prison sentence. Two weeks before his expected release with remission he was transferred to Broadmoor hospital *with* restrictions.

This means that the restriction order will not lapse for another year. Only then will he be entitled to apply for a tribunal.

The patient claims that he was transferred because the prison authorities believe he had assaulted a warden; a fact which he arduously denies.

The Butler Committee dismissed the argument made above as "almost entirely theoretical".[16] The hub of Butler's case is this: most prisoners are transferred to hospital with restrictions on discharge (sections 72/74). However, at the end of a sentence, the prisoner's restriction order automatically lapses. He therefore remains in hospital under section 72, which places him in virtually the same position as a section 26 patient.

There are important problems with Butler's position. First, the restriction order will not lapse until the *full* term of his sentence expires. Had he

†The United States Supreme Court, in *Baxstrom v Herold*, 383 U.S. 107 (1966) declared unconstitutional a statutory provision that had a similar effect to section 72 of the Mental Health Act 1959.

Baxstrom was convicted of assault and sentenced as an ordinary offender to three years' imprisonment. Just over two years later, he was examined by a prison doctor and transferred to a secure mental hospital. At the end of his three-year sentence, two doctors said he was still mentally ill and required treatment. As a result, he was kept in a mental hospital.

The Supreme Court held that, at the end of a penal sentence, if continued detention in hospital is justified, it must be in accordance with the civil procedures applicable to all other persons. The Court said that once a prison sentence has lapsed, the person is like all others, and is entitled to the same safeguards against compulsory confinement as are available to all other citizens.

remained in prison, he would, with good behaviour, have been released with remission after two-thirds of that sentence. For prisoners serving a long sentence, this has more than theoretical significance: for example, a prisoner serving a nine-year sentence would quite probably be released with remission after six years; but if he is transferred to hospital under section 72/74, the restriction order will not lapse until the full nine years have passed.

Secondly, the criteria and procedures for transferring a prisoner to hospital under section 72 are less stringent than those for a civil admission under section 26. An admission under section 26 can be made only if "it is necessary in the interests of the patient's health or safety or for the protection of other persons". These criteria are more exacting than those of section 72, where the Home Secretary need only find that the transfer is 'expedient' in the public interest. Further, the rights of appeal available to a section 26 patient are marginally greater than those of a transferred prisoner. For example, the nearest relative has the right to discharge a section 26 patient; but he cannot discharge a transferred prisoner.

Moreover, an adult suffering from subnormality or psychopathy cannot be compulsorily admitted to hospital under section 26. But he can be transferred from prison to hospital, and detained after his prison sentence has expired. MIND received the following letter from a prisoner who could not have been admitted to hospital under section 26 if he had been allowed to complete his sentence in prison:

"I am very nearly at the end of my prison sentence at Dartmoor. I have been classified as a psychopath, and the recommendation is that I be transferred to one of the special hospitals; which I take to mean either Broadmoor, Moss Side or Rampton. . . . Could you explain precisely what this could mean, and whether there is any time limit within which I must be released from hospital?"

Thirdly, a transferred prisoner is detained in hospital as a result of his offence. He is in the same position as a patient admitted under section 60. He is therefore stigmatised as an abnormal offender, instead of a patient civilly detained under section 26. This stigma may last throughout his detention in hospital, no matter how much time has passed since his conviction.

Finally, most transferred prisoners go to one of the special hospitals. Sheer administrative inertia makes it likely that they will remain there after their sentences have expired. (We have also seen that once a patient is in a special hospital it is difficult to transfer him to a local NHS hospital.) Ex-offenders admitted under section 26 are sometimes sent to special hospitals, but it is less likely.

The choice of the particular institution where the patient receives treatment is very important. Placement in a special hospital is an infringement of his liberty if he does not require treatment under secure conditions. He should not, therefore, remain in a special hospital after his sentence has expired, unless a fresh assessment shows that he requires treatment under secure conditions. Accordingly, we recommend that a transferred prisoner should have the right to apply to a tribunal on what would have been his earliest date of release from prison (see below). The tribunal's power should be extended to include a transfer from a special to a local hospital (see Chapter 7 *infra*). This would have the same effect as a recommendation for the transfer of an unrestricted patient by the RMO; it would therefore require the agreement of the staff at the receiving hospital.

The National Council for Civil Liberties suggests that a transferred prisoner should not remain in a special hospital when his sentence expires, unless two independent medical reports are presented to the hospital managers stating it to be necessary.[17] We think that this is a less effective safeguard than a tribunal hearing, but we would support this proposal if our own is not implemented.

MIND and the NCCL both take the view that, if appropriate, an ex-offender should be given the opportunity to show whether he can benefit from a non-secure therapeutic environment. There should, however, be some implicit undertaking that the special hospital will re-admit the patient if he causes undue disturbance in the local hospital.

We should also note that when the RMO or the tribunal is deciding whether to discharge a patient, they may be more cautious about a transferred prisoner in a special hospital, than about a section 26 patient in a local hospital. The offence for which a transferred prisoner was admitted to prison is often viewed as more important than any offence a section 26 patient may have committed in the past.

The Butler Committee's view

To safeguard the individual against possible abuses of the transfer provisions, the Butler Committee proposes the following two measures:[18]

(a) Every offender who is transferred to hospital under section 72 should have the right to apply for a tribunal hearing when what would have been his *earliest* date of release is reached. (The reader will recall that the right of application for a section 72/74 patient exists at present only when the full sentence has expired, without remission.)

(b) Where the prisoner is transferred with restrictions under section 74, the Home Secretary should review, at the earliest date of release, whether they need to continue.

The first recommendation is highly ambiguous, but potentially significant. It could be interpreted in any of three ways:

The Butler Committee does not recommend (as MIND does) that a restriction order under section 74 should lapse at the *earliest* possible date of release. Yet the Committee appears to be proposing an 'application' to a tribunal at that time. If the Committee is using the term 'application' correctly, this means that the tribunal would have a *right of discharge* at that date* – which would be a significant improvement over the *status quo*. The problem with this interpretation, however, is that the RMO would *not* have the right of discharge at this time. This is evident from the second recommendation, which allows the Home Secretary to continue the restrictions on discharge until the *full* term of the sentence expires.

Alternatively, if the Butler Committee's first proposal is interpreted to mean that a person has the right of *reference* to a tribunal at the earliest date of release, then it makes no significant improvement over the *status quo*. Under the present law, a section 72/74 patient can already have his case referred to a tribunal during specified periods; furthermore, in these cases a tribunal can only *advise* the Home Secretary. We will point out in Chapter 11 that when a tribunal is only acting in an advisory capacity, it is a weak safeguard of the patient's liberty.

A third interpretation is also feasible. It may refer only to prisoners transferred without restrictions under section 72. (The Butler Committee does not mention section 74 in its first proposal, but specifically refers to it in the second.) This recommendation would be virtually superfluous, because if a prisoner is transferred without restrictions, he already has the right to apply immediately to a tribunal.

The Butler Committee's second proposal apparently has very little meaning. It says that the Home Secretary should review the need for a restriction order under section 74 at the earliest possible date of release. The Home Secretary can already remove the restrictions at any time, and it is hardly significant that the Butler Committee should remind him of this and ask him to review the situation. As we understand the present administrative arrangements, the Home Secretary should periodically review a restriction order, to decide whether it need remain in force. In any case, it would be extraordinary if he were to remove a restriction order without the recommendation of the RMO and, under current arrangements, the RMO has a duty to bring to his attention any case where a restriction order is no longer needed.[19]

In view of these arguments, MIND makes the following proposal. At the earliest date of release from prison (i.e. with full remission), the transferred prisoner should no longer be liable to detention under section 72. If the need for compulsory detention continues, this should be effected by a civil order with appropriate safeguards.

If this wider proposal is not acceptable, MIND suggests this alternative: if a prisoner is transferred to hospital under section 72/74, the restriction order should lapse at the earliest date when he would have been released had he remained in prison. He will then continue to be liable to detention under a hospital order without restrictions.

---

*If a person has the right to *apply* for a tribunal, the tribunal has the right to discharge him unconditionally. If he only has the right to have his case *referred* to a tribunal by the Home Secretary, the tribunal can only *recommend* that he be released. This would give the Home Secretary the right to release him on licence.

References and Notes

1. Mental Health Act 1959, s. 72(1)(a).
2. *Ibid.*, s. 72(1)(b).
3. *Ibid.*, s. 72(1).
4. *Ibid.*, s. 72(2).
5. *Ibid.*, s. 72(4).
6. *Ibid.*, s. 72(5).
7. *Ibid.*, s. 74.
8. *Ibid.*, s. 72(3).
9. *The Butler Report*, para. 3.37.
10. Mental Health Act 1959, s. 75(1)(b).
11. *Ibid.*, s. 75(1)(a).
12. *Ibid.*, s. 75(2).
13. *Ibid.*, ss. 72(3) and 63(4).
14. *Ibid.*, ss. 72(3), 63(3) and 43(6).
15. *Ibid.*, ss. 75(3), 75(4).
16. *The Butler Report*, para. 3.42.
17. *Ibid.*, para. 3.41.
18. *Ibid.*, para. 3.43.
19. "Memorandum on Parts I, IV to VII and IX of the Act" 1960, paras. 166, 167.

7. Transfer of patients from special to local hospitals

Exposition of the law and practice

Under section 41 of the Mental Health Act, a patient who is for the time being detained may be transferred to another hospital.[1] The transfer may be authorised by the hospital managers (in the case of the special hospitals, the DHSS acts as the managers)[2] or by any person whom they nominate (in most instances, the RMO). A patient detained under a restriction order cannot be transferred without the consent of the Home Secretary.[1]

Part IV of the Mental Health (Hospital and Guardianship) Regulations 1960 lays down the administrative details for the transfer of patients.[3] Regulation 13(3) states:

"The authority for transfer shall not be given unless the person giving the authority is satisfied that arrangements have been made for the admission of the patient to the hospital to which he is being transferred within a period of 28 days beginning with the date of the authority."

The receiving hospital must therefore be consulted and the necessary formalities completed before the transfer will have legal effect. Thus a patient cannot be transferred unless the receiving hospital is prepared to admit him.

Without prejudice to any of the foregoing provisions, section 99(2) of the Act states:

"The Minister may give directions for the transfer of any patient who is for the time being liable to be detained under this Act in a special hospital into a hospital not being a special hospital."

In practice, a patient will not be transferred from a special to a local hospital until his RMO decides that he no longer requires treatment under maximum security conditions. The RMO submits his recommendation to the Department of Health and Social Security, where it is carefully considered by medical and administrative staff in light of the patient's history and present medical condition.* If they decide that the proposal for transfer can be supported, they send a copy of the doctor's report to the Home Office, and request the Home Secretary's consent. (This step is unnecessary if the patient is not subject to a restriction order.) At the same time, a copy is sent to the health authority for the patient's home area, with a request that the authority allocate him a place in one of its psychiatric hospitals.[4]

---

*It is noteworthy that the DHSS take their role as hospital managers very seriously. In contrast, the managers in local hospitals often delegate their functions, *carte blanche*, to the RMO.

In some cases, the patient has in the past presented a danger to the public and his prognosis has been somewhat uncertain. These cases, which are very few, have been designated as requiring special care in assessment; the Home Secretary therefore seeks the advice of an independent advisory board before agreeing to the patient's transfer, which may cause considerable delay (see Chapter 10, *infra*).

Poor quality of relations between the special and local hospitals

There is increasing evidence of a poor relationship between special and local hospitals. Several consultants in the special hospitals have indicated that on occasion certain local NHS hospitals have refused without good reason to accept some of their patients. Particular allegations have been made against the Wessex and North East Thames Regions and St. Augustine's Hospital and Oakwood Hall Hospital in the South East Thames Region.[5]

The following two cases illustrate some of the problems involved:

Janet's case
The consultant psychiatrist at Moss Side Hospital put Janet on the transfer list in September 1975. Her Liverpool solicitors received this letter (dated 14 April, 1976) from the Department of Health and Social Security: "At present, nursing staff in the Hampshire area, who belong to COHSE, are unwilling to nurse patients subject to restriction orders. However, we are continuing our endeavours to arrange for Janet's transfer to the area, but the situation with the Union is a difficult one and I cannot hold out very much hope that it will be satisfactorily resolved in the future."
Janet is still in Moss Side as of October 1976.

M's case *
Dr. W., a local hospital consultant, gave evidence to the court in the case of M. He recommended that M be sent to Broadmoor under a restriction order without limit of time. But in his report, he said: "I undertake that if and when treatment has controlled his behaviour, I would accept transfer to St. Crispin Hospital in my care."

Two years later, the RMO at Broadmoor recommended M's transfer to St. Crispin, the local hospital in M's catchment area. The DHSS and the Home Office agreed. After some six months of indecision, during which he made no attempt to visit the patient, Dr. W refused to accept the transfer. He said that M was not, in his opinion, ready to be transferred, but did not give his reasons.

This places Broadmoor in a difficult position. During the six months of indecision, the hospital could not try to find an alternative placement. Further, the one other psychiatric hospital in M's catchment area only

*See Chapter 3, *supra*.

takes private patients, and M cannot afford this. Therefore, Broadmoor will have to look for a hospital outside M's catchment area. This will be difficult because local hospitals are reluctant to admit patients whose homes are not in their area. They feel that they have enough trouble stretching their resources to accommodate patients who live near the hospital, without accepting them from other parts of the country. They also feel that it is more difficult to integrate the patient into the community socially if his relatives and friends do not live nearby.

So patients may remain in the special hospitals for long periods, even though their consultants are of opinion that they do not need treatment under maximum security conditions.[6]

It seems that one of the reasons why local hospitals are reluctant to accept transfers is that it will be difficult to have patients re-admitted to the special hospitals if they break down. The local hospitals therefore have the uneasy feeling that once they agree to a transfer, they will be forced to cope with a potentially violent patient for an indefinite period.

The Hospital Advisory Service, in its investigation of Broadmoor Hospital, was emphatic about the poor quality of relations between special and local hospitals:[7]

"One aspect of Broadmoor's isolated and inward-looking culture for which consultants have the primary responsibility, is the relationship with the psychiatric hospitals in the National Health Service. At present, this is bad-tempered and directly hampers Broadmoor's functioning. All in Broadmoor are united in believing that the rest of British institutional psychiatry (90,000 patients, more than 150 hospitals, some 2,000 psychiatrists, and 20,000 psychiatric nurses) dislike them and are actively trying to make their lives difficult. The patients told us that they could not be discharged because 'the counties won't take us'; the nurses said that a main cause of their overcrowding was because 'the conventional hospitals always refuse our patients'; one consultant told us that he was making a collection of letters of refusal from colleagues in the National Health Service."

The deteriorating quality of relations between special and local hospitals has frequently led to the use of a bargaining system. Local hospitals often insist on a 'swopping' arrangement, whereby they will accept a transfer only if the special hospital will accept one of their patients in return. This is of course unsatisfactory, because it places the patient's interests in the background. If the staff at a local hospital happen to consider a patient troublesome, they may make a deal and request that he be transferred. This puts pressure on the special hospital to accept him, although they may not agree that he requires treatment under secure conditions. Alternatively, if the local hospital does not want to 'swop', the patient may remain needlessly in the special hospital. In either case, the patient's well-being is jeopardised by an administrative conflict between two institutions.

Scope of the problem

The following facts and figures show something of the extent of the problem.

(1) Dr David Owen, then Minister of Health, estimated that most of the patients in Rampton and Moss Side hospitals could be treated in hospitals for the mentally handicapped.[4] But it is difficult to effect transfers to the local subnormality hospitals. Accommodation is at a premium, because mental handicap is permanent and the after-care facilities provided by local authorities are at present very limited. Hence not many mentally handicapped patients can be discharged from hospital, and vacancies arise only infrequently. A special hospital patient who is accepted by a local hospital for the mentally handicapped usually has to take his turn on the waiting list, which includes patients awaiting admission direct from the community.

(2) Similarly, many of the patients in Broadmoor could be treated in local hospitals for the mentally ill. Although these hospitals do not usually have such long waiting lists, it has still been very difficult to transfer patients.[4]

(3) In their evidence to the Butler Committee, the special hospitals estimated that 450-500 of their patients could be safely transferred to local hospitals or regional secure units if places were available.[7]

(4) In the two-year period that ended in May 1976, 125 restricted patients were transferred from the special to the local hospitals. The longest time taken to effect a transfer was $2\frac{1}{4}$ years, the shortest was one month, and the average was just under six months.[4]

Observations and proposals for reform

Transferring a patient from a special hospital to an NHS hospital near his home is the first major step towards rehabilitating him. It is important for his individual liberty, because it means much more relaxed security arrangements. It is also an important part of his treatment, because it provides a realistic opportunity to reintegrate him into the community in a sheltered setting. The special hospitals are far away from the population centres, so that the patient is usually isolated from his family and friends, and from developments in the outside world. As the Aarvold Committee has stated, it would be wrong to discharge a patient direct to his family or to casual lodgings; a period of rehabilitation in a local hospital or a hostel is normally far better.[8]

Transfer to a local hospital also ultimately serves the best interests of the community. If an offender-patient is in a local hospital, his behaviour can be monitored; he can be given the chance to make ordinary decisions, and take part in community affairs, only to the extent that he proves himself able to do so. The decision on whether to discharge him can be based on his behaviour when coping with community activities. Clearly, the staff in a special hospital do not have the necessary information upon which to recommend outright discharge. They must rely on the patient's institutional behaviour to predict whether he will adjust successfully in the community; this has been shown to be extremely difficult.[9]

It follows that transfer to a local hospital in the patient's catchment area is essential to an integrated rehabilitation programme. The issue is not *whether* a transfer should take place, but *when*. The staff in local hospitals, and the unions who represent them, should recognise this, and should make every effort to co-operate with the special hospitals in deciding when the transfer should be made.

It is difficult to justify the continued detention of a patient in a high security institution once his transfer has been recommended by the RMO, and accepted by both the DHSS and the Home Office. Thus, if the local hospital proposes to resist the transfer, it should be obliged to follow these procedures: members of its psychiatric and nursing staffs should visit the special hospital to examine the patient and review all the relevant information. They should then be required to submit in writing to the DHSS positive and concrete reasons for their refusal to admit him. They should also give an estimated date when they will review their decision. In addition, the DHSS should (on rare occasions) instruct a local hospital to accept a patient. It should do this only where the hospital authorities have made their decision in bad faith or without reasonable care (see pp. 53-56 *supra*).

The DHSS should undertake to re-admit a patient to the special hospital if he fails to settle in the local hospital within a reasonable period.

We also make the following general proposal. The DHSS should immediately look for ways to reduce the misunderstandings between local and special hospitals. Regular discussions, meetings and visits should take place between members of the various hospitals; the DHSS should liaise with the regional health authorities, the professional bodies and the trade unions; and so forth.

We recognise that the DHSS is already making a genuine effort to improve the relationship between the local and special hospitals. But we think it can do no harm to air some specific advice given by the Hospital Advisory Service in its Report on Broadmoor:

"The managing staff in Broadmoor should be more active in presenting the true facts about the traffic with other hospitals. The consultants should remind the nurses and the patients of the significant numbers who have been transferred rather than continually highlighting those cases where difficulties have arisen.

The consultants of Broadmoor need to cultivate their colleagues of the National Health Service just as the consultants of an ordinary hospital need to work continuously on good relations with their main professional counterparts – the local general practitioners. It is an endless task, but if neglected leads to mutual hostility and mistrust. The present practice of

Broadmoor staff going out to see patients and to advise psychiatric hospitals, and of outside consultants coming to see patients proposed for discharge, should be extended. Broadmoor nursing staff should go out on visits to these hospitals. Visiting consultants should be pressed more vigorously to bring their nursing colleagues.

Other ways of improving the relationship of Broadmoor with its colleagues should be explored. A follow-up letter a year later to the consultant who accepted the patient might dispel the feeling that Broadmoor are only interested in getting rid of people and no longer interested in them after discharge."

References and Notes

1. Mental Health Act 1959, s.41 and Third Schedule.
2. See, for example, the National Health Service Reorganisation Act 1973, s. 40; Mental Health Act 1959, s. 99; Ministry's Memorandum of Guidance, 1960.
3. See generally, A.H. Edwards, *Mental Health Services,* 4th ed., 1975, pp. 145-146.
4. Letter dated 24 June, 1976 to Eric Moonman, M.P., Chairman of the All Party Parliamentary Mental Health Group, c/o MIND, signed by Dr. David Owen, Minister of State at the Department of Health and Social Security, PO(MIH-H) 1801/37.
5. Information obtained directly from Broadmoor Hospital.
6. *Interim Report of the Committee on Mentally Abnormal Offenders,* Cmnd. 5698, July 1974.
7. National Health Service Hospital Advisory Service, *Report on Broadmoor Hospital,* Crowthorne, Berkshire, February 1975, para. 316. Although the Hospital Advisory Service Report is a confidential document, it has been discussed extensively by the media. The most comprehensive coverage was given in *Psychology Today,* vol. 1, no. 6, September 1975.
8. *Report on the Review of Procedures for the Discharge and Supervision of Psychiatric Patients Subject to Special Restrictions,* Cmnd. 5191, January 1973, para. 39.
9. See lectures by Norval Morris, "The Future of Imprisonment", especially, "Prison as Coerced Cure", p. 22 and "Rehabilitating the Rehabilitative Ideal", pp. 11-12 (The Cooley Lectures, University of Michigan, 1974); Dean and Duggan, "Problems in Parole Prediction: A Historical Analysis", *Social Problems,* vol. 15, 1968, p. 450.

Part III
The nature of the institutions

8. The special hospitals

Under section 40 of the National Health Service Reorganisation Act 1973, the Secretary of State for Social Services has a duty to provide and maintain special hospitals for people who, in his opinion, need treatment under conditions of special security because of their dangerous, violent or criminal propensities. The Department of Health and Social Security is directly responsible for the administration of these establishments, which stand outside the ambit of the National Health Service.[1]

At present, there are three such hospitals in full operation:[2] Broadmoor at Crowthorne, Berkshire; Rampton at Retford, Nottinghamshire; and Moss Side at Maghull, Lancashire. A fourth, Park Lane, is being constructed; it stands on the same grounds as Moss Side, and already has a small advance unit in operation.

The special hospitals can admit only 'persons subject to detention';[3] they cannot accept informal patients under the Mental Health Act. Otherwise, any category of patient may be admitted to either a special or a local hospital. (For example, special hospitals are not limited to patients who have committed offences.) The distinction between the patients in the special and the local hospitals is simply that the Secretary of State for Social Services considers the former to require treatment under conditions of special security.* Patients may be admitted to the special hospitals either directly from the community, or by transfer from local hospitals or from prisons.

Table 1 gives a breakdown of the statutory categories of the 2,210 patients who were in the special hospitals on December 31, 1975.

Table 1
Legal status of the patients in the special hospitals on December 31, 1975.

Category	Number of patients total 2,210	Percentage
Mental Health Act, s. 26 (civil admission for treatment)	422	19.1
Mental Health Act, s. 60 (hospital order without restrictions)	287	13.0
Mental Health Act, ss. 60/65 (hospital order with restrictions)	979	44.3

*Local hospitals sometimes admit abnormal offenders. In 1973, of the 185, 672 patients admitted to hospitals for mental illness and mental handicap, 25,437 (13.7%) were compulsory patients; of these, 1,082 (4.2%) were abnormal offenders admitted under section 60, 71 or 72 of the Act.[4]

Mental Health Act, ss. 71, 72 and 73 (detention under Her Majesty's Pleasure, or transferred prisoners)	118	5.3
Mental Health Act, sixth schedule (admitted under Acts prior to the Mental Health Act 1959)	290	13.1
Criminal Procedure (Insanity) Act 1964 (unfit to plead, or not guilty by reason of insanity)	114	5.2

Source: Parliamentary Written Answer by Dr David Owen, *Hansard* PQ 1651/1975/6, Wednesday, 25 February, 1976.

As this table shows, most of the 2,210 patients in the special hospitals are abnormal offenders: that is, they have been placed in hospital as a result of an appearance before a criminal court. This would apply to patients detained under sections 60 (with or without restrictions), 71, 72 and 73 of the Mental Health Act; some patients detained under the sixth schedule of the Mental Health Act; and patients detained under the Criminal Procedure (Insanity) Act.

The 422 patients (19%) detained under section 26 are not offenders (i.e. they are not detained as a result of a conviction for an imprisonable offence).

The 290 patients (13%) admitted before the Mental Health Act 1959 was enacted have been continuously detained in hospital for at least 17 years. These people are detained as if under either section 71 (Her Majesty's Pleasure) or section 26 (civil admission for treatment), depending on which particular provision of law was used in their cases before 1959. *

In 1973 (the year for which we have the most recent breakdown figures) 45.8% of the 2,354 patients in the special hospitals were in Rampton; 35.7% in Broadmoor; and 18.5% in Moss Side (Table 2). In 1980, when Park Lane will be in full operation, it will have bed space for approximately 400 patients.[5] This will make it just slightly smaller than Moss Side, whose grounds it will adjoin. This does not mean that 400 extra beds will be available, since the main purpose of this new hospital is to relieve the overcrowding in Broadmoor.

As the reader can see in Table 3, Broadmoor Hospital specialises in mentally ill or psychopathic patients with an average or above-average intelligence. The other two hospitals specialise in patients with some degree of subnormality or brain damage, although they have a fairly even distribution of patients in each of the diagnostic groups. As the only unit now in operation at Park Lane Hospital (catering for 70 patients) has been opened specifically to cope with the overflow from Broadmoor, it is reasonable to assume that most of its patients also suffer from mental illness or psychopathic disorder.

*The Butler Report (para. 2.33) states that 30% of the special hospital population, as of December 1973, were civilly detained under Part IV of the 1959 Act or corresponding provisions of earlier Acts. We shall return to this particular group of people later.

Table 2
Sex, legal status and mental category of patients in the special hospitals on December 31, 1973*

Legal status	All Special Hospitals					Broadmoor				
	All	Mental illness	Psycho-pathic disorder	Subnormal	Severely subnormal	All	Mental illness	Psycho-pathic disorder	Subnormal	Severely subnormal
All residents	2,354	927	649	383	395	840	609	228	3	—
Detained under:										
Section 26	456	196	37	46	177	76	74	2	—	—
Section 60 or 61	1,280	433	544	270	33	524	320	202	2	—
Section 71(2) 72 or 73	145	88	44	10	3	92	69	23	—	—
Sixth Schedule	373	121	22	51	179	91	89	1	1	—
Other compulsory powers	100	89	2	6	3	57	57	—	—	—

Legal status	Rampton					Moss Side				
	All	Mental Illness	Psycho-pathic disorder	Subnormal	Severely subnormal	All	Mental illness	Psycho-pathic disorder	Subnormal	Severely subnormal
All residents	1,078	225	310	254	289	436	93	111	126	106
Detained under:										
Section 26	266	87	25	25	129	114	35	10	21	48
Section 60 or 61	534	82	252	183	17	222	31	90	85	16
Section 71(2) 72 or 73	40	16	16	6	2	13	3	5	4	1
Sixth Schedule	206	11	17	38	140	76	21	4	12	39
Other compulsory powers	32	29	—	2	1	11	3	2	4	2

*Source: Department of Health and Social Security, Statistical and Research Report Series No. 12. In-patient statistics for the year 1973, pp. 98-99.

Table 3
Percentages of patients in each mental category in the special hospitals on
December 31, 1973*

	Mental Illness	Psychopathic disorder	Subnormal	Severely subnormal
Broadmoor	72.5%	27.1%	0.4%	–
Rampton	20.9%	28.8%	23.6%	26.8%
Moss Side	21.3%	25.5%	28.9%	24.3%

*Compiled from the data given in Table 2.

Interpersonal dynamics in a simulated high-security institution

Professors Haney, Banks and Zimbardo conducted an interesting study which shows the profound effect upon warders and inmates of confinement in a high-security environment.[6] They chose 24 subjects, described as normal, healthy college students. Half of these were randomly assigned to play the role of warders for eight-hour shifts each day, while the others played the role of detained inmates for nearly one week. Neither group was given any specific training for these roles. The warders were free to introduce the inmates into the institution and keep and care for them there. They were, however, expressly told not to use physical punishment or aggression.

The results of the study show that the mere custodial environment had a negative effect on both the warders and the inmates; both groups became more self-deprecating as they internalised the experience. The encounters between these two randomly assigned groups were hostile, affrontive and dehumanising. The inmates adopted a generally passive mode of response, while the warders took the initiative and were quite abusive in the interactions. The experimenters described the situation thus:[7]

> "The most dramatic evidence of the impact of this situation upon the participants was seen in the gross reactions of five prisoners who had to be released because of extreme depression, crying, rage and acute anxiety. The pattern of symptoms was quite similar in four of the subjects and began as early as the second day of imprisonment. The fifth subject was released after being treated for a psychosomatic rash which covered portions of his body."

The students who acted as warders appeared upset when the experiment was prematurely ended: "It appeared to us that they now enjoyed the extreme control and power which they exercised and were reluctant to give it up."[7]

The Haney study suggests that something in the character of a secure institution itself impedes the process of rehabilitation. The typical inmate becomes passive, dependent, depressed, helpless and self-deprecatory.

Some of these elements emerge from the following description of Broadmoor Hospital.

The environment in Broadmoor Hospital

Introductory comment

We have chosen Broadmoor Hospital for this discussion because we have more information about it than about the others. Our chief source of information is the Hospital Advisory Service (HAS) Report on Broadmoor.[8] We were also able to visit the hospital.

We should emphasise at this point that the HAS Report was complimentary about the staff at Broadmoor: "They have not only managed to live reasonably happily with the conflict [between safe security and adequate treatment] but, and this is even more impressive, to have given a great deal of help to many people and to have discharged considerable numbers" (para. 110).

The negative comments in the HAS Report and in this report are directed against the nature of large-scale secure institutions, which by necessity impede rehabilitation. In fact, the Haney study presented above clearly illustrates that it is the secure institution itself, and not the professional staff, which causes many of the problems.

Security

The Hospital Advisory Service Report on Broadmoor stressed the heavy accent on security which is patently obvious to any visitor to the hospital:[9]

"There are locked doors and side rooms, a perimeter wall, checking of patients in and out of areas using radio links, the nursing staff, when not on the wards, wear a dark blue uniform with a peaked cap,* patients' letters are subject to censor, and visiting is carefully controlled. Nor are these physical obstacles the only means by which control can be exercised: the staff operate simple reward and punishment systems to regulate patients' behaviour. The small number of escapes in recent years (5 in the last 10 years) and the low level of violence, suggest to us that control is effective."

The nursing staff belong to the Prison Officers Association, not to any union of hospital employees. As the HAS Report states: "The inward-looking attitude of Broadmoor is at its strongest among the nurses. . . Security is seen as the first consideration, and treatment within that situation varies. The nurses, until comparatively recent times, had a very custodial role to play . . . but it does not seem that a positive treatment role is emerging."[10]

---

*The HAS Report comments in para. 206 that patients come to an environment which puzzles and controls them: "In Norfolk House their handcuffs are taken off and they are given medical and psychological examinations – but they are still locked up for 10 hours every night by people who say they are nurses, but who show by their dress and behaviour that they are also warders." It is worth noting that the staff at Park Lane hospital do not wear uniforms. The patients and staff agree that this promotes a better atmosphere.

Overcrowding

There is severe overcrowding in all the special hospitals, and especially in Broadmoor. The Butler Committee estimated that around 2,000 more beds are needed in secure establishments, of which some 450-500 should be used to relieve congestion in the special hospitals.[11] Broadmoor was built to house 500 patients, but in 1975 the total population was 763.[12]

Descriptions of the overcrowding have come from various sources. In 1968 the Estimates Committee described the conditions as 'appalling'.[13] In 1974, the Interim Butler Report said of the special hospitals:[14]

"We have been astonished and shocked at the overcrowding, particularly at Broadmoor, where in some wards the beds, in rows right across the room, are no more than eighteen inches apart. In these dormitories, the patients, who are by definition likely to be detained for long periods . . . can obviously have no privacy, and as there is no cupboard room, they are living out of suitcases."

The HAS Report on Broadmoor was equally forthright in its descriptions:[15]

(1) Overcrowded dining areas, causing patients to have their meals in the corridors.
(2) Lack of occupation for many patients unable to leave the ward to work elsewhere.
(3) Lack of motivation and increasing apathy among patients who have no occupation or challenging interests.
(4) Feelings of frustration because wards need decorating and upgrading . . .
(5) The toilet and bathroom accommodation is inadequate in most wards . . . Urinals are not screened and are a cause of much embarrassment to both patients and visitors.

The night conditions are even less adequate. Not all wards have toilet access in dormitory areas, and chamber pots have to be used extensively. Many patients have no access to their personal effects at night. Their personal property is often stored in large cases and boxes; this heightens the impression of overcrowding, as well as presenting a fire hazard.

Finally, because of the shortage of dormitory space, some patients have to sleep in the infirmary areas, with the physically sick. Even more unsatisfactory, the Education Department has to be used as a dormitory area at night.[16]

Rehabilitation

Four factors may be considered important when a patient is admitted to a special hospital such as Broadmoor. These are security, control of dangerousness, clinical treatment and rehabilitation. The first three are well accepted by the staff at Broadmoor. The patient is confined behind high perimeter walls, his violence is contained in a rigid and controlled environment, and his pathological condition is assessed and treated. But rehabilitation – the process of enabling him to retain or build up competence to live in the community – is lacking.[17]

Attitudes of staff

The HAS Report on Broadmoor points out that the staff do not see rehabilitation as very relevant in a high-security institution. "It is a fact that Broadmoor staff in general view rehabilitation with some suspicion. They equate it with certain practices which are welcome in an open hospital, but which are incompatible with Broadmoor."[18] Broadmoor staff argue that rehabilitation should be postponed until after transfer or discharge.

The HAS Report therefore concluded that there is "no evidence of a co-ordinated rehabilitation policy for the hospital".

Institutionalism

As was discussed in Volume I of this report,[19] the sheer social poverty of the environment in mental hospitals often produces a functional pathology, which has been labelled 'institutionalism' – the enforced idleness and isolation in which the patients live leads to withdrawal, apathy, and submissiveness, and eventually to acceptance of and reliance on institutional life. This is very damaging to any prospects of rehabilitation into community life.

This danger of institutionalisation is especially severe in the special hospitals. The high-security environment, which involves marching, head-counting, and confinement in small quarters for long periods, all contribute to institutional dependence. The sheer geographic distance of the special hospitals from the home areas of most patients means that they lose close contact with their families and friends, and with community activities. It also impedes communication with the treatment and caring agencies in their home areas. The conclusion drawn by the Hospital Advisory Service on Broadmoor follows:[20]

> "A hospital where early rehabilitation is neglected will rapidly produce institutionalised patients and regimes. There will be under-employment, irrational systems of motivation and denial that patients can rightly be given any personal responsibility. The hospital will be organised to suit staff conveniences rather than patient needs, and patients will know that their work is only a time-filler and that their contribution is not respected."

The danger of institutionalisation is also heightened where there is a high proportion of long-stay chronic patients. According to the HAS Report, the average stay in Broadmoor is $5\frac{1}{2}$ years,[21] and many patients stay for 10 or 20 years or more:[22]

> "During his years in the hospital the patient learns the 'Broadmoor way of life' in the presence of constant observation, control, support and interest. After three to five years here many a disordered unhappy young man is often at terms with himself for the first time in his life. It is almost too successful; after ten years here few wish to return to the unsupported chaotic and threatening life outside. For Broadmoor is a powerful and effective social conditioning process."

Stigma

A patient in a special hospital may find that care-giving professionals are profoundly reluctant to help him, or even to tolerate him. Staff of local hospitals feel that to accept patients from the special hospitals may disturb the 'open-door' spirit they have established, and damage their relations with the community. Social workers in the local authorities feel that they are not properly trained to deal with the problems of abnormal offenders. Thus, because he lives (or has once lived) in a special hospital, the professionals in the patient's home area may not give him the time and care that he so badly needs.

Members of the public are also often intolerant of former special hospital patients. The media give the impression that they are all unpredictably violent – colloquially speaking, they suffer from the dual stigma of being both 'mad' and 'bad'. Thus, it may be very hard for them to find a home, a job, close friends, and so forth. Brian's case illustrates this point:[23]

> Brian was convicted of arson in 1963, and admitted to Broadmoor Hospital under a restriction order without limit of time. Two years ago he was released on licence. He was recalled to Broadmoor after failing to report his change of address to his probation officer. Eight months later he was again released on licence. Brian attempted to find a home, but found very little help: "I tried Islington Council because I was once on their housing list, but they sent me to the Mental Patients' Union in Hackney. They suggested that I contact MIND, and they didn't have any ideas."
>
> Brian has tried to find accommodation himself, but according to the terms of his licence, he is instructed to inform every potential landlord about his stay in Broadmoor. To date, more than 60 landlords have said no to him.

Inward-looking approach

Where staff and patients both live under closed, high-security conditions, tensions are bound to develop.* This frequently leads to complaints: the nursing staff tend to complain to the RMO about troublesome patients,† while the patients often write to organisations such as the NCCL or MIND when they feel they have been unfairly treated by staff members.

---

*See, for example, the Haney study, p.125 *supra*.

†A Broadmoor consultant told MIND about a patient on his ward who was troublesome. The nursing staff did not find him violent, but he was rude and disrespectful. They complained to the consultant. He replied by fully supporting the members of the nursing staff. He authorised them to hold the patient in solitary confinement until such time as *they* thought necessary. The staff refused to release the patient after several days of confinement. The consultant felt uncomfortable about this, but he continued to support the staff. This went on for 12 days, until the nursing staff finally agreed to release him.

The consultant now holds that his decision was correct, because the patient is no longer troublesome; he is fully co-operating with members of staff.

In dealing with complaints from patients, we have found that the following criticism made by the HAS is quite accurate: "Broadmoor has an isolated and inward-looking culture . . . Despite its internal tensions, Broadmoor presents a defensive, and often united, face to the outside world."[24] MIND sometimes receives little co-operation from the hospital authorities when trying to discover facts in order to advise both patients and staff of their rights and responsibilities. The following issues illustrate the kinds of problem that we meet.

Transfer
Broadmoor patients often write to tell us that they have been placed on the transfer list, but their RMO cannot find them a place in a local hospital or hostel. MIND's Social Services Department has information, resources and expertise which, in suitable cases, it is glad to lend to the special hospitals. In some cases, we have found sheltered accommodation when asked to do so by patients. Nevertheless, the hospital authorities have resisted our offers of help. They seem to feel that these matters should be handled exclusively by medical officials. This may perhaps be the proper way to proceed, but it is very time-consuming; patients and their relatives understandably find it hard to accept that transfers must involve such lengthy delays.

Homosexual relations
A Member of Parliament received this letter from a constituent. He did not feel that he could help the patient, but he passed the letter on to MIND:

"I am (not to my shame) a practising homosexual and since being in Broadmoor these last two and a half years, myself and another patient formed a relationship. This relationship was sanctioned by our RMO who stated that he had no objections whatsoever to my partner and I indulging in sexual activities as long as it did not disrupt his ward management. I would like to state that neither my partner or I did misuse this privilege. You see, I was what is termed as a House Parole Patient, which entitled me to certain privileges, for example, to invite another patient to my room. That is how my partner and I could spend our free time together, and the acts that took place between us were done in private, and I can assure you that we *did not* disrupt the ward management.

The doctor said we were both making excellent progress and that we were helping each other, and I agree with that; we were both very happy for two and a half years.

On Thursday last, June 10th, 1976, I was told by the charge nurse that the doctor was splitting us up and that I was being transferred to another ward at once. This came as a great shock to me I can assure you, and it has nearly broken my heart.

From my point of view, this is a case of mental cruelty and I would like you to investigate the incident for me."

This case shows one of the basic problems of running a 'rights' service for patients in psychiatric hospitals. There is no particular legislation which clearly explains how much authority hospital staff have over compulsory patients. The RMO, for example, is defined in section 59(1) of the Act as the medical practitioner in charge of the treatment of a formal patient. Nothing further is said about his authority in the definition section of the Act. (Notably, doctors in high-security hospitals are not given any more special powers than those in local NHS hospitals.) Presumably, section 59(1) empowers the RMO to make decisions about compulsory patients only in relation to positive medical treatment; it does not specifically authorise him to control the patient's social behaviour. Other parts of the Act merely expand upon his basic responsibility to provide care and treatment. He is empowered to grant a leave of absence (s. 39), discharge a patient (s. 47), bar the discharge of a patient by the nearest relative (s. 44), and make statutory reports for the renewal of authority for detention.

The decision of the RMO in the case described above may have been a non-medical decision, which is wrong in law. But given the nature of closed institutions, it is difficult to verify facts as they are described by patients. Moreover, even if these could be verified, it is difficult to find a remedy in law for the alleged injustice.

In this case we have recommended that the MP should write to the doctor. If he receives no satisfactory explanation within a reasonable period, we have recommended that he obtain the patient's permission to refer the case to the Parliamentary Commissioner for Administration (the Ombudsman).[25] The Ombudsman is empowered to investigate complaints by individuals who claim to have "sustained injustice in consequence of maladministration" by central government bodies. The special hospitals are directly administered by the Department of Health and Social Security, so complaints about these institutions or their agents may come within the purlieu of the Ombudsman. The term "maladministration", which was intentionally left undefined, is crucially important here. It includes bias and unfair discrimination, which may bring this case within the Ombudsman's terms of reference. But it does not include unreasonable exercise of discretion.[26] It is therefore important to determine whether the RMO's decision was legitimate within the confines of his clinical discretion as outlined in the Mental Health Act.

Censorship

Under section 36 of the Mental Health Act, the RMO may withhold a postal packet from a patient if he considers that receiving it would be "calculated to interfere with the treatment of the patient or cause him unnecessary distress". He may also withhold from the post any postal packet sent by a patient if he feels that it would be "unreasonably offensive to the addressee, or is defamatory of other persons . . . or would be likely to prejudice the interests of the patient".*

*It is interesting that section 36 applies equally to special hospitals, and there are no extra statutory or administrative provisions to cover their special need for security. Presumably, much of the censorship which does take place in the special hospitals is intended to maintain security. We understand that any post censored for this purpose is considered to come within the terms of section 36(1): "the receipt of the packet would be calculated to interfere with the treatment of the patient".

But if the patient addresses the packet to any of the following individuals, it cannot be withheld: the Minister, Members of Parliament, an Officer of the Court of Protection, the hospital managers, or any other person or authority that has the power to discharge the patient.[27]†

According to subsection 3, these provisions do not authorise the RMO to open or examine the contents of every postal packet sent by patients in his hospital. The general right to send and receive unopened correspondence is not to be infringed unless the RMO determines that the particular patient is "suffering from a mental disorder of a kind calculated to lead him to send such communications as are referred to [above]".[28]

We pointed out in Volume I that the criteria given under section 36 (such as "unnecessary distress" and "likely to prejudice his interests") are extremely broad and ambiguous; freedom of expression is an important constitutional right, which should be interfered with only for narrow and well-defined reasons. Moreover, some of the criteria (such as 'offensive' or 'defamatory') are not medical judgments, and therefore should not properly be made by the RMO.[29]

Although the criteria given in section 36 are vague, they must be reasonably adhered to if a postal packet is lawfully to be read without the patient's consent. But it is interesting to compare the actual practice of censorship in Broadmoor with the statutory guidelines.

There is a person at Broadmoor whom patients refer to as "The Censor"; he is employed solely to read every postal packet sent or received by the patients. He refers anything that could conceivably come within the terms of section 36 to the RMO.[30]

Patients believe that their complaints about the internal affairs of the hospital and their letters asking for information about their rights are all regularly passed on to be read by the RMO. They therefore fear that they will be victimised because of the content of these letters. Hence, they sometimes refuse to explain their problems in the post, and instead ask us to send a MIND representative to visit them personally. Other patients write to MIND, and ask that a duplicate reply be sent to one of their friends outside the hospital. In this way, the patient can 'compare' the letter he receives with the one the friend receives, to see whether the incoming letter has been censored.

One Broadmoor patient claimed that his RMO read his correspondence with MIND about finding a representative for his tribunal hearing. The RMO held a ward meeting to tell all his patients that it was 'unwise' to apply for a tribunal. The reason he gave was the time it took to prepare for the tribunal. This would delay the treatment programme that he had designed, which might mean that the patient would have to be detained longer.

---

†Under the Mental Health (Hospital and Guardianship) Regulations 1960 (reg. 23), a patient can correspond with his solicitor in certain circumstances. Under general powers, the Secretary of State for Social Services has added to the list the European Commission for Human Rights, with which a patient may correspond unimpeded. There is also a movement afoot to include Community Health Councils on the list.

Another Broadmoor patient wrote to MIND complaining that he was not receiving the education he wanted. He claimed that the RMO read the letter and spoke to him about it the next day.

This practice of censorship at Broadmoor is troubling on several levels:

(1) Every letter is evidently read by a hospital employee, and there is no safeguard about what information he passes on to the psychiatric or nursing staff of the hospital. Thus, even if not a single postal packet is actually withheld, the practice itself has a 'chilling effect' on free and vigorous exchange of information by post. The patients fear "The Censor", and this in itself deters open communication.

(2) Apparently, no attempt is made to determine, in accordance with section 36(3), whether the individual patient is "suffering from a mental disorder of a kind calculated to lead him to send such communications as are referred to". Instead, all letters are systematically read as a matter of general hospital policy. Further, if patients' complaints to organisations such as MIND and the NCCL are indeed read by the RMO, this is difficult to reconcile with the criteria given in section 36. Can it be, for example, that the RMO feels that such information may be "calculated to interfere with the treatment of the patient?"

(3) Any decision to censor* a letter is not subject to any kind of scrutiny or review. Even the DHSS, as hospital managers, do not take an active interest in which letters are being censored, and why. Accordingly, there is no way of knowing whether the criteria under section 36 are being followed; this in itself makes them meaningless.

Observations and proposals for reform

The description of Broadmoor hospital given in this chapter shows the profoundly negative impact which a high-security institution may have on the life of a patient:

(1) The regime of the institution may involve marching, head-counting, confinement in small quarters, censorship of post, limitation of visiting hours, lack of privacy and so forth. This promotes institutional behaviour and loss of self-esteem; it also inevitably impedes proper rehabilitation.

(2) Mere residence in a high-security institution necessarily implies that the person may present a danger to others. This places a special burden on

*The Department of Health and Social Security has recently published a consultative document: *A Review of the Mental Health Act 1959.* On page 63 the Department argues that the term 'censorship', as used in volume 1 of *A Human Condition* (pp. 111-114), is misleading, as the Act makes no provision for deleting passages of a letter, but only for preventing the entire letter from reaching the post. While the Department is, of course, correct in its interpretation of the Act, it should be pointed out that a 'censor' is one who judges or assesses the value of written material and then prevents it from being expressed – either in whole or in part. The great English philosopher John Milton, for example, addressed himself to a form of censorship whereby government officials sought to prevent entirely the publication of certain, undesirable books. For a more detailed discussion of the issue see L. Gostin, "Freedom of expression and the mentally disordered: philosophical and constitutional perspectives", *Notre Dame Lawyer,* vol. 50, February 1975, pp. 419-447.

him to show clearly that he is safe for transfer or discharge. The statistics shown in Chapter 5 suggest that patients therefore remain in special hospitals longer than they would in either a local hospital or a prison.

(3) The patient may still be treated as inclined to violence even after his discharge or transfer from a special hospital. This often makes it difficult to find a job, housing and even adequate after-care.

It is interesting to note that one-third of all patients in special hospitals are not offenders.[31]† The same assumptions are made that they are dangerous, and there are also the same implications of prolonged detention and stigma. But there is no conviction by a court of law to rely upon; the reasons for their admission or transfer to a special hospital are passed from one professional to the next by hospital records and correspondence, which are never open to public scrutiny.

MIND knows of a number of patients in the special hospitals who have not, to our knowledge, shown seriously violent behaviour in the past. We do not necessarily question the decision to detain them compulsorily for treatment, but we have serious reservations about the need for special security conditions. In Chapter 5 we cited the case of *Nigel Smith,* where the Court of Appeal itself apparently felt that the criteria under section 40 of the National Health Service Reorganisation Act 1973* were not satisfied.[33] But he is still detained in Broadmoor Hospital, even though there is no concrete evidence that he has a propensity towards violence.

We also know of cases in which non-offenders in local hospitals under section 26 have been transferred to special hospitals as a result of 'troublesome or disturbing behaviour' (which did not, however, amount to violence against the person). In one case, a patient was transferred because he pulled down the curtains in the hospital ward. In another, the patient caused minor property damage by throwing a breakable object against a wall.

The Butler Committee estimated that 450-500 patients in the special hospitals do not need treatment under maximum security conditions.

In sum, the decision to admit or transfer a person to a special hospital involves an important restriction of liberty.‡ It should not be made without

---

†Another 13% of the residents in special hospitals are unrestricted patients, whom the courts did not feel presented a danger to the public.

*Under section 40 of the 1973 Act, the Secretary of State for Social Services may admit any formal patient to a special hospital who, *in his opinion,* requires treatment under conditions of special security on account of his dangerous, violent or criminal propensities.[32] When taking this decision, the Minister need not go through any formal procedures (for example, he does not need two medical recommendations), and there is no appeal against his decision.

‡Arguably, the decision to admit a person to a *special* hospital is more important, from the civil liberties perspective, than the decision to detain him compulsorily. Yet many statutory safeguards surround compulsory admission to hospital, but there are none on the question, "Which hospital?" For example, a person may be admitted under section 26 to The Bethlem Royal and the Maudsley Hospitals, and be quite content with this situation. If he were then transferred to Broadmoor he could conceivably feel aggrieved. Yet he would have no legal remedy against the transfer.

statutory safeguards. These could be created quite economically by extending the powers of the Mental Health Review Tribunals. Currently, they can only decide whether an unrestricted patient should be detained or released – not *where* he is to be detained. We recommend that the tribunal should be authorised to hear evidence on the issue, and to determine whether the patient needs treatment under high security conditions because of his "dangerous, violent or criminal propensities". It should then be empowered to recommend the transfer of an unrestricted patient out of a special hospital or to prevent his entry to it.

Thus, before an unrestricted patient is admitted (other than through the courts) or transferred to a special hospital, he should be provided with a tribunal hearing. This requirement could be waived in emergency only. Then a tribunal hearing should be held as soon as possible after his admission.

Alternatively, the patient should be given the right to apply for a tribunal at any time within the first six months after transfer from a local to a special hospital.

The main advantage of this alternative proposal is that it would be very easy to implement. The local hospital could transfer the patient to the special hospital as usual. He could then apply for a tribunal if he wished, and the tribunal could recommend that he be readmitted to the local hospital. The disadvantage is that once a patient has been transferred to a special hospital, the decision will be very difficult to overturn. The tribunal will be less likely to alter the *status quo,* and the local hospital will be extremely reluctant to readmit.

References and Notes

1. Statement by Mr Eric Deakins, Under-Secretary of State for Health and Social Security, *Hansard,* June 22, 1976, p. 1,564.
2. See generally *The Butler Report,* paras. 2.14-15, 3.9-11; N. Walker and S. McCabe, *Crime and Insanity in England,* vol. 2, 1973, Chapter 1; Ministry of Health Working Party (D. Emery, Chairman), *Special Hospitals,* 1961.
3. National Health Service Reorganisation Act 1973, s. 40.
4. Department of Health and Social Security, *Statistical and Research Report Series No. 12: Psychiatric Hospitals and Units in England,* In-patient statistics for the year 1973, pp. 100-101.
5. Dr David Owen, Written Parliamentary Answer, December 2, 1974, p. 374 (Park Lane will "provide places for 180 patients by the end of 1977, with a further 220 to be added some two years later.")
6. C. Haney, C. Banks and P. Zimbardo, "Interpersonal dynamics in a simulated prison", *International Journal of Criminology and Penology,* vol. 1, 1973, pp. 69-97.
7. *Ibid.,* p.8.
8. National Health Service Hospital Advisory Service, *Report on Broadmoor Hospital, Crowthorne, Berkshire (HAS Report).* Administered by the Department of Health and Social Security. Unpublished, February 1975.
9. *Ibid.,* para. 111.
10. *Ibid.,* para. 347.
11. *Interim Report of the Committee on Mentally Abnormal Offenders,* Cmnd. 5698, July 1974, para. 13.
12. *Community Care,* October 29, 1975.

13. *Second Report from the Estimates Committee Session 1967-68,* paras. 12-13.
14. *Interim Butler Report,* reference 11, para. 4.
15. *HAS Report,* para. 603.
16. *Ibid.,* paras. 201, 605, 607.
17. *Ibid.,* para. 401.
18. *Ibid.,* para. 402.
19. L. Gostin, *A Human Condition,* vol. 1, 1975, p. 13.
20. *HAS Report,* para. 404.
21. *Ibid.,* para. 314.
22. *Ibid.,* para. 207.
23. "No vacancies", *Time Out,* May 14-20, pp. 6-7.
24. *HAS Report,* para. 116.
25. Parliamentary Commissioner Act 1967.
26. See generally S.A. de Smith, *Judicial Review of Administrative Action,* 3rd ed., 1973, pp. 45-52.
27. Mental Health Act 1959, s. 36(2).
28. *Ibid.,* s. 36(3), 36(4).
29. L. Gostin, *op cit.,* Chapter 9.
30. Information received directly from the Department of Health and Social Security.
31. *The Butler Report,* para. 2.33.
32. See Parliamentary Written Answer by Dr David Owen, Wednesday, February 25, 1976.
33. R v McFarlane [1975] 60 Cr.App.R. 320, at 324.

9. Regional secure units

There is an undoubted need for better provision for those people whose needs fall between the services offered by local psychiatric hospitals and special hospitals. These people, because of their difficult and at times violent behaviour, require extra security which is not provided by local hospitals; but they do not require the degree of security found in the special hospitals.

The problems caused by this situation have been set out in detail earlier. Some 500 people in the special hospitals do not require treatment under maximum security conditions. They remain in special hospitals partly because the National Health Service fails to offer appropriate care under less restrictive conditions. This leaves the special hospitals overcrowded, and they are forced to turn away numbers of mentally disordered offenders referred to them from the courts and prisons. Two consequences arise: many special hospital patients are under a more restrictive regime than is necessary for their own well-being, and for public safety; and offenders in need of psychiatric treatment are unnecessarily sentenced to terms of imprisonment.

These problems were first identified by a Ministry of Health Working Party on Special Hospitals in February, 1961.[1] They recommended that some NHS hospitals should specialise in treating more difficult types of patient, and should therefore provide less stringent security arrangements than the special hospitals. But, because a single area may not have enough patients who require these conditions, the services should be planned on a regional basis. The Working Party suggested that before a person was admitted to a special hospital, he should be considered for admission to a regional secure unit, so that his condition and needs could be fully assessed: "Admission to a special hospital should be arranged only when it seems clear that there is no other course open."[2]

The Ministry of Health issued a memorandum to Regional Hospital Boards in July, 1961, advising them on how to implement the Working Party's recommendation – but not a single secure unit materialised. One reason for this may have been the lack of any special financial provisions.[3]

The idea of a medium secure unit was reintroduced in 1974 by the Committee on Mentally Abnormal Offenders in their interim report. The Committee were "astonished and shocked" at the overcrowding in special hospitals. They also pointed to the increasing number of mentally abnormal offenders in prison. They proposed, "as a matter of urgency", the provision of secure hospital units in each regional health authority area. (It was estimated that 2,000 beds would be needed.) The Committee urged the Government to finance the units by allocating funds directly to regional health authorities for this specific purpose.[4]

The Revised Report of the Working Party on Security in NHS Psychiatric Hospitals (chaired by Dr J. E. Glancy) was published at about the same time as the Interim Butler Report. The Working Party also recommended the development of regional secure units; but it proposed only 1,000 beds instead of 2,000.[5]

On July 18, 1974 the Secretary of State for Social Services said in Parliament:[6]

> "I accept the recommendation of both reports [Butler and Glancy] that urgent action should be taken to establish in each health region, secure psychiatric units ... We shall begin by providing a total of 1,000 places and if the need is confirmed by experience, will build up, as and when resources permit, to the 2,000 places recommended by the Committee on Mentally Abnormal Offenders."

The Department of Health and Social Security issued a circular of guidance to the regional health authorities, agreeing to make a direct grant to the regions for the establishment of the secure units.[7] The Department also asked the regions to designate particular hospitals in the interim to provide treatment in security conditions until proper regional units could be set up.

The Department said that it expected a "substantial number" of the 14 regional health authorities to begin work on the construction of the units (by adaptation or new building) in 1975/76, and all regions should have started construction by 1976/77. Yet, as of July 1976 although 10 of the 14 Regions had made interim arrangements,[8] only the Yorkshire, South-Western and North-Western authorities had started to build their units;[9] no Region had as yet established a permanent secure unit.[8]

The design of the units

Location and size

The Butler and Glancy Reports emphasised that regional secure units should be placed in population centres, and should be close to other medical facilities.[10] It was envisaged that the sites would be within the district general hospital complex.[11] If the units were able to share common services and facilities with an existing hospital, then the recommended ideal size would be 50-100 beds. If sharing of facilities were not possible, the units would probably need about 200 beds, in order to justify the expense of equipping them with self-contained resources.[11]

Patients

The White Paper on Mental Illness made a positive statement on which kind of patient should be admitted to a regional secure unit: "patients who are continuously behaviourally disturbed or who are persistently violent or considered a danger to the public, albeit not an immediate one."[12]

138

The units will admit all types of patient:[13] offenders and non-offenders, formal and informal, male and female, in-patients, out-patients and patients being assessed for the courts, adults and adolescents, and so forth. They are not, however, intended for severely mentally handicapped patients; these people should be provided for in ordinary mental handicap hospitals.

Staffing

The Department has strongly advised the adoption of a multi-disciplinary approach in secure units.[14]

The recommended staff ratio is one nurse to one patient. The Department points out that an overall staffing ratio of 1:1 is likely to be 1:4.5 at any one time.[15]

A pay lead of £201 per annum, besides the psychiatric lead to which they are entitled, will be paid to the nursing staff who are employed permanently and exclusively in the unit.[15]

Security

The Department issued a paper entitled "Regional Secure Units Design Guidelines" in July, 1975. It explained the provision of security thus:[16]

"The units will not be expected to emulate the special hospitals or prisons in the degree of security they provide; nor will they be expected to take account of the possibility of outside 'rescue' attempts. They will not be trying to contain the determined absconder nor the type of patient who, if he escaped, would present an immediate and grave threat to the public. The units will be expected to stop patients simply walking out or otherwise leaving on impulse without staff knowledge."

The Department advised a sophisticated and positive use of security. A unit should not require a perimeter wall, although perimeter security may be needed around a particular section of the unit for patients who are particularly dangerous or likely to abscond. There should be different levels of security within the unit, and every effort should be made to apply only that degree of security which is essential to the particular case. The Department warned that the "dangers of falling into a routine use of too much security should not be under-estimated", and measures should be taken to overcome this.[17]

Length of stay

The secure units should aim to keep patients as short a time as possible, and to have a high turnover of patients. Regular reviews should be made in all cases. If no progress is made after 18 months, an alternative placement (such as a transfer to a local NHS hospital, a special hospital, or a prison) should be seriously considered.[18]

Observations

When the government accepted the concept of regional secure units, one author made the following comment: "The circular which followed these two reports [Butler and Glancy] indicates haste bordering on panic in the speed of implementation."[19] Evidently, the government has been so impressed with the well-documented need for improved forensic psychiatric services that it has not fully assessed whether regional secure units will satisfactorily meet that need.

The experience of the special hospitals provides a useful model upon which to assess the value of the proposed units. In the last chapter we examined the situation of the patient in a special hospital: he exists in a regimented and secure environment which necessarily isolates him from the community and impedes his rehabilitation; the attendant stigma makes it difficult to transfer him to a local hospital, and for him to obtain a job or housing in the community.

These are some of the inevitable results of any institution which exists for the express purpose of treating 'special' individuals. Every patient, present or past, is automatically presumed to have dangerous or troublesome qualities.

Despite the considerable problems that have arisen with the special hospitals, the government now proposes to create 1,000 additional places for patients who will be designated as 'difficult' or 'disruptive'. No one seems to have realised that the new units may have similar problems. Indeed, every indication shows that professionals and members of the public are already pre-judging the prospective patients.

Take the situation in Redhill, Surrey.[20] The South-West Thames Regional Health Authority proposed to build a secure unit immediately beside the Royal Earlswood Hospital, which accommodates some 650 mentally handicapped people. Local residents drew up a petition of protest. The Confederation of Health Service Employees (COHSE) described it as a 'dastardly scheme'. Mr George Gardiner, the local Member of Parliament, called it a 'monstrous injustice'. The newspapers referred to the proposed unit as a 'mini-Broadmoor' which was to house the 'criminally insane'.[21] The feelings of the community were summed up by Mr Gardiner: "No site proposed for such a security unit, designed to accommodate criminal elements among others, will ever be greeted with enthusiasm by local residents."

Mr Jim Callaghan, MP (Middleton, Prestwich) was similarly concerned about a proposed unit at Prestwich Hospital.[22] He argued that there was an apparent lack of precision about the type of patient to be housed in the new secure units: "Because of the lack of precision, fears have been expressed locally about the possibility of patients who are dangerous, violent or criminal, being transferred from the special hospitals to the Prestwich security unit." Mr Callaghan noted that the proposed unit had caused "great alarm, anxiety and fear" in the community. "The public needs assuring that the doors, the windows and fencing of the security unit will give maximum security."

In September, 1976 the first permanent secure unit was to have opened at Rainhill Psychiatric Hospital in Liverpool. However, while the nurses belonging to COHSE agreed to staff the unit, NUPE (National Union of Public Employees) refused to do so. Among other complaints, they maintain that the level of security recommended in a confidential report by the Mersey Health Authority indicates that the unit will be a high-security institution on the lines of a special hospital; a 17-foot-high perimeter fence is alleged to be an 'essential physical requirement'. The Union claims that the unit will eventually contain 100 potentially violent criminals who could be a danger to staff and local residents. They have threatened similar industrial action in other units.[23]

David Ennals, Secretary of State for Social Services, expressed disappointment at the 'slow and patchy' progress towards establishing regional secure units. At the instigation of the Trade Union Congress, he set up a working party to explore the difficulties that are arising in each region.[24]

These voices of concern and dissent indicate that the same disharmony which now exists between the special hospitals on the one hand, and the National Health Service and the general public on the other, may well occur with the regional secure units.

The Department of Health and Social Security argues otherwise. It says that the units will develop as an integral part of the psychiatric services of the region, and will not be isolated from ordinary NHS psychiatric services. The treatment of patients is therefore seen as a continuous process during which transfers will be easily effected between special, regional secure and local hospitals.[25] The Department, however, does not indicate how these goals can be achieved, especially in light of the already poor relations between special and local hospitals. It places some faith in the possibilities for 'intensive therapy' in the proposed units, but does not discuss its nature.[26] Nor does it indicate how quality staff can be attracted to these units without draining the already depleted numbers of professionals in the local hospitals.[27]

It is unrealistic to believe that local hospitals will transfer their most troublesome patients to medium secure units and, after less than 18 months of intensive therapy, accept them back. The reverse is more likely to happen. By creating more specialisation in the health service, the government is simply encouraging the local hospitals to delegate their special problems to segregated institutions. At the same time, there is no indication that staff in existing local psychiatric hospitals will be helped to develop rich and sophisticated rehabilitation programmes which could decrease disruptive behaviour and avoid the need for restraint; nor is there any proposal for in-depth training and guidance to help psychiatric nurses to deal with violence on the wards.

No relief for special hospitals and prisons

The Butler Committee states: "Our main concern is that the units are crucial to the greater flexibility in placement needed for mentally abnormal offenders, and to the early relief of the prisons and the special hospitals."[28]

But will regional secure units meet these pressing needs? The research presented in the Glancy Report is probative. The Report pointed out that in 1971 some 13,000 patients (7.6% of all those in psychiatric hospitals) were in wards that were locked during the day. The working party made the following comment:[29]

"We believe that this number includes many patients who do not present continuously difficult or disturbed behaviour and who are therefore not in need of secure accommodation. It includes many people who . . . are commonly held in secure accommodation but not rightly placed therein – the elderly wanderer, the severely mentally handicapped destructive patient, and the patient who is difficult only during an acute phase of illness. There are also a significant number of patients in large wards which are kept locked for the sake of a small proportion of difficult patients. It happens that in some local situations serious staff shortages are compensated by locking in patients who could be managed perfectly satisfactorily in an open situation if there were sufficient staff. Another factor . . . is that of traditional custodial attitudes, where there is reluctance to adopt more open and active treatment methods. We consider that these factors accounted for the great majority of the 13,000 who in 1971 were in regularly locked wards; they are in our view practices which in varying degrees constitute a mistaken and negative use of security."

A survey was conducted to see how many of these patients were considered so difficult that they would be candidates for transfer to regional secure units.[30] In all, 1,258 patients were reported as falling into this category, but the differences between regions, and between the hospitals within regions, were too wide to be accounted for by variation in incidence or in methods of patient management; they may instead reflect different interpretations of the criteria for admission to regional secure units. The Glancy Working Party said that significant numbers of the patients put forward as candidates for secure units were commonly placed in secure accommodation – but were not in need of it. Nevertheless, according to the Working Party, 1,000 people in the local hospitals could legitimately be placed in regional secure units.

The detailed information presented in the Glancy Report suggests the following:

1) *Regional secure units will mainly accommodate patients currently in local hospitals.* There are ample numbers of 'troublesome' patients in the local hospitals to fill the 1,000 beds to be provided in regional secure units. Moreover, given the attitudes of some members of staff in local hospitals, demand for secure beds may continually increase to meet the available supply.* (The Working Party, however, pointed out that "this demand

---

*The Glancy Report (para. 25) stated that the "creation of a secure facility catering for the specific problem of continuously disturbed behaviour may, if care is not taken reduce the tolerance of lesser forms of behaviour in ordinary psychiatric wards. One particular manifestation of this might be increased reluctance to accept patients direct from Special Hospitals."

would not necessarily be one which could or should be met").[31] Thus, the special hospitals and prisons may not receive the relief that the Butler Committee originally envisaged.

Instead, patients who are now housed in community psychiatric hospitals may simply be moved to more secure surroundings. Indeed, Mr David Ennals, Secretary of State for Social Services, in an attempt to allay the anxieties of the unions and the general public, recently stated that "the patients for whom regional secure units are intended are mainly accommodated in the wards of ordinary NHS mental illness and handicap hospitals." He failed utterly to mention that the units were also originally intended to accept patients from the special hospitals and prisons.[32] When Mr Jim Callaghan asked which type of patient would be admitted to the Northern Regional Secure Unit, Mr Eric Deakins, Under-Secretary of State for Social Services, said: "The patients to be admitted to this ward are in the main those already admitted to Prestwich Hospital, who will be brought together in more suitable accommodation."[33]

Thus, it seems very likely that regional secure units will be used mainly for the more difficult types of patient currently in the local hospitals. This may leave very little room for patients from the special hospitals and prisons.

2) *There may be ambiguity in the admission and discharge policy.* The survey in the Glancy Report shows that the psychiatric hospitals vary greatly in their conception of which types of patient are candidates for regional secure units. This is particularly disquieting, because the Department has not proposed any formal standard for admission to and discharge from the units.[19] The Butler Committee said that the units should not accept "aggressive psychopaths or any patients who would be an immediate danger to the public at large".[34] The Glancy Report frankly states that "there is a very real difficulty in defining those who should be admitted to the secure units" – not the "elderly wanderer", the "severely mentally handicapped", or "the patient difficult only during an acute phase of illness".[35]

Moreover, no structure is proposed for monitoring the kinds of individual sent to the secure units. Nor is there any way in which a patient may question whether he is rightly placed there. It may well happen that a patient will remain in the unit, not because he requires treatment under medium secure conditions, but because no local hospital will accept him. This situation currently arises in the case of special hospitals, and there is little which the patient, or indeed the Department, can do to remedy it.

3) *The resources in local hospitals will not be improved.* It was pointed out earlier that in 1971, approximately 13,000 patients in psychiatric hospitals were housed in locked wards. The Glancy Report suggested that this was caused, *inter alia,* by staff shortages and traditional custodial attitudes. These figures are alarming; they merit an investigation into

possible ways of improving the services offered by local NHS hospitals. But it is clear that, whatever one's view of the value of regional secure units, they will do little to improve the resources for the management and care of such patients.[36]

Proposals for reform

Several commentators have suggested that in times of financial stringency it would be better to improve existing services for the care and treatment of disturbed people in local hospitals and prisons, rather than embarking on a new programme which is both expensive and hastily conceived.[19][36] MIND has great sympathy with this view. But we fully recognise that the government has made a financial and political commitment to create regional secure units, and it would be unrealistic to expect the proposals to be withdrawn. Accordingly, we wish to offer certain suggestions to help assure that the units will achieve the high goals† which have been set for them.

We have recommended throughout this report that a patient should be able to question any decision to move him to a more restrictive institution. He should fully understand the reasons for this decision, and be given the opportunity to present evidence which may show he can safely remain in a less secure setting.

This principle could be implemented in any number of ways; but we have specifically suggested that the powers of Mental Health Review Tribunals should be extended to include the authority to recommend transfer. (A recommendation by the tribunal would have the same effect as that stated on pp.118-119 *supra*). The tribunal should make its decisions on the basis of strict behavioural criteria for admission and discharge. For example, the local hospital might have to demonstrate that, by reason of recent overt acts, the patient is dangerous to himself or others. The hospital should also be able to show how often this behaviour occurs. It would therefore be important for each hospital to keep a detailed record of any incident where the patient is alleged to have acted dangerously.

Moreover, the local hospital and regional secure unit should provide a statement on the specific problems which show that the patient needs treatment under conditions of medium security; a description of the treatment goals, with a projected time-table for their attainment; the criteria for transfer to a less restrictive setting; and an estimated date for this transfer.[38]

The patient should, if possible, have the right to be heard by a Mental Health Review Tribunal before he is transferred; in an emergency, the hearing should take place soon after the transfer has been effected. Moreover, since the units are intended as short-term treatment centres, the patient's case should be *automatically* referred to a tribunal after 12-18 months'

†The South West Regional Health Authority claims that its regional secure unit "will contain a cheerful community, therapeutically orientated, combining as much of a homely atmosphere as we can contrive with an unobtrusive barrier restricting the residents' freedom to wander off at will."[37]

detention in a secure unit. If the responsible medical officer intends to keep the patient in the unit, the onus should be on him to prove that continued treatment under medium secure conditions will have a positive and substantial effect.

In addition, we recommend that the Department should set up a Working Party to monitor the effects of regional secure units in their first two years of operation. In particular, the Working Party should examine whether special hospitals and prisons have been able to transfer patients to the units; the numbers and types of patients who are transferred from local hospitals to regional secure units, and the average lengths of stay of patients in the units. The Working Party should use its findings to evaluate the benefits of regional secure units and, if necessary, propose changes to the Department.

References and Notes

1. Ministry of Health, *Report of Working Party on Special Hospitals*, HMSO, 1961, paras. 23-29.
2. *Ibid.*, para. 29.
3. *Interim Report of the Committee on Mentally Abnormal Offenders*, Cmnd. 5698, July 1974, paras. 20 and 21.
4. *Ibid.*, para. 8.
5. *Revised Report of the Working Party on Security in NHS Psychiatric Hospitals* (The Glancy Report), 1974, para. 33.
6. See *Hansard*, Written Answer by Dr David Owen, Minister of State for Social Services, December 2, 1974, pp. 373-74.
7. Health Circular (Interim Series), HSC(15)61, July 1974.
8. *Hansard*, Written Answer by Dr David Owen, June 28, 1976, p. 69. See also the DHSS press statement on a talk given by Mr David Ennals, Secretary of State for Social Services, at Royal Earlswood Hospital, Redhill, September 22, 1976: "The Yorkshire and Northern Regions have had their plans for units at Wakefield and Prestwich approved in principle by the Department. Two other proposals at Middlesbrough in the Northern Region and at Dawlish in the South Western Region are currently being considered. Several other Regions are on the point of submitting proposals, and the remainder are in the process of planning and local consultation."
9. *The Observer*, June 27, 1976.
10. *The Interim Butler Report*, para. 14; *The Glancy Report*, paras. 45-47.
11. *The Interim Butler Report*, para. 16; *The Glancy Report*, para. 48.
12. Department of Health and Social Security, *Better Services for the Mentally Ill*, Cmnd. 6233, October 1975, para. 5.2.
13. *The Glancy Report*, paras. 36-43; Department of Health and Social Security, *Regional Secure Units Design Guidelines*, July 1975, paras. 3.1-3.6; David Ennals' press statement, reference 8.
14. Department of Health and Social Security, *Regional Secure Units Design Guidelines*, July 1975, para. 5.1.
15. *Ibid.*, para. 5.2.
16. *Ibid.*, para. 8.2.
17. *Ibid.*, paras. 8.1-8.9. See also *The Glancy Report*, paras. 49-52.
18. *The Glancy Report*, para. 44.
19. *British Medical Journal*, August 24, 1974, p. 519 (correspondence by M. Bury and J. A. O. Russell).
20. See generally *Hansard*, June 22, 1976, pp. 1558-70.
21. *The Daily Telegraph*, April 23, 1976.
22. See generally *Hansard*, July 14, 1976, pp. 865-76.

23. *The Observer*, September 5, 1976.
24. *Hansard*, Written Answer by David Ennals, Secretary of State for Social Services, July 8, 1976, p. 656. See also *Hansard*, Oral Answer by David Owen, Minister of State for Social Services, June 29, 1976, p. 180; *Hansard*, Written Answer by David Owen, July 8, 1976, p. 653; *Hansard*, Oral Answer by David Owen, March 23, 1976, pp. 178-179.
25. DHSS, *Regional Secure Units Design Guidelines*, paras. 2.1-2.2.
26. *The Interim Butler Report*, para. 9; *The Glancy Report*, paras. 23, 28, 29(3) and 50. See also *British Medical Journal*, January 25, 1975, pp. 205-206 (correspondence by A. Kushlick, G. Cansick, and J. W. Palmer).
27. L. S. Christie, "Are security units really necessary?", *Nursing Mirror*, August 5, 1976, pp. 69-70.
28. *Interim Butler Report*, para. 9.
29. *The Glancy Report*, paras. 18-19.
30. *Ibid.*, paras. 20-21.
31. *Ibid.*, para. 24.
32. DHSS press statement, reference 8.
33. *Hansard*, July 14, 1976, p. 874.
34. *The Interim Butler Report*, para. 10.
35. *The Glancy Report*, paras. 36-39.
36. *The Lancet*, November 15, 1975, p. 986 (correspondence by N. H. Rathod). See also A. Kushlick, G. Cansick and J. W. Palmer, reference 26.
37. South West Regional Health Authority, "Report of a working party to consider the regional forensic psychiatric hospital," October, 1975, Chairman's foreword by G.A. Turner.
38. See generally L. Gostin, *A Human Condition*, vol. 1, 1975, pp. 124-125.

Part IV
Discharge from hospital of patients subject to restriction orders

10. The advisory function of the RMO and the Aarvold Board

We have described in Chapters 4 and 5 the existing provisions for restriction orders made under section 65 of the Mental Health Act, and our recommendations for their reform. This part of the report will more specifically examine the statutory powers of the Home Secretary.

The reader will recall that the Home Secretary must give his consent before a patient subject to a restriction order can be given a discharge, a transfer, or a leave of absence. Also, a restriction order made without limit of time will not lapse until the Home Secretary so directs.[1] He may receive advice on these matters from the responsible medical officer, the hospital managers* or the Mental Health Review Tribunal (MHRT). However, their advice is in no way binding and, as we shall see, he rejects as often as not their recommendations for discharge.

The Home Secretary will not set in motion the normal process for examining whether a restricted patient is fit for discharge until he receives a recommendation to that effect from the RMO or MHRT. A positive recommendation will trigger a complex decision-making process in the Home Office. This will involve, for example, private consultations with the RMO and other professionals, the gathering of additional information about the social setting to which the patient may be discharged, or further assessments of his psychological or medical state.[3]

In certain circumstances, the proposal for discharge may be referred for the opinion of an Advisory Board on Restricted Patients, either because the case has previously been identified as requiring special care in assessment, in accordance with the procedures recommended in the Aarvold Report[4] (see *infra*), or because it is otherwise thought to be especially difficult, and the Home Secretary also wishes to have the benefit of the Board's view. The Butler Committee has now proposed that the Board's purview should be extended to cover all restricted patients in the special hospitals.[5]

The Advisory Board on Restricted Patients does not itself initiate recommendations for discharge; hence it is not asked for advice until the RMO or MHRT makes a positive recommendation.

The Royal Commission on the Law Relating to Mental Illness and Mental Deficiency (Cmnd. 169, 1957, para. 527) envisaged the hospital managers as independent of the RMO: "If he [the RMO] recommends continuation [of detention], his recommendation, explaining his reasons, will be seen by the hospital management committee, who will be able to exercise their own power to discharge the patient; they will themselves interview the patient if either he or they themselves so desire." (Of course, the hospital managers can only *recommend* discharge in the case of a restricted patient.)

In practice, however, the hospital managers have merely acted as a rubber stamp for the RMO – except, perhaps, in the special hospitals, where the views of the Department of Health and Social Security, as managers, are sought before the Home Secretary reaches his decision.[2]

The Home Secretary reaches a decision only after considering the advice of the Board (if the case is within its current purview), of the RMO, and (if there has been a reference to a tribunal) of the tribunal. The final decision is taken by either the Minister or an official of senior or middle grade. Dr Shirley Summerskill, Parliamentary Under-Secretary of State for the Home Department, described the procedure as follows:[3]

"Within the Home Office proposals for discharge or transfer, and advice on such proposals, are considered by Departmental staff and submitted for decision at appropriate levels. In the case of patients convicted or accused of serious crimes of violence authority for discharge or transfer is given only by the decision of a Minister; in the case of other patients the decision may be taken by an official of senior or middle grade. The decision to accept tribunal advice supporting the responsible medical officer's view that the patient is unfit for discharge or transfer may be taken at official level (middle grade). A decision to reject tribunal advice is taken by a Minister. A recommendation from a responsible medical officer, about which reservations are felt, may be the subject of further discussion or correspondence by the Department with the consultant which may lead to some modification, but if after this process the proposal is still thought to be unacceptable the decision not to act upon it is usually taken by the Minister.

The Department of Health and Social Security, as managers of the special hospitals, are consulted on proposals for the discharge or transfer of a patient detained in a special hospital. Indeed, in the case of transfer from a special hospital, the final decision to authorise the move must come from the DHSS as managers: the Home Secretary has no power to direct transfer, only to consent to a proposal to transfer."

The arrangements described above are, in practice, a strong safeguard for the protection of the public. Every indication which we have received (from the Home Office itself, certain consultant psychiatrists in the special hospitals,* and our own casework experience) suggests that the Home Office will not authorise a discharge if any one of the appropriate authorities has advised against it. Dr Summerskill offered this explanation:[3]

"Under the terms of section 65 of the Mental Health Act, the Crown Court makes an order imposing the special restrictions because it appears to the court 'that it is necessary for the protection of the public so to do', and in exercising his statutory functions in respect of restricted patients, the Home Secretary regards the protection of the public as the paramount consideration. . . . [Thus] where there is a conflict of advice, the Home Secretary . . . will tend to prefer the more cautious of the opposing views provided it appears to be well-grounded."

*One special hospital consultant made this statement at a public meeting of the British Association of Social Workers: "In my many years of experience, I have never known the Home Office to discharge a restricted patient against the firm advice of the responsible medical officer."

In the following pages, we shall examine the roles of the various officials involved in the discharge process. First we shall look at those who advise the Home Secretary – the RMO, the MHRT and the Advisory Board – and second, at the Home Secretary himself.

The responsible medical officer

The Butler Committee pointed to two main elements which must be satisfied before a restricted patient is discharged from hospital:[6] "From a medical point of view he must have sufficiently recovered his health; and from the point of view of society there must be, so far as can be assessed, little risk of further serious offending."

A close look at these two elements suggests that it is very difficult for a patient to show that he is suitable for discharge. First, the responsible medical officer must trigger the discharge machinery with a favourable recommendation, or at least must agree with a positive recommendation made by a tribunal. Here it is interesting to note the views of the Butler Committee:[7]

"Those who have the task of advising on the discharge of mentally disordered offenders know full well what a heavy responsibility they bear. They also know that, however careful they are, their opinion of any case may turn out to be wrong. If they have advised in favour of discharge, their mistake may lead to catastrophe and criticism, whereas if they have advised against release, they cannot be faulted; for normally this advice is likely to be accepted, and no one will ever know whether the assessment of the case was right or wrong, since a person who is not released is thereby prevented from demonstrating that if released he would have resettled safely in the community. . . . The tendency (which many members of the public would applaud) will generally be to err on the side of caution, with the result that some people will continue to be detained who, if released, would not commit further violent offences."

Given the generally cautious views of RMOs, one would not expect many disagreements to arise between doctors and the Home Office. Yet, as we discussed in Chapter 5, many consultants have severely criticised the Home Office for the complications and delays that result from the need to inform, consult and satisfy the Home Office before clinical decisions to give a patient a leave of absence, a transfer, or a discharge can be carried out. In fact, the British Medical Association has stressed the encroachment on the doctors' time that this involves, and has recommended that discharge should be settled at a regional level.[8]

The second criterion for discharge presented in the Butler Report suggests that even when medical advice indicates that further treatment will not benefit the patient, the Home Secretary will not discharge him if there is any risk of a further serious offence. The standard set by the Home Secretary appears to be high indeed. MIND asked him why he decided not to discharge a particular patient after a tribunal hearing. The standard for discharge given in the reply was that the Home Secretary must be "assured" that the patient is no longer a risk to the public.*

The Butler Committee fully recognised the difficulties that a restricted patient faces in trying to obtain a discharge, and asked, "What safeguards should be provided for the patient, to protect him from being detained longer than is strictly necessary? Obviously, a long-term psychiatric patient, especially if he has no interested relatives or friends, is not well able to safeguard his own interests."[6]

The Committee proposed two safeguards. First, the RMO should submit annual reports to the Home Office on the patient's suitability for discharge.[9] But, as we have noted earlier, many doctors already do this, and an undertaking was given to Parliament during the passage of the Act that exactly what the Butler Committee is now proposing would be done.[10] Moreover, the RMO is in any case obliged to send in a positive recommendation as soon as it is appropriate. Annual medical reports which do not propose a change of circumstances will not provide any impetus for a fresh review of the patient's case. In fact, since the Home Office has acknowledged that it suffers from severe limitations of staff and great pressure of work,[11] it would not be surprising to find that routine annual reports received little notice from senior officials.

The Butler Committee also discussed the possibility of introducing legislation which would provide guardians or patients' friends for mentally abnormal offenders who have no family contacts or whose families wish only to keep them under detention.[12] This proposal follows the precedent set by section 24(5) of the Children and Young Persons Act 1969, under which persons may be appointed by local authorities to visit, advise and befriend children in community homes who have little or no contact with their parents or guardians. The Butler Committee felt that mentally disordered offenders are in many ways similar to these children. They therefore recommended that statutory provision should be made for the appointment of guardians. They did feel, however, that it would in practice be difficult to find a sufficient number of suitable guardians; hence, the appointment of a guardian should not be mandatory, but should depend on whether a suitable 'independent' person was available and willing.

The task of a guardian is to provide moral support and friendship for the patient; to search for meaningful alternatives to hospital care; to help to arrange for suitable housing, employment and after-care; and to assert the patient's right to treatment under the least restrictive conditions which are necessary in his interests and for the protection of the public.

These services are needed by any vulnerable individual who finds himself friendless in an isolated institution. But since suitable guardians are scarce,

---

*The reader may wish to contrast this standard with the one set in section 66 of the Mental Health Act, where the Home Secretary may direct that the patient shall cease to be subject to special restrictions if he "is satisfied" that it is no longer required for the protection of the public.

one wonders whether offenders should be given priority over other members of the psychiatric population – for example, mentally handicapped or depressed patients, children who are admitted to hospital 'voluntarily' by their parents,[13] and long-stay patients who are in hospital solely because they have no home to go to. Experience has shown us that these patients exercise their rights less often than offenders (see p. 165 *infra*).

The Advisory Board on Restricted Patients

On June 28, 1972 a committee chaired by Sir Carl Aarvold was invited by the then Home Secretary, Mr Reginald Maudling, to advise on whether the procedures for the discharge and supervision of patients subject to special restrictions should be modified within the existing law.[14] (At the same time the Butler Committee was asked to examine the wider question of possible changes in the law.)

The Aarvold Committee came to the following conclusions. Early in the course of treatment certain exceptional cases can be identified which need special care in assessment.[15] Two relevant factors are involved: a clearly unfavourable or unpredictable psychiatric prognosis, and some indication that there is a risk of the patient's harming other persons.[16]

It is the task of the responsible medical officer to identify those patients who need special assessment.[17] The Committee felt that the consultant should be able to reach a decision within three months of a patient's admission to hospital.

Once a patient has been classified as requiring special assessment, the reasons should be recorded and a note made in the Home Office to ensure that special attention is thereafter given to the case. The classification should not be removed.[18]

The Aarvold Committee believed that only a small minority of patients under restrictions need be identified as requiring extra precautions beyond the normal discharge procedures.[19]

The Committee proposed that in a case identified as needing special assessment, a recommendation made by the RMO or MHRT for discharge (or for transfer from secure to open conditions) should not be implemented until an independent advisory body offered a second opinion. The Advisory Board should consist of three members: a legal chairman, a forensic psychiatrist and a representative of the social work profession who has appropriate experience.[20]

These recommendations of the Aarvold Board have been adopted and put into effect. At present, about 5% of all restricted patients in the special hospitals are classified as requiring special care in assessment.[3]

In October 1975, the Butler Committee proposed in its report that these arrangements should be modified and extended.[21] First, all restricted patients in the special hospitals should come within the purview of the Advisory Board. Second, as regards restricted patients in local hospitals or regional secure units, the Board should be available to the Home Secretary and to the RMO, to give an independent opinion in any case where they may find it helpful.[22]

We have several points to make on the arrangements of the Aarvold Committee, and on the extensions proposed by the Butler Committee:

(1) The two Committees seem to contradict each other on the purview of the Advisory Board. The Aarvold Committee firmly stated, "We think it important that the classification should not be too freely applied."[19] On the other hand, the Butler Committee proposes that it be extended to include all restricted patients in special hospitals.

(2) We regard any extension of the purview of the Board as undesirable if no other changes are to be made in the present machinery for the discharge of restricted patients. A MHRT already receives all the information about a patient, and holds an exhaustive hearing. The Butler Committee is proposing that another body – with an almost identical professional composition – should repeat this exercise. The Home Office has already said that at present, when a case comes within the purview of the Board, any decision on discharge is considerably delayed.[3] We also want to point out strongly that this duplication is exceedingly expensive.

(3) The Advisory Board has the special task of considering the risk to the public. Thus, it only reviews recommendations by the RMO or MHRT to discharge or transfer patients. Recommendations for continued detention are not within the remit of the Board. Moreover, the proceedings are completely private: the patient and his representative have no right to give oral or written evidence.[23] It sometimes even happens that patients do not realise that their case is being reviewed.* This article in the *Park Lane News* (written by patients) shows how little they have been told about it:[24]

> "There is something called the 'Aarvold Committee', a safeguard for the public concerning release of patients from special hospitals – I think. . . . The patients know nothing about it, the staff seem to know even less when you ask them. Who are the Aarvold Committee? What are they? What does it consist of? Can patients or relatives see them? Are they advisory to the Home Office, the Ministry of Health or both? How do they fit in as regards Case Conferences and Tribunals? Surely during the past eighteen months, someone could have written something to answer these questions before we needed to ask them."

*Although the patient has no right to appear before the Advisory Board, the members can, if they wish, interview the patient.

References and Notes

1. Mental Health Act 1959, ss. 65 and 66.
2. *Report on the Review of Procedures for the Discharge and Supervision of Psychiatric Patients Subject to Special Restrictions* (The Aarvold Report), Cmnd. 5191, January 1973, para. 13.
3. Letter dated 10 August, 1976 to Eric Moonman, MP, Chairman of All Party Parliamentary Mental Health Group, c/o MIND, signed by Dr Shirley Summerskill, Minister of State for the Home Department.
4. *The Aarvold Report*, paras. 34-38.
5. *The Butler Report*, paras. 4.21-25.
6. *Ibid.*, para. 7.24.
7. *Ibid.*, para. 4.13.
8. *Ibid.*, para. 7.14.
9. *Ibid.*, para. 7.25.
10. A. H. Edwards, *Mental Health Services*, 4th ed., 1975, p. 211.
11. *The Butler Report*, para. 7.17.
12. *Ibid.*, paras. 7.26-28.
13. See generally, L. Gostin, *A Human Condition*, Vol. 1, 1975, chapter 1; S. Herr and L. Gostin, "'Volunteering' handicapped children for hospitals: A case for review", *Oxford Medical School Gazette*, Vol. XXVII No. 2, Michaelmas Term 1975, pp. 86-88.
14. *The Aarvold Report*.
15. *Ibid.*, para. 20.
16. *Ibid.*, para. 21.
17. *Ibid.*, para. 22.
18. *Ibid.*, para. 23.
19. *Ibid.*, para. 24.
20. *Ibid.*, paras. 27-42.
21. *The Butler Report*, paras. 4.19-25.
22. *Ibid.*, para. 4.22.
23. See generally L. Gostin, "The future of the abnormal offender", *MIND OUT*, No. 14, December 1975, pp. 10-11.
24. *Park Lane News*, October 1976, p. 16.

11. The advisory function of Mental Health Review Tribunals

Law and practice

Section 124(1) of the Mental Health Act 1959 empowers the Lord Chancellor to make rules with respect to the making of applications to Mental Health Review Tribunals. He is given a similar power in relation to references by the Home Secretary of the cases of restricted patients under section 66(6), and references by the Secretary of State for Social Services under section 57.[1] The scope of his rule-making power is defined in some detail in section 124(2). Subsection (4) is particularly important in relation to restricted patients, because it provides that rules "may be so framed as to apply to all applications or references . . . of any specified class and may make different provision in relation to different cases".

The rules made in pursuance of the above section are the Mental Health Review Tribunal Rules, 1960.[2] They deal with applications, references by the Secretary of State for Social Services and references by the Home Secretary. Not all the Rules apply to all three cases. Moreover, it is not immediately clear which of the Rules apply to references by the Home Secretary – indeed, the Mental Health Review Tribunal Officers tell us that the tribunals themselves are in some doubt about this.

Rule 19 is the only one which relates specifically to references by the Home Secretary. It reads as follows:

"The tribunal shall consider a reference by the Secretary of State in whatever informal manner they think appropriate and may on any such reference interview the patient and shall interview him if he so requests; and after considering the reference the tribunal shall give their advice thereon to the Secretary of State."

Rule 20, which applies to references by the Home Secretary and by the Secretary of State for Social Services, further states that all proceedings "shall take place in private but the tribunal may, if they think fit, authorise any person to attend."

Most of the rules which specify the procedure to be followed by the tribunal do not apply to restricted cases, for their terms refer only to 'applications'.* It

*It appears to us that the following rules apply both to 'applications' and 'references' by the Home Secretary: rule 1 (Title and commencement), rule 2 (Interpretation), rule 8 (Appointment of tribunal), rule 10(3) (Representation), rule 20 (Proceedings in private), and rule 28 (Transfer of proceedings).

The situation is clearer on references by the Secretary of State for Social Services. Rule 18 states that the "tribunal shall consider a reference by the Minister[3] as if it were an application by a patient who had not requested a formal hearing". Rule 18(a) specifically states that rules 4 and 16 shall not apply. Thus all of the Rules of Procedure are in force where the Minister refers a case to a tribunal, except for Part IV (Formal Hearings), rule 4, rule 16 and rule 19 (References by the Secretary of State).

appears that the conduct of hearings on restricted cases is almost entirely within the discretion of the tribunal. As one Mental Health Review Tribunal Officer put it, the tribunal 'is law unto itself'.

One consequence of this virtually unfettered discretion vested in tribunals when hearing restricted cases is that their practices differ widely from one area to another. No procedure is laid down, so the patient or his representative may be unaware of the informal practices which have developed in a particular area. Thus, they may not know what information is available or how they can obtain it.

Disclosure of documents

In *unrestricted* cases, the disclosure of information to the patient is governed by rules 6 and 13. Rule 6(1) provides that the responsible authority† shall send to the tribunal a statement containing (a) facts about the patient (name, age, date of admission, name of nearest relative, etc.), (b) a medical report, and (c) an after care report.[4] If the responsible authority wishes to withhold certain parts of its statement from the patient on the grounds that its disclosure would be undesirable in the interests of the patient or for other special reasons, it may incorporate those parts in a separate document. The tribunal is then required to send the patient a copy of the hospital's statement, excluding any part contained in a separate document. However, the tribunal is required under rule 13 to make an independent judgment and, except insofar as they consider it undesirable to do so in the interests of the patient or for other special reasons, they are required to make available to the patient any of the authority's statement which has been withheld under rule 6. Rule 13 also requires the tribunal to make available other documents and statements of information.

The practice, however, is very different from the law. The RMO (not the responsible authority) prepares the statement and sends it to the tribunal. We understand that in the Thames regions, the RMO normally objects to the patient's seeing the whole of his medical report, and the tribunal merely rubber-stamps this. Moreover, the RMO often prepares no after care report. RMOs in other areas seem to be more willing to allow patients to see their reports, which are supplied as a matter of course. However, even if the patient is not shown a copy of the RMO's report, it will invariably be supplied to his representative.

In a *restricted* case, the Rules lay down that the proceedings shall be informal, and there is no provision for the disclosure of documents and information to the patient. In practice, it appears that the Home Office supplies all the papers to the tribunal, and the RMO is asked whether his report should be released to the patient. A restricted patient almost never sees his RMO's report. However, the representative will usually be given a copy if he writes to the Home Office. (It will be marked 'confidential', so he cannot show

---

†The responsible authority is defined in rule 2 as the managers of the hospital. (The managers in their turn are defined in section 59(1) of the Mental Health Act.)

it to the patient.) Some representatives do not realise that they may ask the Home Office for a copy of the RMO's report. Others do make a request only to find it refused, because the Home Secretary has been asked not to release the papers by the RMO. Doubts exist as to whether the tribunal may release documents without the consent of the Home Office; but it would seem that they do have this power. If the tribunal does provide the representative with reports on the day of the hearing, he may if he wishes ask for an adjournment so that he can read them and, if necessary, discuss them with the patient.

Representation

Rule 10(1) provides that an unrestricted patient may be represented by anyone except another compulsory patient or a patient at the same hospital. The restricted patient does not have this right. Under rule 10(3) he may be accompanied by another person at the hearing, unless the tribunal directs otherwise. However, restricted patients are in practice permitted to have representatives, who are treated in much the same way as representatives of unrestricted patients.

Formality of hearing

An unrestricted patient can ask for a formal and a public hearing.[5] If this is granted,[6] all those taking part in the proceedings may be present throughout (subject to the tribunal's power to exclude any person).[7] For a restricted patient, on the other hand, the hearing is automatically informal, and usually the tribunal hears witnesses one by one. The patient is normally excluded when a member of his family or the RMO is giving evidence; his representative, however, can usually remain. (We do know of one case where the patient and his representative were both excluded while a police officer was giving evidence to the tribunal.)

Medical examination

In an unrestricted case, the medical member of the tribunal is required by rule 11 to examine the patient or take such steps as he considers necessary to form an opinion of his mental condition. No such requirement is imposed for a restricted case – rule 19 only provides for an interview with the patient, not for a medical examination. But a medical examination is invariably carried out, despite the fact that it is not strictly required.

Advisory function

In a restricted case, as already explained, the tribunal does not reach a decision and then notify the patient. Instead it advises the Home Secretary, and the nature of its advice is never disclosed to the patient or his representative. Moreover, the patient is never told what advice and information the

Home Office receives about him before or after the tribunal hearing from, for example, the hospital and the RMO, the police, or officials of other Government departments. Thus, the patient and his representative are involved in only one stage of the decision-making process.

The duty to observe the rules of natural justice

The rules of natural justice are first, the rule against bias *(nemo judex in causa sua[8])* and second, that the parties must be given adequate notice and an opportunity to be heard *(audi alteram partem).*[9] In order to determine whether Mental Health Review Tribunals have a statutory duty to observe these rules, one must consider first of all the enabling Act – here section 124 of the 1959 Act – and the Rules of Procedure. As we have just seen, many of the rules appear to breach the rules of natural justice,[10] but they cannot be impeached in the courts, provided that they are within the authority of the enabling Act – that is to say, *intra vires.* If the power to make rules is exceeded in some way, a rule which is not authorised by the parent Act is said to be *ultra vires,* and can be challenged in the courts.[11] So far as we can see, there is no question of the Rules of Procedure being *ultra vires* in any respect.

Where a statute or rules of procedure give no firm guidance as to whether a tribunal should observe the rules of natural justice, a court may, in some circumstances, impose such a duty.

The duty to act judicially

The duty to observe the rules of natural justice is often called 'the duty to act judicially'. The courts have considered in a large number of cases whether the functions performed by individuals, ministers, local authorities and various boards, committees and tribunals were judicial rather than administrative. Various tests have emerged by which courts identify whether a function is judicial.[12] For example, if the proceedings and functions of a tribunal closely resemble those of an ordinary court, it may well be that the tribunal is acting judicially. One of the main tests is whether its proceedings terminate in an order or decision which is conclusive and binding on the parties.

So far as we know, no case has occurred since the passing of the 1959 Act in which a court has considered whether a Mental Health Review Tribunal is under a duty to act judicially. But there are strong grounds for saying that a tribunal hearing the case of a patient detained under section 26 or section 60 is under such a duty.[10] The words of Lord Guest are in point here:[13]

"It is reasonably clear on the authorities that where a statutory tribunal has been set up to decide final questions affecting parties' rights and duties, if the statute is silent on the question, the courts will imply into the statutory provision a rule that the principles of natural justice should be applied. This implication will be made on the basis that Parliament is not to be presumed to take away parties' rights without giving them an oppor-

tunity of being heard in their interest. In other words, Parliament is not to
be presumed to act unfairly."

A tribunal hearing the case of a restricted patient does not make a conclusive
and binding decision: it hears evidence, forms recommendations and
submits advice to the Home Secretary. The established view is that such a
body, which cannot do more than advise on the action that another individual should take, is not required to act judicially. "This characteristic
[i.e. conclusiveness of decisions] is generally regarded as one of the essential
features of judicial power, and a body exercising powers which are of a merely
advisory, deliberative, investigatory or conciliatory character, or which do
not have legal effect until confirmed by another body, or involve only the
making of a preliminary decision, will not normally be held to be acting in a
judicial capacity."[14] It seems fairly clear, therefore, that a tribunal hearing a
restricted case is under no duty to act judicially.

This point arose in the mental health field (although before the Mental
Health Act 1959 was enacted) in the case of *R v Statutory Visitors to St.
Lawrence's Hospital, Caterham, Ex. p. Pritchard.*[15] A patient detained in
hospital under the Mental Deficiency Act 1913 applied for *certiorari* to quash
a special report by the visitors whose statutory duty it was to consider the
case, and to state whether in their opinion she was still a proper person to be
detained. The patient's mother wanted to be present at the visitors' meeting
and to be represented by counsel. The visitors did allow her and her counsel
to be present (except when the daughter was examined), but they did not
hear her. The visitors reported their opinion to the Board of Control, whose
duty it was to decide whether the detention order should be continued. The
court said that the visitors were not a tribunal; they were merely an advisory
body which was not governed by any particular rules of procedure. The
visitors therefore had no duty to act judicially.*

The duty to act fairly

In recent years, the courts have developed a new concept: the duty to act
fairly. "In general it means a duty to observe the rudiments of natural justice
for a limited purpose in the exercise of functions that are not analytically
judicial but administrative."[16] The notion of acting fairly was first used by
Lord Parker, Chief Justice, in *Re K(H) (an infant):*[17]

> ". . . . even if an immigration officer is not acting in a judicial or quasi-
> judicial capacity, he must at any rate give the immigrant an opportunity

---

*The patient's application for *certiorari* was dismissed on the grounds that the order would not
lie to quash a report of opinion. However, the remedy of *certiorari* may have been inappropriate.
An alternative procedure would have been to apply for prohibition, to prevent the Board of
Control from acting on the visitors' report, and for *mandamus* to compel the visitors to report
afresh. It should be noted that the procedure of 'case stated' is now available under section
124(5), and it may be more appropriate than *certiorari* where a tribunal is wrong in law. It is
possible that the *St. Lawrence's Hospital* case would not now be followed.

of satisfying him of the matters in the subsection, and for that purpose, let the immigrant know what his immediate impression is so that the immigrant can disabuse him. That is not, as I see it, a question of acting or being required to act judicially, but of being required to act fairly."[18]

Since that case, the courts have imposed the duty to act fairly on various individuals, panels and committees which have advisory or investigative rather than decision-making roles.[19] Lord Denning, Master of the Rolls, in *Selvarajan v Race Relations Board*,[20] described the kind of cases in which there is a duty to act fairly:

"In all these cases [listed at (i) to (iii) in reference 19] it has been held that the investigating body is under a duty to act fairly; but that which fairness requires depends on the nature of the investigation and the consequences which it may have on persons affected by it. The fundamental rule is that, if a person may be subjected to pains or penalties, or be exposed to prosecution or proceedings, or deprived of remedies or redress or in some way adversely affected by the investigation and report, then he should be told the case made against him and be afforded a fair opportunity of answering it. The investigating body is, however, the master of its own procedure. It need not hold a hearing. It can do everything in writing. It need not allow lawyers. It need not put every detail of the case against a man. Suffice it if the broad grounds are given. It need not name its informants. It can give the substance only. Moreover, it need not do everything itself. It can deploy secretaries and assistants to do all the preliminary work and leave much to them. But, in the end, the investigating body itself must come to its own decision and make its own report."

The case of *Selvarajan* suggests that the patient or his representative should know the case which he has to meet. If the responsible authority is recommending continued detention, the patient or representative must know why so that he can present the case for discharge; for it will be upon an analysis of the authority's reasons on the one hand, and of the patient's answer on the other, that the tribunal will tender its advice, and the Home Secretary will decide. But it appears that the substance of the case rather than the complete dossier may be sufficient.†

Advantages of natural justice

In sum, a tribunal acting in an advisory capacity probably has no duty to act judicially – that is, to comply with the formal rules of natural justice. It may

---

†The court in the *St Lawrence's Hospital* case[15] said that hospital reports were "of a highly confidential nature" and "not to be brought out unless the court thinks that a good purpose would be served". It should be noted, however, that the Mental Health Review Tribunal structure is quite different. Parliament has specifically envisaged in section 124(2) (h) and in section 124(3) of the 1959 Act that the patient should have access to relevant information, except for special reasons (see also rule 13 of the Tribunal Rules, 1960). Moreover, there can be no objection to supplying the representative with full information, on condition that it is not disclosed to the patient.

in fact have a duty to act fairly, as suggested in the *Selvarajan* case; but this approach, while expressing sound principles, allows investigating bodies to dispense with many of the rules that normally make those principles effective. For example, the right to a representative is not necessarily part of the duty to act fairly.[20] (In *Frazer v Mudge*,[21] a prisoner was denied a representative when facing a disciplinary charge.) Yet an unrepresented patient may have no access to information which is reasonably necessary to prepare his case.

Although fair standards of natural justice may not be required in law for an advisory Mental Health Review Tribunal, there are sound reasons of policy for amending the Rules of Procedure to provide these standards.* The general principle should be as follows: a patient should have access to all relevant information about his case (including medical reports) and the right to be present during the entire hearing, unless there are clear and particular reasons for withdrawing this basic right.

This general principle is set out – albeit in broad terms – in the Mental Health Act, section 124(2)(h) and in rule 13. Thus the tribunal must make available to the unrestricted patient the authority's statement, unless there are special reasons which in his interests make it undesirable to do so. Yet as we have pointed out, tribunals do not exercise independent discretion in this area, but merely ratify the decisions of the RMO. (Moreover, the doctors themselves do not make an individual assessment – in some areas of the country they agree to release their reports in all cases, while in others, they never do so.) We would stress that tribunal members should abide by rule 13, and make an independent judgment on the disclosure of reports. Perhaps a clarifying amendment in the Rules, or a Departmental Circular, would be appropriate.

At present, a patient whose case is referred by the Home Secretary is routinely denied access to relevant information and excluded from the hearing; he is also not informed of the advice given by the tribunal.† Many of these problems are remedied when the patient is represented by an experienced lawyer or some other professional. However, the Rules give the representative no formal guidance on what information he is entitled to have; who is empowered to supply this information, and at what stage of the proceedings; and what procedural formalities he can expect during the tribunal hearings. These problems have been identified in the *Annual Report of the Council on Tribunals for 1974-75* (para. 71); the Council is pursuing the issue with the Home Office, and will report its findings in 1977.

---

*At the end of this chapter we propose that tribunals in restricted cases should be replaced with a more appropriate advisory body. This body probably would not be under a duty to act judicially, just as an advisory MHRT or the Parole Board has no such duty. Nevertheless, we feel that there are clear advantages of following the rules of natural justice – for example, it provides more complete and accurate information to the advisory body, and it allows the patient to participate in the decision-making process. See *The Annual Report of the Council on Tribunals for 1964,* HMSO, para. 41.

†For more detailed observations and proposals for the reform of tribunal hearings on unrestricted cases, see volume 1 of *A Human Condition,* Part II (pp. 55-99).

We would like to see the Rules amended so that, as far as possible, the same procedural rights are given to restricted as to unrestricted patients.† In our view, a complete and fair exchange of information should help the tribunal to fulfil its statutory role of advising the Home Secretary.

Delay

Concern has been expressed about the length of time that the Home Secretary often takes to decide whether to accept the recommendations of tribunals.[22] He generally accepts unfavourable recommendations, and the patients are notified quickly; the complaints are mainly about delay in notifying decisions on positive recommendations for discharge or transfer.

The time taken by the Home Office to reach a decision on advice from a MHRT is discussed in paragraphs 7.19-21 of the Butler Report, where figures are given showing the interval between the receipt of the tribunal's advice and delivery of the decision in all relevant cases during the two years ending on April 30, 1973. Here are the equivalent figures for 1975:[23]

Intervals between the receipt of tribunal advice and the Home Office decision: figures for 1975
(a) shortest: same day
    longest: 13 months and 3 days

(b) Less than:			Percentage of cases
1 month	223		63.7
2 months	30		8.6
3 months	30		8.6
4 months	30		8.6
5 months	16		4.6
6 months	5		1.4
7 months	5		1.4
8 months	5		1.4
9 months	2		0.5
more than 9 months	4		1.1
	350		

The considerable delays involved in some cases cause the patient and his family great anxiety and may involve substantial injustices. The National Council for Civil Liberties offered the following case as an illustration:[22]

†We would specifically suggest that the patient or his representative should have the right to know what advice the tribunal gives to the Home Secretary (and the reasons for that advice); just as in planning cases, the inspector's report after a public enquiry is made public even though the final decision rests with the Minister. We accept that a tribunal should not always be obliged to disclose the reasons for their advice, but they should refuse to do so only in exceptional cases and for particular reasons.

"One intelligent and well-informed patient wrote to us saying that he was to become eligible for a tribunal hearing on a specific date. He applied before the date due only to have his application returned pointing out that it could not be considered until he was eligible. When he wrote further asking how long it would take for a tribunal to be arranged after his application was accepted, he was most upset to learn that there would be a delay of at least two months before a tribunal could be called. In fact the Tribunal heard his case three months after his application. Other cases show that this is not unusual. As this man was subject to section 65, the Tribunal could only advise the Home Secretary, who then makes the decision. It took the NCCL eight months to find out that the Home Secretary had agreed in principle to discharge this man. Despite persistent attempts to find out why there had been such a long delay, especially as this man had no record of violence or sexual deviation, no satisfactory answer was forthcoming. He was eventually discharged in January this year, nearly 13 months after the tribunal had met, leaving the question open as to why it took the Home Secretary 10 months to agree and make arrangements for his discharge.

In human terms this unexplained delay caused unnecessary suffering to this man and his family. In July 1971 he told us that his father was dying of cancer; he applied towards the end of 1971; his tribunal met in March 1972; his father died in April 1972; he was discharged in January 1973. We could quote several other cases where the delays between a meeting of the tribunal and discharge ran into many months and caused much anguish in the meantime."

The issue of the delay between a tribunal recommendation and the Home Secretary's final decision has been examined by the Parliamentary Commissioner for Administration (the Ombudsman) and by the Butler Committee.

The Ombudsman received a complaint about the time taken by the Home Secretary to decide whether he should discharge a patient from hospital after his case had been considered by a MHRT.[24] On November 20, 1972 the patient formally requested the Home Secretary to refer his case to a tribunal. The tribunal met on February 13, 1973. It forwarded its recommendation to the Home Office on March 2. Some months later the patient asked his Member of Parliament to refer the case to the Ombudsman, as the Home Secretary still had not come to a decision. On September 4 (when the Ombudsman's case was still in progress), the Home Secretary decided that the patient should not be released; he notified the hospital authorities of this decision.

The Parliamentary Commissioner found out that the Home Office had lost the patient's file between March 20 and June 27. The explanation offered by the Home Office was that on March 20, a junior officer had drafted a letter to the RMO. Thereafter he had thought that a senior officer was still considering the draft, whereas the senior officer had in fact approved it, and had marked the file back to the junior officer, believing that the letter was to be typed. The Ombudsman concluded:

"I accept the Department's claim that the Secretary of State cannot be rushed into a decision . . . for, although an individual's liberty is involved, so also is the safety of the public at large. But the fourteen weeks' delay in the middle of the handling of the patient's case was indefensible, and although as it happened, it did not have the effect of depriving the patient of his liberty the complainant is right in saying that this delay kept the patient in suspense unreasonably and for an unreasonably long time. I criticise the Department accordingly."

The Butler Committee emphasised that it is most important to make adequate enquiries and ensure that arrangements are as satisfactory as possible before authorising the discharge of section 65 patients. In the Committee's view, any delays that arise for this reason are justified. The Committee did make the sound recommendation that the patient should be sent an interim communication informing him that his case is being pursued, and telling him the nature of the difficulty to be resolved.[25]

The concept of a 'tribunal'

A Mental Health Review Tribunal* is readily presumed to be a significant safeguard of the liberty of the subject: it is called a 'tribunal', and conducts 'hearings' on the 'cases' brought before it; it is empowered to summon witnesses, administer oaths and receive documents in evidence.[26] In sum, it has all the 'trappings of a court'.

But this image of the MHRT may be positively misleading if it is not examined more closely. Here the duality of the function and power of MHRTs must be emphasized. The tribunal exercising jurisdiction over unrestricted patients is required to apply an objective pre-existing legal standard to its findings, in order to determine definitively whether he shall continue to be detained. Thus it has the power to overrule the detaining authority, and unconditionally discharge the patient.

But with a patient subject to a restriction order, the tribunal is merely advising a Minister of State on how to use his unfettered authority over an individual. It does not in fact function as a 'tribunal', within the proper meaning of that term – i.e. a body "empowered to inquire into and decide an issue".[27] The essential feature of a tribunal is that the performance of its function terminates in a decision which has conclusive effect.[28]

The value of an advisory body can be judged by two standards: How often is its jurisdiction invoked? And more important, how often is its advice accepted by the effective decision-maker? We shall explore these two questions in the next few pages.

*For a complete explanation of the composition, functions and powers of MHRTs, see volume I of this report, pp. 55-99.

Tribunal reference rates†

Of the 2,018 restricted patients in psychiatric hospitals in 1975, some 1,000 were eligible for tribunals.[29] Of these, 32% actually had their cases heard and decided.

These figures illustrate two points of some small significance. First, approximately two-thirds of the patients who are eligible for tribunals do not take the initiative to request a hearing. This may be a result of their lack of information about tribunals, little encouragement from the hospital to request a hearing, isolation or withdrawal due to the patient's own illness, or the effects of psychotropic (mood-changing) drugs. These and other reasons are fully discussed in volume I of this report (Chapter 5).

Second, a higher proportion of restricted than of unrestricted patients ask for tribunals. (The application rate for unrestricted patients is approximately 12%.)[30] Our own casework experience suggests that the special hospitals (which accommodate the majority of restricted patients) are on the whole more careful than the local hospitals to inform patients of their rights. Moreover, special hospital patients tend to be more aware of their rights and more anxious to exercise them. (This is especially true in Broadmoor and Park Lane, where there are relatively few mentally handicapped people.) We receive a disproportionately large amount of correspondence from these patients, concerning all aspects of our 'rights' service.

The value of a tribunal's advice

We have already discussed the fact that the Home Secretary – who is the effective decision-maker in the case of a restricted patient – will not follow the advice of a tribunal if the responsible medical officer is firmly opposed to it. Further, since the RMO may trigger consideration of a discharge or transfer at any time, a tribunal hearing normally (but not always) takes place only when the RMO is opposed to the discharge or transfer. It is not therefore surprising that the Home Secretary rejects a considerable number of tribunal recommendations for change.

Table 1 shows the number of cases referred to MHRTs in the years 1970-1975, together with the number of recommendations for change which were rejected.‡ The figures include a few recommendations for change which may not represent a considerable relaxation of control over the patient – for example, advancement within the hospital, transfer to a special hospital, trial leave of absence, repatriation, and review or reference to a tribunal in no

†The reference rate is defined as the percentage of restricted patients eligible to have their cases referred to tribunals who did in fact receive a tribunal hearing during a particular year. The statistical calculations are explained in volume 1 of this report (Chapter 5 and Appendix I).

‡Some forms of advice (e.g. advancement within the hospital) are not within the Home Secretary's jurisdiction, while transfer is only partly so – his consent is required, but only the hospital managers can carry out the recommendation.

Table 1*
References, recommendations and results of Mental Health Review Tribunals, 1970-1975

	NW Metro-politan RHB		Sheffield RHB Trent RHA		Liverpool RHB Mersey RHA		All other RHBs/RHAs	Totals		Total
	Broad-moor	Local Hospitals	Ramp-ton	Local Hospitals	Moss Side	Local Hospitals		Special Hospitals	Local Hospitals	
1970										
No change advised	84	4	85	3	35		14	204	21	225
Advice for change accepted	26	2	21	1	6		14	53	17	70
Advice for change rejected	9	–	22	2	4		4	35	6	41
Totals	119	6	128	6	45		32	292	44	336
Number of references made										349
Number of restricted patients	641		376		137			1154	742	1896
1971										
No change advised	84	2	89	3	34		21	207	26	233
Advice for change accepted	32	2	27	3	9		10	68	15	83
Advice for change rejected	6		34	1	5		4	45	5	50
Totals	122	4	150	7	48		35	320	46	366
Number of references made										
Number of restricted patients	659		407		139			1205	742	1947
1972										
No change advised	67	1	126	2	38	2	9	231	14	245
Advice for change accepted	17	–	25	2	2		8	44	10	54
Advice for change rejected	4	–	27	1	10		3	41	4	45
Totals	88	1	178	5	50	2	20	310	28	344
Number of references made										361
Number of restricted patients	659		433		168			1260	769	2029

									Total
1973									
No change advised	69	6	89	5	45		8	203	19	222
Advice for change accepted	17	4	42	3	6		14	65	22	87
Advice for change rejected	6		42	1	8		5	56	6	62
Totals	92	10	173	9	59	1	27	324	47	371
Number of references made						1				378
Number of restricted patients	666		453		174			1293	796	2089
1974										
No change advised	78	2	81	2	53	1	13	212	18	230
Advice for change accepted	22		37	–	12	1	17	71	18	89
Advice for change rejected	6		40	2	7		7	53	9	62
Totals	106	2	158	4	72	2	37	336	45	381
Number of references made										390
Number of restricted patients	641		466		169			1307	752	2059
1975 (provisional figures)										
No change advised	67	–	70	1	39	2	23	178	26	204
Advice for change accepted	12	2	27	1	11		12	52	15	67
Advice for change rejected	3		30		4		3	37	3	40
Still under consideration	2		7		–			9		9
Totals	84	2	134	2	54	2	38	276	44	320
Number of references made										327
Number of restricted patients	616		452		*Moss Side* 172	*Park Lane* 60		1300	718	2018

*Source: Unpublished statistics supplied by the Home Office.

Table 2*
Results of references to Mental Health Review Tribunals for restricted patients in 1974 and 1975

Hospital	Discharge		Transfer to a local hospital		Removal of special restrictions	
	Accepted	*Rejected*	*Accepted*	*Rejected*	*Accepted*	*Rejected*
1974						
Broadmoor	2	1	18	5	–	–
Rampton	3	11	30	28	1	
Moss Side	3	4	9	3		
All specials	8	16	57	36	1	–
Locals	15	6	1		1	2
Total	23	22	58	36	2	2
1975						
Broadmoor	3	1	6	2		1
Rampton	4	8	22	21		1
Moss Side	4	1	7	2		
Park Lane			2			
All specials	11	10	37	25		2
Locals	15	1				2
Total	26	11	37	25		4

*Source: unpublished statistics provided by the Home Office.

more than 12 months. The most significant recommendations are for discharge, transfer to a local hospital or removal of a restriction order; the breakdowns of the figures on these three recommendations in 1974 and 1975 are shown in Table 2.

In the years 1970-1975, the Home Secretary rejected the tribunals' advice in 40% of all cases.

One would expect the Home Secretary to reject the tribunals' advice more often for special hospital patients than for local hospital patients. This is strikingly confirmed by the data. In 1970-1975, the rejection rate for special hospitals was 43%, compared with 25% for the local hospitals. The comparative rejection rates for recommendations for discharge only was even more significant: 58% for the special hospitals, as compared with 19% for the local hospitals.†

We have been fortunate to receive a detailed breakdown of every type of recommendation for change made in the Trent Area (which includes Rampton Hospital) since MHRTs first began to hear cases in 1960. The raw data are set out in Table 3, and Table 4 shows in chart form the percentage of recommendations for change that were rejected by the Home Secretary in the Trent Area. The reader will notice that recommendations for discharge and transfer were rejected in more than half of the 411 cases. Furthermore, in Rampton Hospital all 13 recommendations for the removal of special restrictions were rejected; the corresponding rejection rate for all hospitals in the area was 81%.

The substantial rejection rate of tribunal recommendations (which is consistently over 40%) requires some thought. It should be contrasted with the fate of the recommendations of other bodies which serve the same function of advising the Home Secretary on whether to continue to detain offenders – i.e. the Parole Board and the Advisory Board on Restricted Patients.

The Parole Board advises the Home Secretary on the early and conditional release of selected prisoners.[31] Although he is under no obligation to follow its advice, the Home Secretary nearly always accepts it, and acts promptly upon its recommendations.[32] In 1974 3,507 prisoners serving fixed sentences were recommended for parole. The Home Secretary rejected the Board's view in only five cases. Some may argue that it would be fairer to compare patients under restriction orders with prisoners serving life sentences; but even with this type of prisoner, recommendations for parole were rejected in only 4% of cases.[33]

The picture is similar with the Advisory Board on Restricted Patients. As of September 1976, the Board had advised on 24 cases; and the Home Secretary has never rejected the advice given.[23]

Why does the Home Secretary place such a low value on the advice of MHRTs, as opposed to that of other advisory bodies? The Butler Committee maintains that there is an inherent contradiction between the functions of

---

†There is also a wide difference between the discharge rates of the three special hospitals for the years 1970-1975. In Rampton and Moss Side Hospitals, 52% and 45% respectively of all recommendations for change were rejected. In Broadmoor Hospital, the figure was only 21%.

Table 3*
Results of References to Mental Health Review Tribunals in the Trent Area from 1960 to 1975*

Nature and result of recommendation	Rampton		Other Hospitals		Total	
	1975	1960-75	1975	1960-75	1975	1960-75
References heard	156	1,406	4	54	160	1,460
Number of recommendations for changed conditions	113	592	4	34	117	627

Home Office decisions on recommendations	Rampton Considered		Other Hospitals Considered		Total Considered	
	1975	1960-75	1975	1960-75	1975	1960-75
Recommendation for discharge						
Accepted	4	55	1	6	5	61
Not accepted	6	62	—	3	6	65
Awaiting reply	3	3	—	—	3	3
Recommendation for transfer to local mental hospital						
Accepted	24	141	1	2	25	143
Not accepted	15	142	—	—	15	142
Awaiting reply	20	20	—	—	20	20
Recommendation for removal of restriction order						
Accepted	—	—	—	5	—	5
Not accepted	—	13	—	8	—	21
Recommendation for advancement within present hospital						
Accepted	32	42	1	6	33	48

Recommendation for transfer to other special hospitals						
Accepted	1	20	–	–	1	20
Not accepted	2	10	–	–	2	10
Awaiting reply	2	2	–	–	2	2
Recommendation for trial leave						
Accepted	–	1	–	2	–	3
Not accepted	–	4	–	–	–	4
Awaiting reply	–	–	–	–	–	–
Recommendation for repatriation						
Accepted	–	6	–	–	–	6
Not accepted	–	1	–	–	–	1
Awaiting reply	–	–	–	–	–	–
Recommendation for review or reference to tribunal in no more than 12 months' time						
Accepted	2	44	–	1	2	45
Awaiting reply	1	1	–	–	1	1

*Source: unpublished statistics supplied by the Mental Health Review Tribunal Officer for the Trent Area.

Table 4
Rejection rates by the Home Secretary of MHRT recommendations in the
Trent Area, 1960-1975†

Nature of recommendation	Percentages rejected		
	Rampton	Other hospitals	Total
All recommendations for change in present conditions	43%	33%	42%
Recommendations for discharge	53%	33%	52%
Recommendations for transfer to a local hospital	50%	–	50%
Recommendations for removal of restriction order	100%	62%	81%

†Source: unpublished statistics supplied by the Trent Area Mental Health Review
Tribunal Officer. The raw data are shown in Table 3.

MHRTs and the Home Office: tribunals exist as a safeguard for the patient
against unjustified detention, whereas the primary responsibility of the
Home Secretary is the protection of the public.[34] It is therefore inevitable
that the advice of MHRTs will be viewed with caution.

The Butler Committee's explanation is perhaps too simple, and does not
describe those characteristics of the tribunal which affect its credibility. It is
interesting to observe that the professional composition of a tribunal (a legal
chairman, a medical member and a lay member with experience of the social
services) is markedly similar to that of the Advisory Board. (There is also
some similarity to the Parole Board.)* The most important difference,
however, is the way in which the members of the various advisory bodies are
appointed. As we pointed out, MHRTs are modelled on the concept of a
proper tribunal, and have many of the 'trappings' of a court. Their members
must be independent and impartial, and are therefore appointed by the Lord
Chancellor. There is no consultation with the Home Office. Moreover, the
Home Secretary has no meaningful communication with tribunal members;
hearings are conducted in all regions of the country, and he has no personal
contact with the majority of members.

The Home Office is also well aware that many tribunal members have had
little experience of hearing cases, especially those that involve offenders. At

*The Parole Board for England and Wales has 30 members. It includes judges, psychiatrists,
probation officers, criminologists and lay persons with special experience of offenders. The
Board works in panels of about five members, each with a different background. The chair-
manship rotates among all members and the proceedings are informal, to allow for full and frank
discussion.[35]

the time when the Mental Health Act was introduced it was not clear how many cases tribunals might be called upon to hear. Experience has shown that there have been far fewer than the 7,000-8,000 cases then expected annually. In fact, the largest number has been 1,515 in 1967, and since then the numbers have fallen as low as 843 in 1971. As a result of the original overestimate, far too many members were appointed. Although the panels of members have now been reduced by resignations and deaths, the current number of approximately 580 is still very high. This means that some tribunal members get very little casework experience[36] – indeed, the majority will not hear more than a few cases each year. In some regions members are unlikely to serve more than once a year.[37] The situation is still worse when one considers that substantially less than half of all cases heard are referred by the Home Secretary; hence tribunal members have even less experience with offenders.

With the Parole Board and the Advisory Board, the situation is wholly different. The members of these advisory bodies are selected by the Home Secretary. In the case of the Parole Board, some members (in particular the probation officers) work for services run by the Home Office. As one author put it, "Any serious possibility of conflict of aims between the Board and the Home Secretary would seem unlikely to arise, although in practice the individuals selected are independent-minded and far from 'yes men'."[32]

There is a significant amount of communication, liaison and consultation between the chairman and secretariat of the Parole Board on the one hand, and the appropriate Home Office Department on the other.[38]

Parole Board members also have a considerable amount of experience, although they do not normally remain members for more than three years, in order to guard against the danger of entrenched attitudes.[39] During 1973 panels of the Board met on 163 occasions to consider cases for parole or recall from licence. These meetings were normally held in London, Birmingham and Manchester, and they averaged three each week.[40] (Members of the Advisory Board on Restricted Patients are drawn from panels small enough to ensure that experience and expertise are built up rapidly. Moreover, the Home Secretary chooses individuals who have considerable experience with offenders. The Advisory Board meets in London.)[41]

It is also worth pointing out that while the decisions of tribunals are secret, the Parole Board publishes thorough annual reports, with statistics and justifications of its policy. The Parole Board also receives considerable feedback about the effects of supervision and support on individuals who have been released on licence, whereas the tribunals have no way of assessing the progress of people who have been conditionally released.[42]

In sum, the Home Secretary is more likely to follow the recommendations of the Parole Board (and the Advisory Board) than the tribunal, because he has more control over the selection of members, closer communication and liaison with them, a better understanding of the overall policy considerations of the Board, and more trust in the competence of the members, owing to their extensive knowledge and experience with offenders.

Proposal for reform

There are two clear functions which are served by a Mental Health Review Tribunal hearing restricted cases. The primary function is that it gives advice to the Minister. Here, it is questionable whether tribunals provide a satisfactory safeguard against unjustified detention of the offender-patient. There are severe shortcomings in any advisory body whose advice is not strongly relied on by the statutory decision-maker. Moreover, the existence of a body called a 'tribunal' may wrongly suggest that the restricted patient has a remedy against unnecessary confinement.

The secondary function of the Mental Health Review Tribunal is that it re-focuses attention on the patient. A tribunal hearing normally means that the RMO must examine the patient and write a report; social workers must make fresh investigations about housing, jobs and treatment in the community; relatives are invited to the hearing and usually attend. Thus, it provides an opportunity to review and sometimes renew a patient's contacts with the world outside the hospital. Moreover, it may give a patient a sense that he is contributing to and participating in the decisions made about him.

We mentioned earlier the Butler Committee proposal that the Aarvold Board should review every recommendation for discharge or transfer made by the tribunal or RMO. This proposal reflects the distrust shown of tribunals. It requires two advisory bodies, with virtually identical professional compositions, to hold separate full-scale hearings on the same case. Presumably, the Mental Health Review Tribunal and the Aarvold Board would review the same evidence, interview the same people, and abide by similar criteria.

We consider that in times of financial restraint, this duplication is unnecessary. Moreover, the use of two advisory bodies engenders significant delay and does not ensure that the ultimate decision will be more accurate.

It would have been politically very difficult for the Butler Committee to propose the abolition of a 'tribunal' – substituting for it another body such as the Parole Board or Advisory Board. (Instead the Committee chose the road of compromise by suggesting *both* the MHRT and the Advisory Board). But it is clear that the Mental Health Review Tribunal cannot be a decision-maker in one case and an influential adviser in another: in the former it must be independent of the detaining authority; in the latter it cannot be so independent that the Home Secretary lacks confidence in its judgments.

The Parole Board provides a useful model. Its members are appointed by the Home Secretary, so he has confidence in their abilities, but they make their decisions in an impartial and independent manner.

Dr. Nigel Walker, Professor of Criminology at the University of Cambridge and a member of the Butler Committee, made the following suggestion:[42]

"Those who feel that the offender-patient who is under a restriction order needs a more adequate safeguard might well consider the suggestion that the Parole Board would be preferable. It has more experience of assessing offenders' careers than any Mental Health Review Tribunal could acquire in a decade of sittings. It includes psychiatrists and criminologists (as well as judges) amongst its members. And it pays close attention to the circumstances in which the offender will be living if he is given his freedom."

The Butler Committee did not accept this proposal, presumably because the restricted patient should not be so directly associated with the penal system. However, the Committee did propose that the purview of the Advisory Board should be extended. We go further by proposing that the Advisory Board should completely take over the function of Mental Health Review Tribunals in respect of restricted cases. The Home Secretary currently relies on the judgments of this Board; he would be expected to do so in the future, save for exceptional cases.

This proposal, of course, suggests that the Advisory Board should no longer act exclusively as a safeguard to the public; its jurisdiction should be invoked by an application to the Home Secretary, just as in the case of advisory tribunals.

The issue will arise whether the basic rudiments of natural justice should apply to the Advisory Board. We mentioned earlier that an advisory body probably has no duty to act judicially, but only to act fairly. In this regard, it is of some small significance that the Parole Board need only accept written evidence from the offender.[43] Nevertheless, we feel that it would be advantageous to allow the patient and his representative to participate fully in the deliberations of the Advisory Board. This would ensure that the Board made its decisions on the basis of full and accurate information.

References and Notes

1. Mental Health Act 1959, s.124(3).
2. Mental Health Review Tribunal Rules 1960, S.I., 1960, No. 1139 (hereinafter cited as MHRT Rules).
3. Where the Mental Health Act 1959 and the MHRT Rules 1960 refer to 'the Minister', they mean the Secretary of State for Social Services, and where they refer to 'the Secretary of State', they mean the Home Secretary.
4. MHRT Rules, second schedule.
5. *Ibid.*, Rule 3(3) and Rule 24(1).
6. *Ibid.*, Rule 23.
7. *Ibid.*, Rule 24(3).
8. See generally S.A. de Smith, *Judicial Review of Administrative Action*, 3rd ed., 1973, ch. 5.
9. *Ibid.*, ch. 4.
10. See generally L. Gostin, *A Human Condition*, Vol. 1, Chapter 7.
11. S.A. de Smith, *op cit.*, pp. 83-84.
12. See generally *Halsbury's Laws of England*, 4th ed., Vol. 1: *Administrative Law*, 1973, paras. 64-65; S.A. de Smith, *op cit.*, pp. 68-77.
13. Per Lord Guest in Wiseman v Borneman [1969] 3 All E.R. 275, at 279.
14. S.A. de Smith, *op cit.*, p. 69.
15. R. v Statutory Visitors to St Lawrence's Hospital, Caterham, Ex parte Pritchard [1953] 1 W.L.R. 1158.
16. S.A. de Smith, *op cit.*, p.208.
17. Re K (H) (an infant) [1967] 1 All E.R. 226, at 231.

18. In fact, the distinction between the duty to act judicially and the duty to act fairly is not always so clear. Some judges differentiate between the two, but others seem to use the expressions interchangeably.
19. See for example:
    (i) R v Gaming Board for Great Britain, ex parte Benaim [1970] 2 All E.R. 528. (It was the Gaming Board's function to consider suitability of applicant for gaming licence, before applicant applied to licensing justices).
    (ii) Re Pergamon Press Limited [1970] 3 All E.R. 535.
         (Inspectors investigated the affairs of a company and then reported the results of their inquiry to the Board of Trade).
    (iii) Wiseman v Borneman [1969] 3 All E.R. 275.
         (A tax tribunal had to determine whether there was a *prima facie* case).
    (iv) Selvarajan v Race Relations Board [1976] 1 All E.R. 12.
         (The Race Relations Board's function was to investigate complaints in order to determine whether discrimination had occurred).
    (v) *Halsbury's Laws of England,* 4th ed., Vol. 1: *Administrative Law,* 1973, para. 66.
20. Selvarajan v Race Relations Board [1976] 1 All E.R. 12, p.19b to d.
21. Frazer v Mudge [1975] 3 All E.R. 78.
22. National Council for Civil Liberties, *Evidence to the Butler Committee,* October 1973, paras. 4.1.-4.4.
23. Letter dated August 10, 1976 to Eric Moonman, MP, chairman of All Party Parliamentary Mental Health Group, c/o MIND, signed by Dr Shirley Summerskill, Minister of State for the Home Department.
24. *First Report of the Parliamentary Commissioner for Administration,* Session 1974, HMSO, pp.92-94.
25. *The Butler Report,* paras. 7.19-7.22.
26. MHRT Rules, Rule 14.
27. *The Universal Dictionary of the English Language* (H. C. Wyld, ed.).
28. S. A. de Smith, *op cit.,* pp.68-70, 203-206.
29. The number of references to Mental Health Review Tribunals, and the number of restricted patients in psychiatric hospitals, are shown in Table 1.
30. L. Gostin, *A Human Condition,* Vol. 1, ch. 5 and Appendix 1.
31. See generally Criminal Justice Act 1967, ss.59-64.
32. D. J. West (ed.), *The Future of Parole,* 1972, p.15.
33. *Report of the Parole Board for 1974,* HMSO, May 22, 1975, pp.1-3.
34. *The Butler Report,* para. 7.20.
35. *Report of the Parole Board for 1973,* HMSO, June 17, 1974, para. 32.
36. Department of Health and Social Security, *A Review of the Mental Health Act 1959,* HMSO, para. 8.10.
37. L. Gostin, *A Human Condition,* Vol. 1, pp.58-60.
38. *The Report of the Parole Board for 1973,* ch. 5.
39. *Ibid.,* para. 33.
40. *Ibid.,* para. 77.
41. *Report on the Review of Procedures for the Discharge and Supervision of Psychiatric Patients Subject to Special Restrictions* (The Aarvold Report), Cmnd. 5191, January 1973, para. 37.
42. N. Walker and S. McCabe, *Crime and Insanity in England,* Vol. 2, 1973, p.201.
43. Criminal Justice Act 1967, s.59.

12. Statutory Powers of the Home Secretary: The Exercise of Discretion

The lawfulness of detention

The lawfulness of the detention of a restricted patient can be challenged in two ways. First, the patient may in certain circumstances appeal against the Crown Court's decision to make an order under sections 60 and 65 of the Mental Health Act. Second, he may apply for *habeas corpus*. The procedural and substantive provisions of appeal and of *habeas corpus* are reviewed below.

Appeal

A hospital order with restrictions on discharge is no more than a particular type of sentence passed by the Crown Court.[1] Accordingly, an offender may obtain leave of the Court of Appeal[2] or of a single judge[3] to appeal against it.[4]

Notice of appeal or application for leave to appeal must be given to the Registrar of Criminal Appeals within 28 days from the date on which sentence was passed.[5] The time for giving notice may be extended, either before or after it expires, by the Court of Appeal.[6] However, substantial reasons for the delay are required before an extension is allowed,[7] and the case must have such merits that the appeal would probably succeed.[8] If an application for extension of time is refused by a single judge, it may be reviewed by the full court.

An appellant may abandon his appeal or application for leave to appeal before the hearing by serving notice on the Registrar of Criminal Appeals; it is then treated as having been dismissed or refused by the court.

An appellant may withdraw his notice of abandonment of appeal only where the abandonment can be regarded as a nullity. "This will only arise in exceptional circumstances where, e.g. some vital mistake of fact or fraud or possibly wrong advice from a legal adviser, has resulted in an unintended, ill-considered decision to abandon the appeal."[9] The court generally has no jurisdiction, where, for instance, an appellant abandons his appeal because of a misapprehension as to the law or the powers of the court.[10]

If an appeal is heard, the Court of Appeal can dismiss it, or "if they consider that the appellant should be sentenced differently for an offence for which he was dealt with by the court below may:

(a) quash any sentence or order which is the subject of appeal; and

(b) in place of it pass such sentence or make such order as they think appropriate for the case and as the court below had power to pass or make when dealing with him for the offence;

but the court shall so exercise their powers under this subsection that, taking the case as a whole, the appellant is not more severely dealt with on appeal than he was dealt with by the court below."[11] We have already noted in Chapter 4 that a hospital order, with or without restrictions, is not considered 'more severe' than a prison sentence of whatever length.

Section 23 of the Criminal Appeal Act 1968 provides that the Court of Appeal may, if it thinks necessary or expedient in the interests of justice, order the production of any document, order any witness to appear, or receive evidence.

The court can take into account changes which have occurred since the date of the trial, for the question before it is whether at the date of the hearing of the appeal a hospital order with restrictions is an appropriate sentence. In particular, the court can hear up-to-date medical evidence which was not available at the date of the trial.[12]

Thus, an appellant can argue that on the basis of evidence available to the Crown Court, orders under sections 60 and 65 are inappropriate, or he can present new evidence to show that the sentence should be changed – for example, that an order should not be made under section 65.

M's case (see Chapter 3, p.38) provides an illustration of the procedures for appeal:[13]

M was made the subject of a hospital order with restrictions by the Birmingham Crown Court on July 30, 1973. A favourable psychiatric report by his Royal Navy psychiatrist was not submitted to the court, so he sought leave to appeal against the section 65 order. Leave was denied on March 22, 1974; Judge Watkins said that the appeal was misconceived. On April 4, M renewed his application to appeal, but on April 28 he abandoned it. On June 3, before a five-member Court of Appeal, he sought to withdraw abandonment of appeal. It was submitted that he was induced to abandon it by the words of Judge Watkins, which indicated that the report of the Royal Navy psychiatrist (which was new evidence) was inadmissible. The judge had overlooked the provisions of section 11(3) of the Criminal Appeal Act 1968, which empowers the Court of Appeal to quash or substitute an appropriate sentence on material that has become available since the original sentence. In addition, his RMO at Broadmoor actively dissuaded him from appealing – he said that the appeal would divert M's attention from his programme of treatment at Broadmoor. Despite these arguments, and his generally vulnerable position, the court held that he could not withdraw abandonment of appeal.

Habeas corpus

"The prerogative writ of *habeas corpus ad subjiciendum* has for many centuries been one of the most important safeguards of individual liberty, and is still regarded as the ultimate weapon of defence for the oppressed".[14] An individual who considers that he is *unlawfully* imprisoned or detained, or another person acting on his behalf, may apply to the Queen's Bench Division of the High Court to challenge the legality of the detention.

In the past, it was not uncommon for a person detained in a mental institution to apply for a writ of *habeas corpus* to secure his release. For example, in the case of *R v Turlington*[15] a writ was issued on behalf of a woman detained in a mad-house after a medical expert had examined her and declared that she was not mentally disordered. However, such cases date from the time when there were no formal, statutory procedures for compulsory admission.[16] Since the passing of the Mental Health Act 1959, there appear to have been no reported applications for *habeas corpus* by mental patients.* It is possible that Mental Health Review Tribunals provide, to some extent, an alternative remedy.†

In theory a patient detained under sections 60 and 65 can apply for a writ of *habeas corpus*, but in practice it seems unlikely that a court would find grounds for granting such an application. *Habeas corpus* is not a significant safeguard for the restricted patient.

The writ of *habeas corpus* may not be used as a means of appealing against the decision of the Crown Court.[17]

It seems reasonably clear that a writ would be issued if some irregularity or want of jurisdiction in the court making the orders under section 60 and 65 were to affect the legality of the patient's detention – for example, if a magistrates' court made an order under section 60 in respect of a person convicted of a non-imprisonable offence, or if a Crown Court made a section 65 order without hearing oral evidence from at least one medical practitioner.

If, on the face of it, all the procedures laid down in the Mental Health Act have been strictly observed by the Crown Court, it seems that the detention of the patient is lawful. The Divisional Court has refused to issue a writ of

---

*But see *R v The Governor of Broadmoor, ex parte Clifford William Argles,* not reported. Judgment given June 28, 1974. Mr Argles applied for a writ of *habeas corpus* in an attempt to secure his discharge from Rampton Hospital, where he was detained under section 26 of the Mental Health Act. The patient claimed that the Mental Welfare Officer did not consult his nearest relative – his brother – as required by section 27(2), before mailing the application, but merely stated on the application form: "In my opinion it is not reasonably practicable before mailing this application to consult a Mr Argles of Wendover, Bucks." The patient argued that the Mental Welfare Officer was not justified in saying this and that he could easily have contacted his brother, who would have objected to the application. The validity of one of the medical recommendations was also questioned.

The hearing was adjourned for further investigation of these two points, but we understand from DHSS that the application was eventually refused. However, the words of Lord Justice Melford Stevenson are worth noting as indicating the attitude of the courts in such cases: " . . . here is a Section 26 order which on the face of it seems to have been regularly made in the sense that the necessary material is written out on the forms. It may be that there is a terrible hinterland which demonstrates that it should not have been done, but at the moment this detention seems to me to be effective under Section 26 . . ."

†The essential difference between *habeas corpus* and Mental Health Review Tribunals is that the former is concerned with the *lawfulness* of detention (i.e. whether the statutory procedures were observed at the time of admission) while the latter are concerned with the medical and social *justification* for detention at the time of the tribunal hearing.

habeas corpus to a person serving a prison sentence passed by a court of competent jurisdiction.[18] *In Re Featherstone,* The Lord Chief Justice, Lord Goddard, said:

> "The court does not grant, and cannot grant, writs of *habeas corpus* to persons who are in execution, that is to say, persons who are serving sentences passed by courts of competent jurisdiction. Probably, the only case in which the court would grant *habeas corpus* would be if it were satisfied that the prisoner was being held after the terms of the sentence passed on him had expired."

The same principle would probably apply to an application by a mental patient who had been properly admitted to hospital by a Crown Court acting within its jurisdiction.

The Home Secretary

A patient who is lawfully detained under sections 60 and 65 of the Mental Health Act is subject to the unfettered authority of the Home Secretary. Thus, "if he thinks fit", the Home Secretary may order a conditional or absolute discharge from hospital;[19] and he "may at any time" during the continuance of a restriction order recall to hospital a patient who has been conditionally discharged.[20] (A restriction order without limit of time will continue in force until the Home Secretary "is satisfied" that it is no longer required for the protection of the public.)[21] It is also of some small interest to note that he may, "if satisfied . . . it is desirable in the interests of justice", direct that the patient be taken to any place in Great Britain and kept there in custody.[22]

The Act does not require the Secretary of State to follow any procedures or criteria in the exercise of these powers. Thus he need not hear evidence on the issue or follow any advice which is rendered. Furthermore, he need not give reasons for his decision, and no appeal is available.

The absolute discretion given to the Home Secretary, together with the 'closed-door' decision-making process, appears to insulate the Minister from justified complaints by the patient or others acting on his behalf. Governments are prone to assert that the individual is protected by the doctrine of ministerial responsibility, because the Home Secretary is accountable to Parliament, and ultimately to the public, in the exercise of his statutory powers.

Ministerial responsibility is reinforced by the use of the parliamentary question. Any Member of Parliament may question the Home Secretary in the House of Commons about any decision taken by him or by any official under his control. For example, if an MP feels that a patient in his constituency should not be detained under a restriction order, he is free to enquire about the patient. This system has many merits, but it is not an effective means of holding the Minister accountable in respect of a particular individual. Professor Harry Street observes:[23]

"Question time is short and progress so slow that a Member will be lucky if he can confront a Minister at all. A Minister can refuse to answer a question and often does refuse. When he does answer, the civil servant, who has drafted his reply, will have taken every care to give away as little information as possible, and to protect the reputation of the Minister. . . . The further defect is that the Member of Parliament does not know what questions to ask – he has no access to departmental files, and a Minister will not disclose the contents of files in the course of answering a question in Parliament. There is a simple explanation why the myth of the effectiveness of this device has persisted: it suits Ministers because it appears to be subjecting them to control by Parliament, although the reality is quite different; it flatters the ego of back-bench MPs who wish to feel that they are more than rubber-stamps for their party."

Any solicitor, MP or voluntary organisation who has asked the Home Secretary to justify his decisions on restricted patients will know that there are very standard forms of reply: "Having considered the case in light of medical advice the Home Secretary is of opinion that Mr X is not well enough to leave Broadmoor. I should like to assure you, however, that Mr X's case will continue to be regularly reviewed and he will be detained in Broadmoor for no longer than is necessary in his own interests and those of the general public."

We realise that the decision to release a section 65 patient necessarily involves considerations of public safety which are properly the Home Secretary's responsibility. He also has to decide, on similar grounds, whether ordinary offenders can be placed on parole, or released on licence from life sentences.

Yet we have suggested two important safeguards against the unfettered authority of the Home Secretary. The first of these is the right to a hearing before the Advisory Board on Restricted Patients. The recommendations of the Board have been accepted in the past, and we would expect the Home Secretary to accept them in the future, save in exceptional cases. More importantly, we have suggested that a restriction order (as opposed to a hospital order without restrictions) is a penal sanction, which should be governed by ordinary principles of criminal justice – for example, the duration of the order should reflect the gravity of the offence. Accordingly, the trial judge should be required to set a time limit on the order, within the statutory maximum for the particular offence. (He could, of course, make an order without limit of time for a life-carrying offence.) At the end of this period the patient need not be discharged from the hospital if his condition still warranted psychiatric treatment. His detention could then be effected by civil procedures under Part IV of the 1959 Act, or by the termination of the restriction order itself (leaving the patient on a hospital order). Neither of these methods requires the Home Secretary's approval for discharge. For the offence itself is in the past, and no longer justifies his involvement.

The following case illustrates many of the problems presented in this report:

Mary's case

On May 8, 1970 Mary was convicted of theft at Southampton Magistrates' Court and, on committal to the court of Quarter Sessions (it would now be the Crown Court) for sentence, she was placed on probation. The circumstances of the offence were that she approached the Captain in charge of a Church Army Hostel for a plaster to cover a cut on her arm. While he was out of the room, she took a bottle of Mysoline tablets and hid them.

On September 29, 1970 she was again committed to Quarter Sessions for breaching the conditions of her probation order. There were two medical reports before the court – both quite short – which stated that she was suffering from a depressive illness. One report stated that Mary was "in need of psychiatric treatment in a hospital for a period of time. In view of the fact that she absconded on several occasions from Knowle Hospital, I feel that admission to Rampton Hospital is necessary. Unfortunately, this request has been rejected by the DHSS." Subsequently, the Department changed its mind and offered a bed in Rampton Hospital. The other medical report stated:

"There is a vacancy in Rampton Hospital if the court is mindful of implementing section 60 of the Mental Health Act, and in view of her propensity to abscond, a restriction order under section 65 of the Act may appear to the court to be necessary in this case."

The court made an order under section 60 and a restriction order without limit of time. Mary was admitted to Rampton Hospital and some two years later was transferred to Moss Side Hospital.

Mary applied to the Home Secretary to have her case referred to a Mental Health Review Tribunal and the hearing took place on October 4, 1974. As a restricted patient, she was not allowed to see any of the reports submitted to the tribunal by the Home Office and the hospital. She was also not told what recommendation the tribunal made to the Home Secretary. She was eventually informed by a member of the hospital staff that the Home Secretary had decided not to discharge her or transfer her to a local hospital.

In September 1975, Mary was put on the transfer list to be moved from Moss Side to Knowle Hospital. Not only her RMO, but also the consultant at Knowle Hospital, the DHSS and the Home Office, were of the opinion that she no longer required treatment under maximum security conditions.

She remained on the transfer list for over a year, although there were several vacancies at Knowle Hospital. Nursing staff who belong to COHSE were unwilling to accept any restricted patients.

In the summer of 1976, Moss Side Hospital considered the possibility of recommending the removal of the restriction order, to expedite her transfer to Knowle Hospital. They were informed that the Union had also placed a ban on all patients under hospital orders without restrictions.

On November 8, Moss Side Hospital held a staff conference on Mary's case. The RMO at Knowle Hospital informed Moss Side that there would be a vacancy for Mary in their new Forensic Unit which would open early the next year. A representative of the DHSS, however, was not informed of this development; in any event, he was sceptical because of the delays and misinformation which had occurred in the past.

MIND advised the hospital not to rely on the offer of a place in the Forensic Unit. Instead, we suggested that a recommendation should be made to the Home Secretary to lift the restriction order. Thereafter, the hospital should transfer Mary to Knowle Hospital as an informal patient. It would then be left to her new RMO to implement the procedures of Part IV of the Mental Health Act, if he felt it necessary.

The case conference accepted this view and Mary was duly transferred to Knowle Hospital. It was fortunate that they did not rely on the offer of a bed in the Forensic Unit, because we have now discovered that the Unit is not accepting female patients.

European Commission on Human Rights
We have filed a brief with the European Commission on Human Rights in respect of Mary's case.[24] We made the following observations:

(1) The Court of Quarter Sessions should not have made a restriction order without limit of time. An order under section 65 of the Act can only be made if it is "necessary for the protection of the public". The facts of this case do not meet this standard.

(2) The Union refused to accept Mary as an offender-patient. But they were quite willing to accept the same person under a different part of the Mental Health Act. The emphasis is on satisfying rigid policy considerations, rather than assessing the individual qualities of the patient involved.

(3) Section 65 of the Act may violate the provisions of Article 5(4) of the European Convention on Human Rights: "Everyone who is deprived of liberty by arrest or detention shall be entitled to take proceedings by which the lawfulness of his detention shall be decided speedily by a court and his release ordered if the detention is not lawful."

Francis Jacobs, Professor of European Law at the University of London, offered the following analysis of Article 5:[25]

"To commit a person to detention for an indefinite period with no fixed maximum, or for a very long period, may involve a serious infringement of the right to personal liberty. The solution to this problem under the Convention may be as follows. Detention of a person which was initially lawful, because for example he was of unsound mind, may subsequently become unlawful if his condition improves. In that event, even if a previous application has been rejected, he may make a fresh application. This application must not be 'substantially the same' as his previous one, or it will be inadmissible under Article 27(1)(b); but if he or his representatives can substantiate any new grounds for showing that he ought now to be released, his application will be admissible. . . . In all these cases, whatever may be the position under domestic law, there is in effect under the Convention a right to a periodical review."

Thus, there are two issues which are important in considering Article 5 of the Convention. The first is the lawfulness of the initial detention, which is a matter of domestic law, not the law of the European Convention. Here, Article 5(4) does not apply where detention has been ordered by a court following proper judicial procedure. It follows that Mary's initial detention was probably lawful under Article 5. It is also noteworthy that if the initial detention were not lawful, she would have a domestic remedy – i.e. a writ of *habeas corpus*.

The second issue which is important in considering Article 5 is the lawfulness of the continued detention – i.e. the substantive justification of detention. Here, the issue is whether there are appropriate means of periodic review under domestic law. In fact, the Government of the United Kingdom conceded this point in their brief to the European Commission in Mary's case:

"Unsoundness of mind, together with most of the other conditions referred to in Article 5(1)(e) is subject to gradual amelioration or deterioration and it is therefore reasonable and desirable that the cases of persons detained under those heads should be re-assessed at intervals appropriate to the nature of each case."

But the United Kingdom further asserted that a "court is not an appropriate body to determine whether the degree of recovery or risk of relapse of the patient suffering from mental illness is such as to justify his conditional or unconditional release into the community".

It is merely stating the obvious to suggest that, if a court is incapable of determining whether a person needs psychiatric treatment, so too is the Home Secretary. Moreover, periodic reviews by the Home Secretary do not satisfy the requirements of Article 5. In the *Neumeister* case, the European Court held that the term 'court' in Article 5 suggests that the authority called upon to decide must be independent of both the executive and the parties to the case.[26] The term 'court' also implies that there should be minimal standards of procedure, depending on the circumstances of the case – for example, that the person detained should be informed of the reasons for detention and given an opportunity to respond.

Our submission to the European Commission was that the Home Secretary is not independent of the executive; that he is not compelled to accept the advice of the tribunal or the RMO; that he hears evidence in private and does not disclose the reasons for his decisions; and he cannot, therefore, be an appropriate authority under Article 5 to determine whether the continued detention of the patient is lawful.

References and Notes

1. Criminal Appeal Act 1968, s. 50(1): "In this Act, 'sentence', in relation to an offence, includes any order made by a court when dealing with an offender (including a hospital order under Part V of the Mental Health Act 1959, with or without an order restricting discharge)...."
2. *Ibid.*, s. 11(1).
3. *Ibid.*, s. 31.
4. *Ibid.*, ss. 9 and 10.
5. *Ibid.*, ss. 18(1) and (2). See also the Criminal Appeal Rules 1968, S.I. 1968, No. 1262.
6. *Ibid.*, s. 18(3).
7. R v Rhodes [1910] 74 J.P. 380.
8. R v Marsh [1935] 25 Cr.App.R. 49.
9. *Halsbury's Laws of England*, 4th ed., para. 648
10. R v Sulton (Philip) [1969] 1 W.L.R. 375; R v Noble [1971] 55 Cr.App.R. 529; R v Peters [1974] 58 Cr.App.R. 328; R v Medway [1976] 62 Cr.App.R. 85.
11. Criminal Appeal Act 1968, s.11(3).
12. R v Bennett [1968] 2 All E.R. 753.
13. R v Medway [1976] 62 Cr.App.R. 85.
14. D.C.M. Yardley (ed.), *Introduction to British Constitutional Law*, 4th ed., p. 88. See also, S.A. de Smith, *Judicial Review of Administrative Action*, 3d ed., 1973, pp.507-526.
15. R v Turlington [1761] 2 Burr. 1115.
16. For a more recent case, see R v Board of Control and Others, ex. p. Rutty [1956] 2 W.L.R. 822; 1 All E.R. 769.
17. Ex parte Corke [1954] 2 All E.R. 440; 1 W.L.R. 899; Ex parte Hinds [1961] 1 All E.R. 707; 1 W.L.R. 325.
18. R v Featherstone [1953] 37 Cr.App.R. 146; R v Governor of Parkhurst Prison, ex. p. Philpot [1960] 1 W.L.R. 115.
19. Mental Health Act 1959, s. 66 (2).
20. *Ibid.*, s. 66(3).
21. *Ibid.*, s. 66(1).
22. *Ibid.*, s. 66(5).
23. H. Street, *Justice in the Welfare State* (Hamlyn Lectures, 25th series), 1968, pp. 114-115.
24. European Commission on Human Rights, Application No. 7099/75.
25. F. Jacobs, *The European Convention on Human Rights,* 1975, p.58.
26. *Ibid.*, p.73.

Appendix 1:
Mental disorder at the time of the offence

There are five instances where the mental state of the accused at the time of the offence is material. These are the special verdict, diminished responsibility, drunkenness, non-insane automatism and infanticide. Strictly speaking, the last four categories stand outside the scope of this report, since the courts do not necessarily make a treatment order on conviction in these cases. The special verdict requires the trial judge to send the accused to hospital under a restriction order without limit of time. Thus it is within the purview of this report. But the special verdict is rarely asked for; in 1974 it was returned in only three cases.[1]

The Butler Report made a thorough and satisfactory assessment of these five categories, so MIND has decided not to make any major new recommendations in these areas. For the sake of completeness, however, this Appendix gives a brief exposition of the current law, and of the Butler Committee's proposals.

We should emphasise here that we specifically endorse the Butler Committee's proposal that the trial judge be given greater discretion in disposal where the special verdict is returned, or where the person is found guilty of murder.

The special verdict
The special verdict, which results in acquittal on the grounds of insanity, was first made law by the Criminal Lunatics Act 1800, though it had long been recognised that "if a person was, at the time of his unlawful act, mentally so disordered that it would be unreasonable to impute guilt to him, he ought not to be held liable to conviction and punishment under the criminal law".[2] The special verdict was incorporated into the Trial of Lunatics Act 1883.[3] It was amended in the Criminal Procedure (Insanity) Act 1964, section 1, which reads:

"The special verdict required by section 2 of the Trial of Lunatics Act 1883 (hereinafter referred to as a 'special verdict') shall be that the accused is not guilty by reason of insanity; and accordingly in subsection (1) of that section for the words from 'a special verdict' to the end there shall be substituted the words 'a special verdict that the accused is not guilty by reason of insanity'."

Thus, the current form of the special verdict is 'not guilty by reason of insanity', which suggests a causal link between the insanity and the crime; while in many instances this link does indeed exist, the Committee on Mentally Abnormal Offenders feels that the form should be 'not guilty on

187

evidence of mental disorder', which means this connection need not be proved.[4]

The special verdict relates to mental disorder at the time of the offence charged, and the health of the accused at the time of the trial has little relevance. The issue before the court is the degree to which he was responsible for his alleged criminal behaviour.

Criteria

The legal and medical definitions of insanity differ: a person who suffers from a medically recognised mental illness may still be legally responsible for his actions. The test of legal responsibility was formulated in the M'Naghten Rules, drawn up by the judiciary in 1843 after the case of M'Naghten[5], who shot Sir Robert Peel's secretary, thinking him to be Sir Robert. M'Naghten was acquitted on the grounds of insanity, but the case caused such controversy that the judges felt that rules must be laid down for cases where the defendant's responsibility for his acts was in question. The Rules state that:

"To establish a defence on the grounds of insanity, it must be clearly proved that at the time of the committing of the act, the party accused was labouring under such a defect of reason, from disease of the mind, as not to know the nature and quality of the act he was doing, or, if he did know it, that he did not know he was doing wrong."[6]

This definition of insanity, which is a very narrow view, has caused many problems of interpretation. Quite possibly, a person may 'know the nature and quality of the act' and 'know he was doing what was wrong', and yet be classified by psychiatrists as severely mentally disordered and in need of treatment. As early as 1874 criticism was levelled at the Rules, and in the Minutes of Evidence to the Select Committee on the Homicide Law Amendment Bill (1874, Q.186) Lord Bramwell said:

"I think that, although the present law lays down such a definition of madness, that *nobody is hardly ever really mad enough to be within it,* yet it is a good and logical definition." (Italics added.)

What, one is prompted to ask, is good about a definition that can rarely be used? In 1953, the Royal Commission on Capital Punishment stated:

"The gap between the natural meaning of the law and the sense in which it is commonly applied has for so long been so wide, it is impossible to escape the conclusion that an amendment of the law, to bring it into closer conformity with the current practice, is long overdue."[7]

The Commission proposed that either (a) the Rules should be extended to include cases where the accused is labouring (as a result of disease of the mind) under an emotional disorder which makes him incapable of preventing himself from committing an act, even though he is aware that it is wrong and capable of appreciating its nature,[8] or (b) the Rules should be entirely abrogated and the jury given total discretion to determine whether he was so insane as not to be responsible for his actions.[9]

No amendment was made on the basis of these proposals, and the only major change in the law on the mentally disordered offender was the inclusion of the doctrine of diminished responsibility in the Homicide Act 1957 (s. 2(1)).[10]

Where the issue of insanity is raised, it must be shown that the alleged criminal behaviour arose from a defect of reason caused by disease of the mind; it is not enough to show merely that the accused did not use his reason in a moment of confusion or absent-mindedness.[11] In *Kemp's* case,[12] 'disease of the mind' was held to include physical illness that resulted in impaired mental faculties. A man suffering from arteriosclerosis (hardening of the arteries) was charged with causing grievous bodily harm to his wife; evidence was brought to show that arteriosclerosis could lead a sufferer to act violently when he was in fact not conscious, and Mr Kemp was found to be 'guilty but insane' (the form of the special verdict before the 1964 Act). During the judgement, Lord Devlin said that temporary insanity is sufficient to satisfy the M'Naghten Rules: "It does not matter whether it is incurable and permanent or not." He further stated: "The law is not concerned with the brain but with the mind, in the sense that 'mind' is ordinarily used, the mental faculties of reason, memory and understanding."[13]

The phrase 'nature and quality of his act' refers to its *physical*, not its moral or legal nature and quality.[14] If the act was prompted by a delusion (for example, if the accused felt that he was being attacked), and that delusion is a symptom of mental disorder, then the special verdict applies, and the defendant is liable to be detained in a mental hospital.[15]

If the accused did know 'the nature and quality' of the act, then it must be shown that he was incapable of appreciating that he should not have perpetrated it. Here, evidence that he knew that his acts were illegal is enough to negate the defence of insanity within the M'Naghten Rules. Furthermore, even if he did not know this act was illegal, he is still not considered insane under the Rules if he knew it was wrong 'according to the ordinary standard adopted by reasonable men'.[16]

The recommendations of the Butler Committee

The Butler Committee maintains that the M'Naghten Rules are based on obsolete beliefs which are no longer held by the medical profession,[17] and proposes a new formula for the special verdict: 'not guilty on evidence of mental disorder'. The grounds for this would include two elements:

(a) a *mens rea* element, which would incorporate the cognitive aspect of the Rules ('Did he know what he was doing?')
(b) specific exemption from conviction for defendants found to be suffering (at the time of the act or omission) from severe mental illness or severe subnormality.[18] The Butler Committee accepts the definition of severe subnormality given in section 4 of the Mental Health Act; in paragraph 18.35, the Committee attempts to define 'severe mental illness'.

Procedure

Burden of proof
As a finding of 'not guilty by reason of insanity' is exculpatory, the defence raises the issue. There appears to be no provision under which the court can raise the question of the defendant's mental state at the time of the offence. However, section 6 of the Criminal Procedure (Insanity) Act 1964 does state that where, in a trial for murder, the defence raises the issue either of insanity at the time of the offence or of diminished responsibility, then the prosecution may "adduce or elicit evidence tending to prove the other of those contentions".

The issue arises as evidence for the defence, and there are no special requirements for early notification either of the prosecution or the court. The Butler Committee feels, however, that where the defence intends to present medical evidence of insanity, it should give advance notice to the prosecution, in order that they may prepare any rebuttal.[4] In all criminal trials, innocence is presumed; so is sanity, and where the defence wishes to rebut that presumption, it bears the onus of proof (that is, of the insanity issue only). However, while the prosecution has to prove beyond a reasonable doubt that the prisoner is guilty, the defence only has to show that on a balance of probabilities, he is not responsible for his actions.[14]

The role of the jury
While the medical evidence is very important in cases where the issue of insanity is raised, it is ultimately up to the jury to decide whether the accused is responsible for his actions. However, should the jury reach a decision which entirely contradicts the medical evidence, that decision will be upset.[19]

Effect

The Criminal Procedure (Insanity) Act 1964 states that where the special verdict is returned, the accused shall be admitted to a hospital specified by the Home Secretary, and the order admitting him to hospital shall carry restrictions on his discharge without limit of time.[20] Thus the Court has no option but to order his indefinite detention in a specified hospital.

The Butler Committee recommended that the trial judge should be given a much wider discretion in such cases. This proposal is similar to the one made for disability in relation to the trial (see pp. 27-28 *supra*.) MIND specifically endorses this proposal. For the special verdict, the Butler Committee also proposes that a new order be set up, to be used at the discretion of the trial judge. The order would allow the offender to live in the community; but he would be on licence and subject to recall, in the same way as a restricted patient conditionally discharged from hospital.[21] MIND agrees with this recommendation, but suggests the following modification: the licence should not be unlimited in point of time (unless the offender is charged with a life-carrying offence). Instead, it should lapse after a specified period, which should be proportional to the gravity of the offence.

Diminished responsibility

The doctrine of diminished responsibility was introduced into English law by the Homicide Act 1957, section 2(1), which states:

> "Where a person kills or is party to the killing of another, he shall not be convicted of murder if he was suffering from such abnormality of mind (whether arising from a condition of arrested or retarded development of mind or any inherent causes or induced by disease or injury) as substantially impaired his mental responsibility for his acts and omissions in doing or being a party to the killing."

The section goes on to state that the burden of proof (on the balance of probability) shall be on the defence,[23] and that a verdict of manslaughter shall be returned where the plea is successful.[24] Since the introduction of this plea, the number of cases in which a verdict of 'not guilty by reason of insanity' has been asked for or returned has dropped significantly – from an average of 20% of all persons committed for trial for murder between 1947 and 1956, to 0.7% between 1971 and 1973.[25] If the jury finds that there is evidence of diminished responsibility, but that the accused did commit the act or omission charged, they will find him guilty of the lesser offence of manslaughter. Diminished responsibility may be pleaded only where the charge is murder.

Diminished responsibility is raised by the defence during the course of its evidence. However, where the defendant contends that at the time of the offence he was insane, the prosecution may give evidence that he was not insane but was suffering from diminished responsibility.[26]

Criteria

The plea of diminished responsibility includes all cases which fall under the M'Naghten Rules, but it carries a much broader interpretation of insanity than those rules, and so includes many instances which they do not cover. Most significantly, it covers those cases where the accused knew what he was doing and intended the consequences, yet was not fully responsible.[27] The wording of section 2 is very broad, and has led to some problems of interpretation; however, the courts have held that "abnormality of mind" means "a state of mind so different from that of ordinary human beings that the reasonable man would term it abnormal".[28] "Substantially impaired" has been held to mean an impairment that is "more than trivial but less than total".[29]

Diminished responsibility has been held to include cases in which the accused suffered from an "inability to exercise willpower to control physical acts";[30] this would appear to include the concept of "irresistible impulse". It is most often pleaded in cases of mercy killing,[31] causing the death of one's own children,[32] and inter-marital killing;[33] that is, where there is some element of jealousy, compassion or depression.

Disposal

Since a successful plea of diminished responsibility leads to a verdict of manslaughter, a large number of disposals are open to the judge, ranging from a life sentence or a hospital order with restrictions, to a psychiatric probation order or an absolute discharge. In the four years from 1970 to 1973, 12.1% of the 290 offenders found guilty of manslaughter under section 2 were given probation orders, 52.8% were given hospital orders (82.4% of these with restrictions), and 31.7% were sentenced to prison.[34]* Thus the judge can decide each case on its own merits – which he cannot do where the accused is found either not guilty by reason of insanity or unfit to plead. In these cases he must make a hospital order with restrictions.

Recommendation of the Butler Committee

Section 2 of the Homicide Act is not without its problems. The criteria laid down in the Act are vague and undefined, and often it is difficult to show that the criminal behaviour of the accused stemmed from some abnormality of mind. For instance it is difficult, if not impossible, to distinguish objectively between an impulse which *could* not be resisted and one which merely *was* not resisted. The Committee on Mentally Abnormal Offenders suggests various ways of overcoming these problems. Their main recommendation is that the mandatory life sentence for murder should be abolished. This would remove the need for the plea of diminished responsibility, by giving to the judge the same wide range of disposals in any case of homicide as he now has in cases of manslaughter.[35] They also suggested that if the mandatory sentence and section 2 are removed, the jury should be empowered to return a verdict of murder (or manslaughter) 'by reason of extenuating circumstances', while leaving those circumstances totally undefined. This would undoubtedly simplify the whole field of insanity and legal responsibility, and would remove most of the problems of definition which the courts have faced in the past; it would allow greater discretion in dealing with offenders, so that less restrictive sentences could be passed in appropriate cases. Accordingly, MIND agrees with the Butler Committee's proposal and recommends its adoption into legislation.

Infanticide

Infanticide is a special offence which was first introduced by the Infanticide Act 1938.[36] It deals with the special case of a mother who causes the death of her child within the first year of its life. It must be shown that at the time of

---

*The Butler Committee (para. 19.6) was told in evidence by the Home Office that a man given a life sentence for manslaughter after a finding of diminished responsibility may be detained longer, because of the doubts cast on his mental condition, than a man given a mandatory life sentence for murder.

the crime, the woman's mind was disturbed "by reason of her not having fully recovered from the effect of giving birth to the child or by reason of the effect of lactation consequent upon the birth of the child".

A person found guilty of infanticide may be dealt with as if she were convicted of manslaughter rather than murder. The statute, which was passed long before diminished responsibility was introduced as a plea in mitigation, allows the courts to deal leniently with a woman suffering from puerperal psychosis that does not amount to insanity under the M'Naghten Rules.

The Butler Committee recommends[37] that the offence of infanticide should be removed from the statute book, and that such cases should instead be dealt with under the legislation on diminished responsibility. This would remove some of the anomalies of this statute (for instance, that it does not apply to a mother who, under the influence of a later birth, kills an older child) and yet would still allow compassion to be shown in such cases.

Drunkenness

Drunkenness at the time of an offence never of itself constitutes a defence, but it may be relevant if the defence shows that the accused was so drunk as to be incapable of forming the necessary intent to commit the crime.[38] Basically, where drunkenness is relevant, the substantive defence is mistake, and the fact of intoxication makes the error more credible. One example of this was quoted by Lord Denning:[39] a nurse got so drunk at a christening that she put a baby on the fire, mistaking it for a log of wood.

Where the crime is one of strict liability, drunkenness can never afford a defence. Should the evidence show that excessive drinking has led to insanity (for example, that the accused suffers from *delirium tremens*), then the M'Naghten Rules will apply, as in any other case where the issue of insanity is raised.

The Butler Committee [40] suggests that the problems of cases involving intoxication could be removed by creating the offence of 'dangerous intoxication'. In the first instance the prosecution would not charge this offence, but an offence under the ordinary law. If evidence of intoxication were given at the trial, and the jury found that the defendant committed the act, but owing to the intoxication they are not sure he did so with intent, they would be directed to return a verdict of not guilty of that offence but guilty of dangerous intoxication.

Non-insane automatism

Criminal acts done while sleepwalking, in a hypoglycaemic episode or under concussion are examples of non-insane automatism. In such cases the jury must be directed not to convict unless satisfied beyond a reasonable doubt that the act was voluntary.[41] Automatism is confined, according to Lord

Denning, [42] "to acts done while unconscious and to spasms, reflex actions and convulsions".

Finally, it should be noted that the courts are reluctant to exempt a defendant from liability for an involuntary act if it was caused by drink or drugs voluntarily taken. [43]

References

1. *Criminal Statistics for England and Wales*, HMSO, Cmnd. 6168, 1974, pp. 154-162.
2. *Royal Commission on Capital Punishment*, HMSO, Cmnd. 8932, para. 278.
3. Trial of Lunatics Act 1883, s.2.
4. *The Butler Report*, para. 18.18.
5. M'Naghten, 10 Cl. and F. 200.
6. *Ibid.,* p.210.
7. *Royal Commission on Capital Punishment, op cit.,* para. 291.
8. *Ibid.,* para. 296.
9. *Ibid.*
10. See generally H. Fingarette, "Diminished mental capacity as a criminal law defence", *Mod. L. Rev.,* vol. 37, 1974, p.264.
11. R v Clarke [1972] 1 All E.R. 219.
12. R v Kemp [1957] 1 Q.B. 399.
13. *Ibid.,* p. 407.
14. J. C. Smith and B. Hogan, *Criminal Law,* 3rd ed., 1973, p. 141.
15. *The Butler Report*, para. 18.4.
16. R v Codere [1916] 12 *Cr. App. R.* 21, p.27.
17. *The Butler Report*, para. 18.6.
18. *Ibid.,* paras. 18.17 and 18.18.
19. Smith and Hogan, *op. cit.,* p.143.
20. Criminal Procedure (Insanity) Act 1964, s. 5(1)(a) and 1st schedule 2(1).
21. *The Butler Report*, para. 18.45.
23. Homicide Act 1957, s. 2(2). See also R v Dunbar [1958] 1 Q.B. 1.
24. *Ibid.,* s. 2(3).
25. *The Butler Report*, p.316. See also A. Samuels, "Mental stress and criminal liability", *Medicine Science Law*, vol. 15, 1975, p. 198.
26. Criminal Procedure (Insanity) Act 1964, s.6.
27. R v Rose [1961] 45 Cr.App.R. 102.
28. R v Byrne [1960] 1 Q.B. 396, p. 403.
29. R v Lloyd [1967] 1 Q.B. 175.
30. R v Byrne, *op cit.,* p.404.
31. R v Morris [1961] 45 Cr.App.R. 185.
32. R v Bastian [1958] 1 All E.R. 565.
33. R v Din [1962] 46 Cr.App.R.269.
34. *The Butler Report*, para. 19.6.
35. *Ibid.,* para. 19.11.
36. See generally J.C. Smith and B. Hogan, *op cit.,* p. 271-272; *The Butler Report*, paras. 19.3, 19.22-27.
37. *The Butler Report*, para. 19.26.
38. See generally Smith and Hogan, *op cit.,* pp. 151-157; A.H. Edwards, *Mental Health Services,* 4th ed., 1975, pp. 194-195.
39. A.G. for Northern Ireland v Gallagher [1961] 3 All E.R.299, p.313.
40. *The Butler Report*, para. 18.54.
41. See generally Smith and Hogan, *op cit.,* pp. 34-37.
42. R v Bratty [1961] 3 All E.R. 532.
43. See generally Smith and Hogan, *op cit.,* p. 37.

Appendix 2:
Psychiatric treatment as a condition of probation

Probation was introduced into English law by the Probation of First Offenders Act 1887, which allowed non-custodial supervision of first offenders for an unlimited period. The Probation of Offenders Act 1907 extended this to include other offenders, and mentioned their mental state as a possible reason to choose probation rather than any other form of disposal.[1] The 1907 Act set the maximum probation period at three years.

The next major step was taken with the Criminal Justice Act 1948, which in section 4 defined much more precisely the criteria under which psychiatric treatment could be made a condition of probation. The 1948 Act has now been consolidated into the Powers of Criminal Courts Act 1973.

Probation orders in general

Where a person aged 17 or over is convicted of an offence (other than one for which the sentence is fixed by law, such as murder), the court may place him under a probation order. This means he will be under the supervision of a probation officer for a fixed period specified in the order, of not less than one year and not more than three years. The court must consider that under the circumstances, including the nature of the offence and the character of the offender, it is expedient to place him under a probation order rather than to sentence him.[2]

A probation order may require the offender to comply with such conditions as the court considers will secure his good conduct or prevent him from committing further offences.[3] The 1973 Act also makes specific provisions for probation orders that require attendance at a day training centre[4] or treatment for a mental condition[5] (the Butler Committee calls this a psychiatric probation order).[6]

Before making a probation order, the court must explain to the offender in ordinary language what effects it will have. It must inform him that if he fails to comply with its requirements or commits another offence, he will be in breach of the order and liable to a sentence for the original offence. The court cannot make the order unless he states that he is willing to comply with its requirements.[7] Should he not fully understand its implications, it may be revoked on appeal.[8]

Probation order on condition of psychiatric treatment

The court may place the offender on probation on condition that he agrees to be treated by or under the direction of a qualified medical practitioner, with a view to improving his mental condition. The court must have evidence from one medical practitioner* (approved under section 28 of the Mental Health Act as "having special experience in the diagnosis or treatment of mental disorder") to the effect that "the mental condition of the offender is such as requires and may be susceptible to treatment but not such as to warrant his detention in pursuance of a hospital order under Part V of that Act".[9]

The offender may be at liberty during his probation, so the order is used only where there is little danger that he will commit further serious offences.[10] Although the order is not usually made for particularly violent offences, the courts have on occasion used it in serious cases – such as attempted murder,[11] attempted rape,[12] arson,[13] and indecent assault.[14]

The court may specify any one of three kinds of treatment:[15]
(a) treatment as a resident patient in a hospital or mental nursing home (but not a special hospital);
(b) treatment as a non-resident at an institution specified in the order;
(c) treatment by or under the direction of a qualified medical practitioner specified in the order.

Modification, variation or cancellation of the order

Schedule I, paragraph 4 of the Powers of Criminal Courts Act 1973 states that the medical practitioner may report to the probation officer if he considers that: (a) treatment should be continued beyond the period originally specified; (b) different treatment is needed (of a type that the court can specify under a probation order); (c) that the offender is not susceptible to treatment; (d) that no further treatment is required; or (e) that the medical practitioner is for some reason unwilling to continue giving it. The probation officer must then apply to the court for a variation or cancellation of the order. The probationer's agreement to the amended requirements must be obtained if the order is to be varied.[16]

Breach of order

If the offender does not comply with the requirements, the supervising court may summon him to appear at a specified place and time or, if the information is given in writing, issue a warrant for his arrest.[17] If the court is satisfied that there has been a breach, it may then: (a) impose a fine of up to £50; (b) make a community service order; (c) make an attendance centre order (under certain conditions only); or (d) impose any sentence that could have been passed at the time of conviction.[18] The use of either (a) or (b) does not imply that the order has ceased.[19]

---

*The Butler Committee recommends that the doctor who gives medical evidence to the court should, wherever possible, carry out the treatment (para. 16.11).

In relation specifically to a requirement for psychiatric treatment, section 6(7) states that the probationer shall not be deemed to have breached the order if he refuses "to undergo any surgical, electrical or other treatment" and his refusal is considered reasonable under the circumstances of the case.

References

1. Probation of Offenders Act 1907, s. 1. See also N. Walker and S. McCabe, *Crime and Insanity in England*, vol. 2, 1973, p. 64.
2. Powers of Criminal Courts Act 1973, s. 2(1).
3. *Ibid.*, s. 2(3).
4. *Ibid.*, s. 4.
5. *Ibid.*, s. 3.
6. See generally *The Butler Report*, chapter 16.
7. Powers of Criminal Courts Act 1973, s. 2(6).
8. R v Marquis [1974] 2 All E.R. 1216.
9. Powers of Criminal Courts Act 1973, s. 3(1).
10. R v Greedy [1964] *Crim. L. Rev.* 669; R v Cave, [1965] *Crim. L. Rev.* 448. A psychiatric probation order is also appropriate where the diagnosis is uncertain; see R v Docherty [1962] *Crim. L. Rev.* 851.
11. R v Hill [1963] *Crim. L. Rev.* 525.
12. R v Smith, not reported. Judgment given October 18, 1966.
13. R v Rideout, not reported. Judgment given March 16, 1968.
14. R v James [1965] *Crim. L. Rev.* 252; R v Tedham [1965] *Crim. L. Rev.* 322.
15. Powers of Criminal Courts Act 1973, s. 3(2).
16. *Ibid.*, schedule 1, para. 5.
17. *Ibid.*, s. 6(1).
18. *Ibid.*, s. 6(3).
19. *Ibid.*, s. 6(8).

Appendix 3:
Section 73 of the Mental Health Act 1959

Section 73 of the Mental Health Act 1959 authorises the Home Secretary to direct the transfer from prison to a mental hospital of prisoners who are *not* serving sentences of imprisonment. It operates in the same way as section 72, which applies to prisoners who *are* serving sentences of imprisonment. The only difference between the two is that section 72 authorises the transfer of persons suffering from mental illness, psychopathic disorder, subnormality or severe subnormality, while section 73 applies only to persons suffering from mental illness or severe subnormality.

A transfer direction will have the same effect as a hospital order under section 60. The Home Secretary may further direct that the person be subject to the special restrictions set out in section 65; and where the transfer is ordered of any person described in subsections (a) to (d) below, the Home Secretary has no choice but to place him under special restrictions. With any of the subsections, the transfer directions are effected in the same way as for subsection (a), described on p.18 *supra*. However, subsections (a) to (c) are subject to the further provisions of section 76, subsection (d) to those of section 77, and subsection (e) to those of section 78. These further provisions are explained below.

Subsection (a) applies to persons committed in custody for trial at the Crown Court (see the discussion on p.18 *supra*).

Subsection (b) which applies to persons committed in custody to the Crown Court, has the same provisions as subsection (a).

Subsection (c) applies to persons remanded in custody by the Crown Court to await a judgment or sentence which has been respited (delayed). It has the same provisions as subsection (a).

Subsection (d) applies to persons remanded in custody by a magistrates' court. It has the same provisions as subsection (a), except that the further provisions of section 77 apply, rather than those of section 76.

Section 77 provides that the transfer direction will cease to have effect when the period of remand expires, unless the person is committed in custody for trial at the Crown Court (in which case section 76 may apply). Where the transfer of a person thus remanded has been directed, the court may exercise its powers without bringing the patient before it; and whether or not he is brought before the court, if he is further remanded, the remand period cannot be deemed to have expired for the purposes of section 77.

Where a transfer direction for such a patient ceases to have effect, then unless the court before which he is brought on the expiry of remand passes sentence or makes a hospital or guardianship order, he will continue to be liable to be detained in the same hospital as when he was under the transfer direction, as if he had been admitted on the date when the transfer direction expired in pursuance of a civil admission for treatment under section 26 of the Act.

Subsection (e) applies to civil prisoners (that is, persons committed by a court for a limited term). Persons committed for contempt of court fall into this category. An 'order for committal' has replaced the 'writ of attachment' referred to in the Act. This does not apply to those committed for contempt for an indefinite period.

Section 73(e) is further governed by section 78, which provides that any direction for the transfer of a civil prisoner shall cease to have effect when he would, but for his removal to hospital, be released from prison. When this occurs, it is deemed that on the day of expiry he entered the hospital under Part IV of the Mental Health Act; and the provisions of that Part apply.

Subsection (f) concerns aliens detained in a prison (or other institution to which the Prison Act 1952 applies) in pursuance of the Aliens Order 1953, or any order amending or replacing that Order. The Aliens Order 1953 (S.I. No. 1671) and subsequent statutory instruments no longer operate, since the Aliens Restriction Act 1914 (the enabling act) was replaced by the Immigration Act 1971. This section presumably applies to those detained under the 1971 Act.

Appendix 4
MIND'S Legal and Welfare Rights Service

Acknowledging the particular difficulties which must arise out of dealing with cases with a mental health component, we have brought together the expertise of lawyers, psychiatrists and social workers in a Legal and Welfare Rights Service. Since its inception a year ago, it has received a large number of requests for help on both mental health and children's legislation. The calls have come from a wide variety of sources, including Members of Parliament, Citizens' Advice Bureaux, Community Health Councils, Regional and Area Health Authorities, solicitors, professionals in the psychiatric services, relatives and patients. The very volume of requests from these diverse groups shows the need for a specialist service.

While most of the enquiries are dealt with by staff, cases which require detailed legal consideration are often referred to members of our lawyers' group – twenty barristers and solicitors who give their time on a voluntary basis. These lawyers have attended training sessions provided by MIND staff and have had other specialised experience with mental health and children's legislation.

The Legal and Welfare Rights Service has defended patients and ex-patients in cases concerning housing, employment, community care, enfranchisement, access to courts, consent to treatment, education and compulsory admissions. Several of these cases are presented in *A Human Condition*:* *Pountney's* case (Volume 1, pp. 106-110), *Robert's* case (Volume 2, pp.89-90), *M's* case (Volume 2, pp. 38, 76, 116-117, 178), and *Mary's* case (Volume 2, pp. 182-184).

Examples of other important cases, not reported in either volume, are described here.

The right to vote †

On November 28, 1975 the provisional electoral register for Warrington was published. It included the names of 574 inmates of the Winwick Hospital, a mental hospital on the outskirts of Warrington. All 574 had been assessed by the hospital staff as having the mental capacity to vote. Objection was taken

---

*The real names of patients are not used unless they have already been disclosed in the press or in a law report.

†For a more detailed account of the voting rights case, see L. Gostin, "Electoral reform for patients in mental hospitals", *Community Care*, May 26, 1976, pp. 12-14; L. Gostin, "The right to vote for mental patients", *Poly L. Rev.*, Volume 2, No 1, Autumn 1976, pp. 17-21.

to their inclusion on the register by the liaison officer of the Newton Constituency Conservative Association on the grounds that the hospital was "an establishment maintained wholly or mainly for the reception and treatment of persons suffering from mental illness or other mental disorder", as section 4(3) of the Representation of the People Act 1949 provides that patients in such an establishment shall not be treated as resident there for electoral purposes. Thus the inmates could only register to vote if they had other residences.

The Electoral Registration Officer, acting in accordance with regulation 19 of the Representation of the People Regulations 1974, decided to delete their names from the register. He held a hearing to consider the objections of five of them under regulation 17. MIND represented the patients, but the Electoral Registration Officer turned down their objections.

MIND appealed to the Warrington County Court (section 45, Representation of the People Act 1949 and regulation 66, Representation of the People Regulations 1974). The grounds included the assertion that the five were not "patients" within the meaning of section 4(3). The court selected a test case (*Wild and others v Electoral Registration Officer for Warrington and another*) and the appeal was heard on June 15, 1976.

The judge ruled that the five were not "patients" and therefore were entitled to vote. He based his decision on evidence which showed that the appellants were in hospital only because they had no home to go to.

The Department of Health and Social Security considered this case of major importance. They issued a health circular to all Area Health Authorities, informing them of the judgement. It was estimated that the decision could effectively enfranchise 50,000 mental patients.

The right to education

Dwight Francis, aged 14, was classified as educationally subnormal and excluded from school some five years ago. Since that time he has had virtually no education or care.

On January 21st, 1976 we made a complaint under section 99 of the Education Act 1944. Section 99 requires the Secretary of State for Education and Science to find a local education authority in default, if they have failed to discharge any duty imposed upon them under the 1944 Act. We made the following submissions:

" . . . These facts appear to constitute a default in the duties of the Northamptonshire Education Authority (NEA) to provide Dwight Francis with an education. The NEA has not made available, under the provisions of section 8 of the Education Act 1944, sufficient schools to provide Dwight with 'full-time education suitable to his requirements'.

The NEA must specifically provide special educational treatment for children suffering from any mental or physical handicap. In accordance with section 8(2)(c), the NEA must have particular regard 'to the need for securing that provision is made for pupils who suffer from any disability of mind or body'. Further, under the provisions of section 34(1), the NEA has a duty to ascertain what children require special educational treatment, and, under section 34(4), they should provide such treatment.

The Education (Handicapped Children) Act 1970 repealed those provisions of the Education Act 1944 and the Mental Health Act 1959 which permitted children to be classified as 'unsuitable for education at school'. Your Department expressed the intent of that legislation in your Circular 15/70 which states that 'no child within age limits for education . . . will be outside of the scope of the educational system'. This also appears to be the Parliamentary intent as provided in section 1 of the 1944 Act.

In sum, the approximate 24 hours of individual tuition and two weeks' residential training which Dwight has received in the past 5 years cannot be consistent with the express and implied provisions of the 1944 and 1970 Acts . . ."

A considerable amount of correspondence on this case passed between the Department and MIND. The final result was that the Secretary of State held that the NEA was not in default of its duties; however, they would make arrangements for Dwight to be admitted to a local psychiatric hospital as an in-patient. Although this will be of considerable help to Dwight and his family, we feel that it does not necessarily meet the requirements of the 1944 Act. We have good evidence that many mentally handicapped people who are placed in hospital do not receive "full time education suitable to [their] requirements". Accordingly, we are now bringing an action against the Department of Education and Science in order to secure for Dwight, and other mentally handicapped children, the education to which they are entitled by law.

Mental Health Review Tribunal representation

In Volume 1 of *A Human Condition* we emphasised the value of a representative for patients at Mental Health Review Tribunals (MHRTs). The patient may be unable to defend his interests for several reasons. His ability to communicate may be impaired by psychotropic drugs, or by his mental disorder. But inarticulateness does not itself mean that he cannot live in the community. Often a patient has become inarticulate and over-dependent through sheer institutionalisation – but that will not improve by his staying in hospital. Moreover, because he is detained, he cannot make all of the necessary preparations for the hearing. He is often denied access to the hospital report, his prognosis, and other information which the tribunal must consider. Hence he cannot refute inaccuracies and state his own case fully. He also cannot make enquiries in the community about a home, a job, after-care and so forth. This is all vital if the tribunal is going to discharge him.

In Volume 1, we also expressed our concern that too few patients are represented. Moreover, representatives who are legally trained may have an insufficient knowledge of community resources to arrange for care, shelter and employment. On the other hand, representatives who are trained in social services may not fully understand the intricacies found in the Mental Health Act and Tribunal Rules of Procedure. They may also lack cross-examination skills and a healthy scepticism for unproven facts.

In order to meet the need for fully qualified representatives, we are holding a series of training courses for lawyers, social workers, nursing officers, teachers, community workers, and other interested people. These courses are intended to provide intensive training in MHRT advocacy.

Indexes to Volumes 1 and 2

Index to Volume 1

police powers, 32
receiving hospital, 45
PLACE OF SAFETY, 25, 26
POCKET MONEY, 102, 149
POST. *See* Expression and Association
PRIVACY. *See* Dignity and Privacy
PSYCHIATRIC DIAGNOSES,
  reliability of, 37-39
    cultural factors, 38
    sex factors, 38
  research, 48-51
  social conformity, 43
  unlimited opinions, 42
  validity of, 39-42
    mental disorder, 39
    overcautious, 39, 40, 41
    prediction of dangerousness, 39-43

RECEIVING HOSPITAL, 45-46
RECORD. *See* Hospital Record
REHABILITATION,
  defined, 16 (footnote)
RELATIVE. *See* Nearest Relative
REMOVAL TO ANOTHER PART OF
  UNITED KINGDOM, 102-103
RESPONSIBLE MEDICAL OFFICER
  (RMO),
  barring certificate, 43
  censorship of post, 111-114
  defined, 23 (footnote)
  discharge by, 44-45
  mental health review tribunals, 82-83,
    84-87
  reclassification, 23
  renewal of detention, 26
RIGHT TO REFUSE TREATMENT. *See*
  Treatment
RIGHT TO TREATMENT. *See* Treatment

SOCIAL WORKERS,
  application for admission, 24
  disagreements with doctors, 36

ill-treated and neglected person, 25
power to inspect premises, 25
proposals for reform, 36-37, 77, 144
STERILISATION. *See* Treatment

TRANSFER TO ANOTHER
  HOSPITAL, 152
TRIBUNALS AND INQUIRIES ACT
  1958 and 1966, 94, 95. *See also* Mental
  Health Review Tribunals
TREATMENT. *See also* CORR
  admission for observation, 122
  admission for treatment, 122
  behaviour modification, 115-116, 118
    (footnote), 119, 135
  consent to, 116, 117, 121-124, 152
  electro-convulsive therapy, 115, 117,
    119 (footnote)
  explained, 102-103, 115-116
  goal of, 116
  group therapy, 115
  hospital record, 149
  individual therapy, 115
  individual treatment programme,
    117, 121, 124-125, 150-151, 154
  irreversible, unpredictable, or
    hazardous, 116-117
  milieu therapy, 115
  modecate, 124
  physiological therapy, 115
  right to, 119-121, 150-152
  right to refuse, 116, 117, 121-124, 152
  seclusion, 117, 149
  sterilisation, 126-129

VEXATIOUS LITIGANT. *See* Access to
  Courts
VOTING, 101

WEAR OWN CLOTHES. *See* Expression
  and Association
WORSHIP. *See* Expression and Association

Table of Cases for Volume 1

Index to Volume 2

219

PSYCHOPATHIC DISORDER. *See*
Psychiatric Diagnosis

RAMPTON HOSPITAL. *See also* Special
Hospitals
referred to, 2, 19, 23 and footnote, 24
(footnote), 25, 31, 38, 39, 40, 76, 93, 105,
111, 118, 122, 179 (footnote), 182
statistics, 82, 123, 124, 125, 166-168, 169
and footnote, 170-172
REGIONAL HEALTH AUTHORITIES.
See Regional Secure Units
referred to, 53, 54, 59 (ref. 57), 119, 137,
140, 200
REGIONAL SECURE UNITS
as place of safety, 63 (footnote)
Butler Committee recommendation
[Interim Report], 46-47, 63 (footnote),
137-138, 140, 141, 143
compared with special hospitals, 140-141
design of, 138-139
discussed, 137-145
Glancy Report, 138, 139, 140, 142-144
history of, 137-138
length of stay in, 139
location and size of, 138
MIND proposals, 47, 144-145
observations on, 140-144
patients in, 138-139
referred to, 45 (footnote), 53, 118, 153
"Regional Secure Units Design
Guidelines", 139
security in, 139
staffing of, 139
REHABILITATION, 83-91, 96, 118-119,
125, 126, 127-128, 133, 140, 141
RELATIVE. *See* Nearest Relative
REPORT OF COMMITTEE ON
MENTALLY ABNORMAL
OFFENDERS. *See* Butler Report
REPORT OF ROYAL COMMISSION ON
CAPITAL PUNISHMENT, 17, 29 (refs. 1
and 12), 194 (refs. 2, 7, 8 and 9)
RESPONSIBLE MEDICAL OFFICER
(RMO)
Aarvold Board, 153
advising Home Secretary, 148-152
barring discharge by nearest relative, 131
censorship of post, 131-133
consultation with, 22
defined, 2, 131
discharge by, 6, 8, 13, 33, 43, 44, 62, 71,
87, 108, 112, 113, 131, 153
duty to identify patients for special
assessment, 152
duty to report on restricted patients, 60,
62

Mental Health Review Tribunals, *See*
Mental Health Review Tribunals
powers (generally), 16, 18, 109, 112, 131
power to grant leave of absence, *See*
Leave of Absence
power to transfer or recommend transfer,
62, 87, 115, 119, 130, 153
reclassification, 68
referred to, 25, 39, 44, 86, 93, 115
(footnote), 116, 129, 130, 131, 145, 178,
182, 183, 184
relationship with hospital managers, 148
(footnote)
renewal of hospital order, 33 and
footnote, 67, 131
report of, 53 (footnote), 67, 95
RESTRICTED PATIENT. *See* Hospital
Order with Restrictions
RESTRICTION ORDER. *See* Hospital
Order with Restrictions
RIGHT TO EDUCATION, 201-202
RIGHT TO REFUSE TREATMENT. *See*
Treatment
RIGHT TO TREATMENT. *See* Treatment.
ROYAL COLLEGE OF NURSING, 51
(footnote), 52 (footnote)
ROYAL COMMISSION ON THE LAW
RELATING TO MENTAL ILLNESS
AND MENTAL DEFICIENCY. *See*
·Percy Report

SECRETARY OF STATE FOR SOCIAL
SERVICES. *See* Department of Health
and Social Security
SECURITY. *See* Regional Secure Units;
Special Hospitals
SENTENCE FOR MURDER
Butler Committee recommendation, 30
(footnote), 187, 192
MIND proposal, 30 (footnote), 187
SOCIAL WORKERS
conveying patients to hospital, 33, 66
referred to, 19, 25 (footnote), 42
(footnote), 56, 129, 152, 174, 200
social inquiry reports by, 28
SPECIAL HOSPITALS. *See also*
Broadmoor Hospital; Hospital Order with
Restrictions; Moss Side Hospital; Park
Lane Hospital; Rampton Hospital;
Regional Secure Units
admission to, 1, 31, 45, 53, 77 and
footnote, 122
Butler Committee comment on, 134
compared with prison, 84
discharge from, 2, 44, 64, 78
discussion of (particularly Broadmoor),
122-135

explained, 2
length of detention in, 79 (footnote), 80-82, 104-105
managers of, *See* Department of Health and Social Security
MIND proposals, 133-135
Ministry of Health memorandum to Regional Hospital Boards, 137
Ministry of Health Working Party on, 137
no bed available in, 46-48
nurses in, 51, 52 (footnote)
overcrowding of, 47, 78, 127, 137
poor relations with local hospitals, 116-117, 141
referred to, 25 (footnote), 38, 42, 45 (footnote), 46, 47, 48, 51, 52, 56, 57 (footnote), 61, 63, 75, 77, 79, 80, 88, 94, 108, 111, 112, 131, 137, 148, 149, 152, 165, 169, 196
statistics, 79-82, 100-106, 122-125
SPECIAL VERDICT. *See* Not Guilty by Reason of Insanity
STUDY BY PROFESSORS HANEY, BANKS AND ZIMBARDO, 125, 126, 129 (footnote), 135 (refs. 6 and 7)

TRANSFERS. *See also* Mental Health Act 1959, ss. 72, 73 and 74
from regional secure unit, 139, 141
of restricted patient, 148, 150, 152
referred to, 8-9, 68, 123, 144, 165
to hospital before trial (s. 73)
    Butler Committee recommendations, 11
    explained, 198-199
    referred to, 6, 11, 17-20, 62 (footnote), 100-101
to hospital of prisoner serving sentence (s. 72),
    Butler Committee recommendations, 15, 98 (ref. 34)
    exposition of law, 108-109
    MIND proposals, 110-112
    NCCL proposals, 112
    referred to, 1, 8-9, 15, 16, 32, 46, 86, 100-101, 122, 198
to hospital of prisoner subject to restrictions (s. 74),
    Butler Committee recommendations, 16, 110, 112-113
    exposition of law, 108-109
    MIND proposals, 110-112
    referred to, 8-9, 11, 16, 18-20
to local from special hospital,
    case study, 182-183

exposition of law and practice, 115-116
MIND proposals, 118-120, 135
poor relations between local and special hospitals, 116-117
referred to, 79 (footnote). 100-101, 111, 112, 140, 169
statistics, 118, 168
to special from local hospital,
    MIND proposals, 135
    referred to, 100-101, 122, 130, 134 and footnote
TREATMENT
for patient subject to hospital order, 83-91, 96, 127
for person unfit to plead, 23, 26, 27
offender not susceptible to, 32
right to, 52
right to refuse, 84, 85 and footnote, 89-90, 200

UNFIT TO PLEAD
appeal, 21-22
Butler Committee recommendations, 12-13, 17, 20 and footnote, 22, 27
case study, 23 (footnote)
criteria, 20-21
disposal, 27-28, 192
effect of a finding, 22
explained, 6, 17
jury, 21
mental disorder in relation to, 20
MIND observations and proposals, 23-27
powers of Home Secretary, 17, 22-23, 25
procedure, 21-22
statistics, 6 and footnote, 17, 100-101, 123
summary of points relating to, 12-13
triviality of offences, 28 (footnote)

VOLUME 1 OF *A HUMAN CONDITION*, 1, 28 (footnote), 36 (ref. 39), 54, 58 (ref. 17), 85 (footnote), 98 (ref. 51), 128, 132, 133 (footnote), 136 (refs. 19 and 29), 146 (ref. 38), 154 (ref. 13), 161 (footnote), 164 (footnote), 165 and footnote, 175 (ref. 10), 176 (refs. 30 and 37), 200, 202. *See also* Index and Table of Cases to Volume 1.
VOTING, 200-201

WALKER AND McCABE, 3 (ref. 5), 7, 9 (ref. 14), 35 (ref. 8), 36 (ref. 24), 42 (footnote), 58 (ref. 16), 61, 72 (ref. 10), 74, 75, 79 (footnote), 97 (refs. 9, 10, 11 and 21), 98 (refs. 25 and 49), 135 (ref. 2), 176 (ref. 42), 197 (ref. 1)

YOUNG, GRAHAM, 2, 44, 78 (footnote), 79

Table of Cases for Volume 2

R v Dunbar [1958] 1 Q.B. 1, p. 194 (ref. 23).

R v Farrel [1967] *Crim. L. Rev.* 185, p. 35 (ref. 14).

R v Farrell, *The Times, The Guardian, The Daily Mail,* January 30, 1976, p. 47.

R v Ford [1969] 53 Cr.App.R. 551, pp. 91, 92.

R v Gaming Board for Great Britain, ex p. Benaim [1970] 2 All E.R. 582, p. 176 (ref. 19).

R v Gardiner [1967] 1 All E.R. 895, pp. 41, 42, 60, 61 (footnote), 87, 98 (ref. 49).

R v Gills [1967] *Crim. L. Rev.* 247, pp. 36 (ref. 26), 57 (ref. 5).

R v Governor of Broadmoor, ex p. Clifford William Argles, not reported. Judgment given June 28, 1974, p. 179 (footnote).

R v Governor of Parkhurst Prison, ex p. Philpot [1960] 1 W.L.R. 115, p. 185 (ref. 18).

R v Greedy [1964] *Crim. L. Rev.* 669, p. 197 (ref. 10).

R v Greenburg [1964] *Crim. L. Rev.* 236, p. 35 (ref. 14).

R v Gunnee [1972] *Crim. L. Rev.* 261, p. 9 (ref. 13).

R v Gunnell [1966] 50 Cr.App.R. 242, p. 36 (ref. 24).

R v Harvey and Ryan [1971] *Crim. L. Rev.* 644, pp. 36 (ref. 24), 37 (footnote).

R v Hatt [1962] *Crim. L. Rev.* 647, p. 9 (ref. 12).

R v Higginbotham [1961] 45 Cr.App.R. 379; [1961] 3 All E.R. 616, pp. 36 (refs. 24 and 25), 58 (ref. 35).

R v Hill [1963] *Crim. L. Rev.* 525, p. 197 (ref. 11).

R v Horan [1974] *Crim. L. Rev.* 438, p. 36 (ref. 25).

R v James [1965] *Crim. L. Rev.* 252, p. 197 (ref. 14).

R v James [1961] *Crim. L. Rev.* 842, p. 35 (ref. 23).

R v Kemp [1957] 1 Q.B. 399, p. 189.

R v King's Lynn Justices, ex p. Fysh ("D.M.F's case"), *Times Law Report,* November 20, 1963, p. 38.

R v Lattimore, not reported. Judgment given 1975, pp. 23, 25-26.

R v Lloyd [1967] 1 Q.B. 175, p. 194 (ref. 29).

R v Marquis [1974] 2 All E.R. 1216, p. 197 (ref. 8).

R v Marsden [1968] 2 All E.R. 341, p. 46.

R v Marsh [1935] 25 Cr.App.R. 49, p. 185 (ref. 8).

R v McBride [1972] *Crim. L. Rev.* 322, p. 9 (ref. 12).

R v McFarlane [1975] 60 Cr.App.R. 320, pp. 58 (refs. 33 and 34), 77, 136 (ref. 33).

R v Medway [1976] 62 Cr.App.R. 85, p. 185 (refs. 10 and 13).

R v Morris [1951] 1 K.B. 394, p. 35 (ref. 3).

R v Morris [1961] 2 Q.B. 237; [1961] 2 All E.R. 672; [1961] 45 Cr.App.R. 185, pp. 36 (refs. 24 and 25), 58 (ref. 35), 194 (ref. 31).

R v Moylan [1969] 53 Cr.App.R. 590, p. 98 (ref. 48).

R v Nicholls, not reported. Judgment given April 16, 1973, pp. 36 (ref. 26), 45, 57 (ref. 5).

R v Noble [1971] 55 Cr.App.R. 529, p. 185 (ref. 10).

R v Officer, *Times Law Report,* February 20, 1976, pp. 46, 48.

R v Parker, Griffiths and Rainbird, not reported. Judgment given March 21, 1975, p. 58 (ref. 33).

R v Peters [1974] 58 Cr.App.R. 328, p. 185 (ref. 10).

R v Podola [1960] 1 Q.B. 325, p. 29 (refs. 13 and 17).

R v Rafi [1967] *Crim. L. Rev.* 715, p. 35 (ref. 14).

R v Rhodes [1910] 74 J.P. 380, p. 185 (ref. 7).

R v Rideout, not reported. Judgment given March 16, 1968, p. 197 (ref. 13).

R v Robertson [1968] 3 All E.R. 557, p. 29 (ref. 14).

R v Rose [1961] 45 Cr.App.R. 102, p. 194 (ref. 27).

R v Ryan, *The Guardian,* June 15, 1975, p. 47.

R v Smith, not reported. Judgment given October 18, 1966, p. 197 (ref. 12).

R v Smith (Nigel Gordon), not reported. Judgment given July 30, 1974, pp. 31, 40, 76-78, 134.

R v Smith (Margaret), *The Guardian,* January 14, 1976, pp. 48, 58 (ref. 33).

R v Statutory Visitors to St. Lawrence's Hospital, Caterham, ex p. Pritchard [1953] 1 W.L.R. 1158, pp. 159, 160 (footnote).

R v Suchodolski, *The Times,* December 9, 1975, p. 48.

R v Sulton [1969] 1 W.L.R. 375, p. 185 (ref. 10).

R v Tedham [1965] *Crim. L. Rev.* 322, p. 197 (ref. 14).

R v Toland [1974] 58 Cr.App.R. 453, p. 41.

R v Turlington [1761] 2 Burr. 1115, p. 179.

R v Turner, *The Times,* October 23, 1974, p. 40.

R v Twigger, *The Times,* February 7, 1976, p. 48.

R v Webb [1969] 2 Q.B. 278, p. 29 (ref. 20).

R v Witt, not reported. Judgment given
December 16, 1974, p. 58 (ref. 23).
R v Wooland [1967] 51 Cr.App.R. 65, pp. 36
(ref. 26), 57 (ref. 5).
R v X (an infant), *Times Law Report*, July
21, 1969, p. 58 (ref. 23).
Re Featherstone [1953] 37 Cr.App.R. 146,
p. 180.
Re K(H) (an infant) [1967] 1 All E.R. 226,
p. 159.
Re Pergamon Press Limited [1970] 3 All
E.R. 535, p. 176 (ref. 19).
Re Wring [1966] 1 W.L.R. 138, p. 97 (ref. 6).

Robert's case, pp. 89-90, 94, 200.

S
Selvarajan v Race Relations Board [1976]
1 All E.R. 12, pp. 160, 161, 176 (ref. 19).

W
Wild and others v Electoral Registration
Officer for Warrington and another, not
reported. Judgment given June 15,
1976, p. 201.
Wiseman v Borneman [1969] 3 All E.R. 275,
p. 175 (refs. 13 and 19).

Table of Statutes for Volume 2

care – understanding – action

As a national mental health charity with 136 local groups and 3 regional offices, we are on the frontline of concern and provision for the needs and rights of the mentally ill and mentally handicapped.

MIND
- provides a casework service for patients, families and professionals.
- provides the only legal and welfare rights service for mental health patients.
- runs a comprehensive information service.
- organises courses and conferences for all those interested in mental health, illness and handicap.
- advises government, members of parliament and official bodies on matters of policy.
- researches and investigates the quality and quantity of care available through the mental health services.
- through its local associations, runs group homes, hostels, day centres, social clubs and sheltered workshops, all run by volunteers and providing practical assistance in the community.

MIND campaigns vigorously on behalf of the people it represents but in order to continue and expand its many services **MIND NEEDS MONEY.**

The MIND 'Turn Sympathy into Action' leaflet, obtainable from the Appeals Department at MIND, explains how you can help. A gift by DEED OF COVENANT will ensure that some of the tax you have paid comes to MIND as an Inland Revenue refund, increasing the gift at no further cost to you. Donating by Deed of Covenant allows YOU to CHOOSE how some of your income tax is spent.

EVERY PENNY COUNTS – PLEASE HELP

MIND (National Association for Mental Health)
22 Harley Street, London W1N 2ED. Tel: 01-637 0741
Northern Office: 4 Park Lane, Gateshead, Tyne & Wear NE8 3LZ. Tel: Low Fell 875600
Yorkshire Office: 155/157 Woodhouse Lane, Leeds LS2 3EF. Tel: 0532 453926
Office in Wales: 7 St. Mary Street, Cardiff CF1 2AT. Tel: 0222 395123